AF530397

FUNDAMENTALS OF PUBLIC ADMINISTRATION

FUNDAMENTALS OF PUBLIC ADMINISTRATION

By
Saroj Kumar Jena
Lecturer, Department of Political Science
D.A.V. Jr. College, Koraput (Orissa)

ANMOL PUBLICATIONS PVT. LTD.
NEW DELHI - 110 002 (INDIA)

ANMOL PUBLICATIONS PVT. LTD.
4374/4B, Ansari Road, Daryaganj
New Delhi-110 002
www.anmolbooks.com

Fundamentals of Public Administration

© Author

First Edition 2001
ISBN 81-261-0998-X

[All rights reserved. No part of this publication may be reproduced, stored in a retrieval system or transmitted, in any form or by any means, mechanical, photocopying, recording or otherwise, without prior written permission of the publisher.]

PRINTED IN INDIA

Published by J. L. Kumar for Anmol Publications Pvt. Ltd., New Delhi-110 002 and Printed at Tarun Offset Press, Delhi.

In the hands of my mother

who successfully shaped me out of moral chaos and intellectual scepticism and incessantly drove me to ride to the castle of professional scholasticism in the lounge of scientific metamorphism.

CONTENTS

Preface xi

1. CONCEPTUALIZING THE ELEMENTARY CONCEPTS 1
   1. Administration – Aspects and Definitions
   2. Public Administration – Meaning, Definitions, Nature & Scope
   3. Public Administration Vs. Private Administration

2. APPROACHING PUBLIC ADMINISTRATION 18
   1. Factors of Growth of Public Administration
   2. Importance of Public Administration in Modern Policy
   3. Public Administration – Science or Art
   4. Approaches to the Study of Public Administration

3. PHYSIOLOGY OF ADMINISTRATION 29
   1. Organization – Meaning, Definitions
   2. Aspects of Organisation – Formal and informal
   3. Bases of Organisation – Purpose, Process, persons, place
   4. Principles of Organisation – Hierarchy, Span of Control, Unity of Command, Delegation, Centralization, Decentralization
   5. Typology of Organization—Line, Staff and Auxiliary, Their Differences

4. ADMINISTRATIVE STRUCTURES 67
   1. Department—Its bases, its structural patterns

Headquarter and field, their organizational patterns, Fields-Headquarter relationship

2. Public Corporation—Factors of Growth; Definitions Characteristics, its Distinction from Joint Stock Company, Private Enterprises, Public Undertakings and Government Departments, its Role in Modern States; Control over Public Corporations, Working of Public Corporations in India, Committee on Public Undertakings

3. Independent Regulatory Commissions—Meaning Definitions, Feature, Functions, the Case in India

5. ADMINISTRATION AT WORK 104

1. Chief Executive—Types, Functional, Chief Executive as General Manager

2. Legislature—Meaning, Functions, Legislature as Board of Directors

6. ADMINISTRATIVE PROCEDURE 113

1. Administrative Law—Meaning, Definitions, Nature, Origin of the concept, Dicey's Views, Its Rejection, Salient Features of Administrative Law, Its Importance

2. Delegated Legislation—Meaning Definitions, Principles of Delegated Legislation, Cause of Growth of Delegated Legislation, implications of delegated legislation, Safeguards in Delegated legislation

3. Administrative Adjudication—Meaning, Definitions, Features, Its Distinction from Judicial Adjudication, Advantages and Disadvantages, Suggestions for Improvement

7. NEW ASPECTS OF ADMINISTRATION 136

Development Administration—Historical Legacy, Definitions, Meaning, Nature, Features, Role of Bureaucracy in Development Administration, People's Participation in Administration. Working of Development Administration in India

8. FINANCIAL ADMINISTRATION IN INDIA 153

1. Budget—Its importance, Features of a good budget

2. Budgetary Process in India—Preparation of Budget, Budget in India, its Aspects

3. Enactment of Budget—Appropriation Bill, Finance Bill

4. Execution of Budget

5. Control over Finance—Executive Control—Audit, the Role of Comptroller and Auditor General of India, Legislative Control—Public Accounts Committee, Estimates Committee

9. PERSONNELS IN ADMINISTRATION 186

1. Civil Service—Meaning, Definition, Types, Civil Service and Bureaucracy, Historical Legacy of Civil Service, Characteristics, Shortcomings, Civil Service in India

2. Recruitment—Meaning, purpose, methods—direct and indirect recruitment, procedures of recruitment, Role of Union Public Service Commission in Recruitment

3. Training—Meaning, Definition, Types, Importance of Training

4. Promotion—Meaning, Types, Bases of Promotion, Significance of Promotion

5. Conditions of Service of Civil Servants, Discipline, Morale

6. Relations between Civil Servants and Ministers

7. Relations between Civil Servants and Public

10. ADMINISTRATION AND PEOPLE 244

1. Redressal of Citizen's Grievances—Lokpal and Lokayukta System

2. District Administration—Meaning, District level Organization, Role of Collector

3. Panchayati Raj in India—Meaning and Evolution, Panchayati Raj in Independent India, Balwantrai Mehta Committee, Gram Panchayat, Panchayat Samiti, Zilla Parishad

Index 278

PREFACE

Public Administration today is one of the most fascinating academic disciplines, that has established its credentials in the field of social science research. One of the most distinguishing marks of the subject is that it exists and do exist for the people only and exclusively. With a touch of human values, it wants to ensure a total quality management of life of the people at large through gradual eradication of mass miseries. It do exist to solve the human problems by necessarily relating the human masses to their societal environment. With the twin task of solving the multifarious human problems on the one hand and reshaping and rejuvenating the civil societies on the other, it has set itself to provide a basic minimum way of civilized life to the great mass of citizenry who had hither to been struggling to keep up their identity amidst urbanization, globalization, liberalization and privatization. It provides up an individual not only with an insight to his own role as an active participant in politico-administrative scenario of the State but also the far sight of judging the governmental performances in the light of the expectations of the society at large. By constantly unfolding the coordinated and collective efforts of the general public, Public Administration aims at narrowing down the differences between the *people* (for the sake of whom administration exists), the *political authority* (from whom emanate all major policy decisions) and the *bureaucratic structure* (by whom administration is carried on to its logical conclusion) and there by bridge a sluice gate among them channelizing the free flow of communication without which Public Administration would have been only dead letters signifying nothing but a literary expression.

There is no death of writings on the subject eulogizing the importance of Public Administration in the life of man and the society. A number of scholars of repute have wrote extensively on the subject. But these are not accessible and understandable to the students who have just started to know the a, b, c, of public administration at their graduate level. Hence before going into the details of the complexities of administrative procedure, one requires to have a conceptual clarity on the subject. Recognizing the importance of the basic fundamental knowledge on the subject, I have set myself to the stupendous task of writing on the *'Fundamentals of Public Administration'* which will suit the needs of the general students who have just started showing their interest in the study of the subject. Keeping in view the handicaps on the path of the self starters on the subject, I have tried my level best to provide, as precisely and as lucidly as possible, a picture of the subject that not only attune to the requirements of the students but also generate interest among them on the subject and build up a sense of confidence. The subject matter presented in the book has been collected from various sources and no originality as such is claimed.

I am very much grateful to all those authors whose works I have freely drawn upon with aim of providing the students with the best available and the most relevant material for their studies. I am thankful to my student friends who had been pressing hard on me to write such a book over the last couple of years. I also extend my heartfelt thanks to all my friends who have been providing me with all sorts of inspiration to write down such a book for the benefit of the students fraternity. I also owe my allegiance to the library staffs of Adivasi College, Balliguda, who by their timely help have provided me with all relevant books and journals that are retrieved and explored thoroughly for the purpose. I am really indebted to my parents whose timely inspiration have made my task easy. In this occasion, it would be a great pleasure on my part to thank my wife who stood all along my side all through the days I wrote the manuscript, inspiring me to devote whole heartedly on the topic without whose advice I would have not been able to complete the book in time. Last but not the least, I would be failing in my sense of gratitude if I would not convey my sincere thanks that I owe to Shri Kripal D. Joshi, Production Manager, Anmol Publications Pvt. Ltd., New Delhi who took the risk of publishing the manuscript so humbly and materialized my wishes into a reality.

—Saroj Kumar Jena

Koraput
21.05.2001

Chapter I

CONCEPTUALISING THE ELEMENTARY CONCEPTS

WHAT IS ADMINISTRATION?

Man is a social animal. The social instinct of man compelled him to live in the society with other fellow beings. Whatever man thinks or does, has a direct bearing with the society. Man cannot fulfil his desires by himself. For the satisfaction of his wants, he depends on others. Thus, there is always a co-operative instinct in man that essentially made him a social creature. Beside these co-operative instinct, man is also governed by self interest. Every individual try to maximize his self interest in relation to others, even at the cost of others. This leads to conflict of ideas in the society. In order to avoid such conflict, there comes the role of authority. The authority is one which gives everyone in the society equal advantage to maximize his interest and helps them in their co-operative efforts, to lead a better, prosperous and progressive life. The technique by which the conflict is resolved and collective activity is maximized, is called administration.

Thus, administration, understood in the above situation involves the art of management—the management of conflict or crisis and the technique of ensuring collective efforts to achieve a desired goal, the goal being peaceful co-existence that leads to progress and prosperity.

The term 'administration' etymologically, is derived from the Latin word '*ad*' and '*ministiare*' which means 'to serve'. Then what is the purpose of administration? The answer is simple. Administration stands for serving the people and help them in achieving their desired goal. However, for achieving the desired objective, a technique is required to be adopted – the technique of managing the affairs of the people in such a way that will help in achieving the goal.

Thus, administration is a technique which is applied by the authority in power to serve the purpose for which people are united, to spread collectivism and to eradicate conflicts by successfully managing the affairs of the people, by emphatically caring for and looking after the people's interest.

Aspects

Administration is both positive and negative. In the positive sense, administration implies the technique to ensure collective and cooperative efforts to achieve the goal. In the negative sense, administration implies not to take any action that will prove detrimental for the society.

People are very often confused with administration and management and consider both the terms as synonymous and thereby interchangeably use them. However, both of them differ from each other in degree. Administration includes all those activities that deals with formation and implementation of policies, establishment of the organisational structure and providing necessary resources for the realization of desired goal, supervising and coordinating the efforts in a collective manner to maximize the objective. On the other hand, Management is confined itself only with the framework of policy, structure and resources. It wants to guide to organisation towards success within the framework set up by administration. Thus, while administration refers to the top level management, management deals only with the bottom level administration.

Administration try to integrate the man with his environment to achieve its objective. It is based on the belief that where man live together, they have to work together and where they work together, they have to be properly arranged in such a way as to facilitate the realization of the objective smoothly. So administration is a process which takes into account the complex web of social relationship as a factor for realizing the goal. As such it is a technique of harmoniously combining the men and material for the attainment of the objective.

Administration is, thus, a rational activity that relates man and material towards the achievement of specific goal. The success of administration depends on the capacity of the authority in 'Organisation' and 'Management'. For instance, there is a construction of building. For the said purpose both men and materials are required. The power applied by the authority to arrange the persons effectively for the construction work constitutes the 'Organisation' and the technique to mobilize the resources effectively for the said purpose constitutes the 'management'. Thus, 'organisation' and 'management' are the basic ingredients of administration. Thus we may define administration as 'technique of rational organisation and management of man and material through collective co-operation towards the attainment of desired objective.'

Definitions

Administration has been defined variously by different scholars. Some of the definitions are follows:

(a) **Z.A. Vieg** — "In simplest terms, administration is the determined action taken in pursuit of a conscious purpose."

(b) **F.M. Marx**—"It is a systematic ordering of affairs and the calculated use of resources aimed at making those things happen, which we want to happen."

(c) **Felix A. Nigro** — "Administration is the organisation and use of man and materials to accomplish a purpose."

(d) **Herbert Simon** – In its broadest sense, Administration can be defined as the activities of groups cooperating to accomplish common goals."

(e) **Marshall E. Dimock** – "Administration is concerned with the 'what' and 'how' of the government. The 'what' is the subject matter and 'how' is the technique of management."

(f) **Luther Gullick** – "Administration is getting things done. It is concerned with the accomplishment of defined objectives."

(g) **E.N. Gledden** – "In its simplest term, Administration is defined as to take some of people for managing the affairs and actions taken in pursuit of common conscious purpose."

(h) **Pfiffner** – "It is the organisation and direction of human and material resources to achieve desired end."

(i) **L.D. White** – "Administration is the direction, coordination and control of many persons to achieve some purpose."

Although administration is a collective activity, yet all the collective activities do not constitute administration. For instance the collective activities of the thieves do not constitute administration. Rather, only those types of collective activities which involve the rational organisation and management of men and materials are called administration.

Viewed from the above said angle, administration is found in any group, whether big or small. On the basis of sphere of influence of these groups in the society, administration can be divided into two broad divisions, such as private administration and public administration. The administration in small groups such as family, club, society, school, universities and small companies covers only a limited part of the society. Thus, it is called private administration. But on the contrary, the administration found in large groups such as state, central, regional and local governments as well as big corporations, engulfs a large chunck of society. As such it is called public administration.

PUBLIC ADMINISTRATION

After a clear understanding of the term 'administration', we are now clear that 'public administration is merely the name given to one of the broad divisions of administration. It refers to the administration present in large groups.

The term 'public administration' makes the term 'administration' more complicated by adding the prefix 'public'. However, the term 'public' itself is quite clear. It refers to the 'people's administration'. However, the term 'people's administration' is nebulous and may lead to various meanings in various situations. In reality, it refers to the administration carried on for the people. But by whom? Naturally, the answer is the authority or the 'government'. Thus, 'Public Administration', in its simplest meaning refers to the governmental administration or the administration carried on by the government for the people only and exclusively. It is the general people at large, which is the objective of public administration.

However, another problem lies before us as to the interpretation of the term 'government'. In a broad sense, 'government' is divided into three wings such as legislative, executive and judiciary. So the question before us is that whether the activities of all the three branches of the government constitute public administration?

Two groups of people held quite contrary views as to the correct interpretation of the term 'government'. These two groups are divided into two schools such as the integral school and the managerial school. The scholars from integral school held that public administration is a comprehensive term that includes all the activities of the government whether falling in the executive, legislative and judicial branch. Thus, to them, public administration studies the integral activities of executive, legislative and judicial wings of government.

On the other hand, the advocates of managerial school of thought held that public administration is not concerned with all the activities of all the three branches of government, rather it is concerned only with the activities of the executive branch which involves both the organisational and managerial technique.

Thus, in political science, the term *public administration* is used in two senses. In its broader sense, it denotes the integration of the activities of executive, legislative and judicial branches of the government. In the narrow sense, it denotes only the activities of executive branch which is concerned with policy formulation and policy implementation task.

As the votaries of public administration are divided into two lines of thought i.e. the managerial school and the integral school, the nature of public administration varies from one school to that of another.

A clear analysis of the concepts hold by both schools led us to conclude that if we take the managerial school for granted, it would give rise to a too narrow picture of public administration as it emphatically laid stress on the activities of authorities in relation with the development of managerial technique only. However, administration is concerned not only with the managerial technique but also is concerned with the policies and programmes of the executive and their execution in the society to achieve the goal.

Definitions

Scholars have attempted to define public administration both from integral point of view as well as from managerial point of view. We would like to discuss them at length as follows:

The integral view of public administration is advocated by the scholars like L.D. White, Woodrow Wilson, Marshall E – Dimock and Percy McQueen. On the contrary, the managerial view of public administration is held by Luther Gullick, Herbert Simon, Messon and Henri Fayol.

(a) **L.D. White** – "Public administration consists of all those operations having for their purpose the fulfillment or enforcement of public policy."

(b) **Woodrow Wilson** – "It is the detailed and systematic application of law, every particular application of general law is an act of administration.

(c) **Marshall E. Dimock** – "Public Administration is the fulfillment or enforcement of public policy as declared by the competent authority. It is law in action.'

(d) **Percy Mcqueen** – "it is the administration related to the operations of government, whether central or local."

(e) **Pfiffner** - "Public administration consists of getting the works of the government done by coordinating the efforts of the people so that this can work together to accomplish their set tasks."

(f) **E.N. Gladden** – "Public administration is concerned with the administration of the government.'

(g) **Duguit Waldo** – "Public administration is the art and science of management as applied to the affairs of the state."

(h) **Luther Gullick** – "Public administration is that part of the science of administration which has to do with the government and thus concerns itself primarily with the executive branch where the work of the government is done."

(i) **Herbert Simon** – "By public administration, is meant, in common usage, the activities of the executive branches of the national, state and local government.'

(j) **Merson** – "As the science of politics is an inquiry into the best means where by the will of the people may be organized, so the science of administration is an inquiry as to how policies may best be carried into operations."

(k) **Henri Fayol** – "Public administration is the determined action taken in pursuit of a conscious purpose. It is the art and science of management applied to the affairs of the state."

(l) **Harvey Walker** – "Public administration is the work done by the government to give effect to a law."

Nature

The above definitions of public administration also reveal, to a great extent, the nature of public administration. However, one is always confronted between the two broad views i.e. the 'integral' and the 'managerial' views as to what is the real nature of public administration. A clear understanding of the nature of public administration depends on an indepth analysis of the broad views regarding the subject.

The integral view held that public administration is the sum total of all the activities—manual, clerical, managerial, technical, operational and so on. This view is so vast and wide that it engulfs the activities ranging from the manager of an enterprise to that of sweeper in their coordinated efforts to serve the enterprise as administration. Prof. **L.D. White** shares this view when he says that "public administration consists of all those operations having for their purpose the fulfillment or enforcement of public policy."

However, this view is too much wide and so vast that it does not lend itself easily to study. It poses a vague and unscientific view of public administration and as such, **F.M. Marx** feats the danger of disappearance of the subject as a recognizable focus of study.

The managerial view, on the other hand, advocates that only those activities of persons engaged in performing managerial functions in an enterprise, constitutes administration. Thus, it laid stress on the technique of management by the authority to unite, control, coordinate and supervise the operations undertaken in an enterprise. This look like the whole process of activities as an integrated effort.

Luther Gullick subscribes to this view who he held that "administration has to do with getting things done with the accomplishment of common objectives."

However, this view is also not free from flaws. It is criticized for being abstract, arbitrary and misses the real substance of administration it is abstract because it concentrates its attention only on the managerial functions and disregard the subject matter completely. It is arbitrary because it excludes the non-managerial activities i.e. the technical and operational activities from the clutches of administration and by emphasizing on only one group of administrative activities i.e. on managerial view only try to build of the theory of institution. The building up a theory by necessarily highlighting the managerial point of view only resembles the construction of a building without proper base or edifice. Therefore, the managerial view misses the real substance of administration.

Then what is the nature of public administration? The answer is the direct outcome of the environment. Public administration is something which is planned, organized, co-ordinated and directed. The real core of administration is not the method of management, but the service that it renders to the people. Thus, it gives equal emphasis on technical and operational factors along with the managerial functions.

The real nature of public administration is that it stands for the service of the people. It is a sociological, moral and ethical activity which is meant for the society of human beings, materials and resources for the attainment of desired end.

Duncan and **Mitchells**, therefore, have rightly observed that "public administration is a study of intricate and complex network of human relationships and forms of organisation which is designed to enable the people to live together in society."

Therefore, public administration is a means to achieve an end, but it is not an end in itself. It is a social instrument to achieve the social goal. It provides a cement to the social organisation. It is a public tool used for the well-being of the people. Its primary objective is the achievement of social objective and therefore it is concerned with the non-political aspects of administration.

Dimock, Dimock and **Koening** has summed up the nature of public administration in the following words:

> "As a study, public administration examines every aspect of government's efforts to discharge the laws and to give effect to public policy; as a process, it is all the steps taken between the time for the fulfillment of public policy; and as a vocation, it is organizing and directing the activities of others in a public agency."

Scope

The duality of outlook as to the nature of public administration very often confused an ordinary citizen as to the real scope of public administration. The scope means the area of operation or the periphery of the subject. In simplest term we can say scope means the subject matter of public administration. What, therefore are the subject matter of public administration? The curiosity can be solved if we go deep into the subject.

Viewed from the integral angle, public administration would include the whole complex of activities undertaken to accomplish any common purpose. So the scope of public administration based on integral view would be so vast and wide that it might lose its temper as a scientific investigation and therefore, shunt the development of the discipline as a distinct academic subject.

The managerial point of view, on the other hand, postulates that administration is the organisation of man and material in the pursuit of common objective. As such, the scope of public administration, basing on this view, would include only those subjects which involve the technique of management and which are common to all sorts of organisation.

Luther Gullick, therefore, prescribed a formulae to

represent the scope of public administration on the basis of the technique of management. The formula stands as POSDCORB in which each letter has a meaning of its own such as Planning, Organisation, Staffing, Direction, Coordination, Reporting and Budgeting.

Planning implies the working out in broad outlines, the things to be done and the methods to be adopted for accomplishment of the purpose. Thus, it is a preparation for action.

Organisation stands for creating the formal structure of authority through which the entire work to be done. This edifice of administrative structure has its numerous subdivisions, each arranged, defined and coordinated in a systematic way.

Staffing means recruitment of suitable candidates to various posts in the organisation, their training, and maintenance of favourable conditions of work.

Direction stands for decision making at the authority level and issuing orders to staffs as a guideline to accomplish the purpose in a collective capacity.

Coordination stands for harmonizing and interrelating various parts of the work as well as eliminating overlapping and conflicts.

Reporting means keeping both the superior and the subordinate informed of what is going on in the organisation and making arrangements for the collection of information through inspection, research and records.

Budgeting represents the whole of financial administration i.e. preparation, passing and execution of the budget.

Although Luther Gullick valiantly attempted to define the scope of public administration, yet he overlooked the fact that different agencies are faced with different administrative problems which are peculiar to the nature of service they render and the functions they perform. For instance, the problem in military department would definitely be different from that of education department. But **Gullick** failed to reconcile this problem. So the POSDCORB view is only one of 'technique oriented' rather than 'subject oriented.'

Lewis Merriam, by recognizing this defect in Gullick's view, held that "public administration is an instrument with two blades like a pair of scissors. One blade may be the knowledge of the field carried by POSDCORB; the other blade is the knowledge of subject matter in which these techniques are applied. Both blades must be good to make an effective tool."

Realizing the importance of both subject matter and technique, Marshall E. Dimock held that "public administration is concerned with the 'what' and 'how' of the government. The 'what' is the subject matter and the 'how' is the technique of management.

According to **Henri Fayol**, the scope of public administration consists of five principles—Planning, organisation, command, coordination and control.

However, **Pfiffner** have attempted to determine the scope of public administration by two broad divisions – such as:

(a) the principle of public administration; and

(b) the sphere of public administration.

The principle of public administration includes organisation, personnel management, methodology, material, public finance and administrative accountability.

On the other hand, the sphere of public administration includes the central government, the state government, the local governments as well as public corporations.

However, credit goes to **Harvey Walker** who had given a comprehensive account of scope of public administration. To him, Public administration consists of two parts–

(a) Administrative theory; and

(b) Applied administration.

The administrative theory laid stress on the theoretical

aspect of public administration which includes the study of structure, organisation, functions and methods of public authority engaged in carrying out administration at national, state and local level; it also includes the study of control over administrative machinery – both internal and external.

Applied administration refers to the systematic application of administrative theories to the administrative structures. He classified applied administration under 10 heads such as political, legislative, financial, defensive, educational, social, economic, foreign, imperial and local.

Felix A. Nigro, on the other hand, held that the scope of public administration includes the following:

(a) Organisation and structure of executive branch;

(b) Formulation and implementation of public policy;

(c) Organisational structure and machinery of administration;

(d) The administrative process;

(e) The role of bureaucracy; and

(f) Interaction between the organisation and their environment.

In short, we can say that the scope of public administration is a comprehensive subject. It includes the following:

(1) Organisation – their structures and functions

(2) Principles of organisation – Hierarchy, delegation, unity of command, span of control, decentralization.

(3) Theories of organisations

(4) Bases of organisation, their types etc.

(5) The role of bureaucracy – recruitment, training, promotion, conditions of service, relation with the ministers, relation with the public, neutrality and anonymity.

(6) Interaction between organisation and their

environment—ecology of administration, comparative administration, development administration.

(7) Applied administration—local administration, Panchayati Raj system.

(8) Financial administration—preparation and enactment of budget.

(9) Control over administration—legislative control, executive control, judicial control etc.

(10) Public corporations—their structure and functions.

PRIVATE AND PUBLIC ADMINISTRATION

After conceptualising the concept of public administration one is still left with an obsession as to the relation between public and private administration. As I told earlier, public administration aims at the general well-being of the people at large; on the other hand, private administration laid stress on the all-round development of a particular person or group of persons. It never looks after and care for the majority of the people in the society. Every private enterprise has its own administration and therefore private enterprise differs from one enterprise to that of another. In general, we can say that public administration deals with the organisation of activities by public authorities, whereas private administration deals with the organisation of activities by private enterprises.

However, both public and private administration show some elements of similarities and exhibits also some amount of dissimilarities. However, the difference between the public and private administration lies only in degree, nor in kind.

Similarities

The similarities between public and private administration are as follows:

(a) Both the public and private administration have a goal of their own.

(b) Both of them apply the same technique of management for the realization of their goals.

(c) The same type of work is done with more or less same produce by the same personnel in both public and private administration. For instance, the work of an engineer is same in both public and private enterprise.

(d) Both public and private administration feed and being fed by each other in the same manner and a systematic coordination in both the enterprises help the state to progress.

(e) The responsibility of public official is, in a sense, the same as that of an official in a private enterprise. Because each of them aims at achieving the goal in their respective fields by systematically using the man and material available to them.

Dissimilarities

Although both public administration and private administration show same degree of congruence, yet they also deviate from each other in some other angles. The dissimilarities between them are as follows:

(a) While public administration is subject to political direction from authorities, private administration is free from any such political direction except, in some urgent situations. As a result, while public administrators has to carry out the orders of political executive, private administrators are free to pursue their own method to achieve the goal.

(b) Public administration aims at general well-being of the people at large and as such it has a philanthropist motive to serve the people. But the private administration is very much egoist and operates only with the consideration of profit motive.

(c) Public administration functions on a comprehensive scale. It deals with the various types of needs of the people ranging from social to that of political need. But on the otherhand, private administration only aims at the economic needs of the life.

(d) Public administration is directly or indirectly responsible to the public for all acts of their commission. But private administration owes no such responsibility and allegiance to the people at large. Thus, are also not at all answerable to any body for any of their activities.

(e) The records and accounts of public enterprise is subject to public scrutiny and as such there is transparency in financial matters in public administration. But no such transparency exists in any private enterprise.

(f) While public administration works on cooperative basis with the help of people and the coordination of the employees, private enterprises run exclusively on competitive spirit. Therefore, there is a cut-throat competition witnessed in private administration but no such competition is ever dominate public administration.

(g) There is consistency in procedure and dealing in public administration. It operates on the principle of equal treatment to all irrespective of any differences be it physical, economic or political. On the contrary, private administration is characterized by preferential treatment to the persons.

(h) In matter of efficiency, the private administration remains a step ahead of public administration. While public administration is characterized by political domination, bureaucratic red-tapism and slow moving, these features are conspicuously absent in private administration which are often characterized as non-political and business-like. In private administration, the incentive of more profit impels an individual to devote himself whole-heartedly to his business. But such type of incentive is taking in public administration.

(i) There is a strong external control in financial matters over public administration. The executive does not control the finance. Rather the legislature does so. Not a single pie can be spent in the public enterprises without the consent of the legislature. Thus, public money is spent meticulously according to strict legal norms. But such type of external control over finance is absent in private administration. Although there is internal audit in private enterprises, yet the finance is controlled by the executive authority.

(j) There is also a strong psychological difference between public and private administration. Employment in public enterprises carries greater social prestige, security of service and better working conditions than employment in private enterprises. Hence public administration commands more respect than private administration.

However, to conclude, although there is a difference between the public and private administration, yet their cooperative efforts for strengthening the social norms and coordination in various fields help the state to achieve development more rapidly than ever.

Chapter II

APPROACHING PUBLIC ADMINISTRATION

FACTORS OF GROWTH

In present day, we are, by and large, helped by public administration in one way or another. It has come to play a vital role in the life of modern man. Certain factors have contributed significantly for the growth of Public administration. They may be summed up as follows:

Firstly, the industrial revolution of 19th Century and technological development thereof paved the way for large scale production. The common man became a cag in this large-scale industry and is exploited by the capitalists very carefully. Here came the role of modern state in general and public administration in particular to rescue the people from such a chaotic situation.

Secondly, the concern of state for the common man led to the development of welfare state. Public administration is significantly emphasized in such a modern welfare state which started ameliorating the problems of the people through staged planning.

Historical Growth

The origin of Public administration can be traced back to

1887 when Woodrow Wilson published his "The Study of Administration". It was followed by Frank J. Goodnow's "Politics and Administration" (1900). It laid stress on politics-administration dichotomy.

However, Public Administration as a distinct discipline developed only with L.D. White's publication of "Introduction to the study of Public Administration" (1926). The subject was thereafter highlighted in the writings of W.F. Willoughby's '*Principle of Public Administration* (1927), followed by Mary Parker Follet's *Creative Experience*, Henri Fayol's *Industrial and General Management*, Mooney's *Principle of Organisation*. Later on, Public Administration was highlighted in the writings of Luther Gullick, Herbert A. Simon, L. Urwick, Robert Dahl, Cyret, James G. March and a host of others.

Importance of Public Administration in Modern Polity

The importance of Public administration in modern polity cannot be overlooked. It has paved the way to material, moral, physical, economic, social, political and cultural development of man. It shapes the basic orientation of man in the society towards the political structure. It also provides him with an opportunity to study the system of organisational structure and behavior of modern states and their functions in providing the best possible development to the man.

Secondly, public administration acts as an instrument of social change. It undertakes for itself the most stupendous task of removing economic inequalities, providing for a socialistic pattern of society devoid of exploitation and starvation, spreading education, removal of untouchability, and the progressive growth and guidance of the state towards industrial development.

Thirdly, Public administration acts as a great stabilizing force in the society. It socialise the people in the particular political culture of the state and thereby helps in transmitting political culture successfully from generation to generation and maintaining the status quo. It, therefore, provides an element of unity among diversity and continuity between traditional and modern.

Fourthly, Public administration assists the legislature and political executives in the formulation of policies and also implementation of the same with their expert knowledge and experience. It also helps in spreading women education for controlling population explosion. It regulates infant morality by coercion and force. By raising literacy rate, public administration helps in raising the economic standards of the people.

Fifthly, Public administration acts as an instrument of solving various socio-political and economic issues that are confronted with the society. It advises the government about the rate of spending on defence. It regulates trade relations, state control over economic activities and energy crisis. By implementing the policies it try to solve the problem of pollution through scientific and technical means. By providing different types of employment or methods of self determination, Public administration helps in checking poverty and eradicating economic inequalities. It also provides a minimum standard of persistence without removing the incentive to personal enterprises.

Sixthly, Public administration fills the details of legislation through rule making or delegated legislation. As the modern legislature is left without time to go deep into each and every legislation, it delegated its power to the administrators. The administrators fill up the details of legislation by taking into account the needs of the people and the gravity of the situation.

Finally, Public administration attempts to distribute the ownership and control of material resources of the community to subserve the common good. By graduating higher taxation, it redistributes the income. It also provides social security assistance to the people in times of undeserved wants such as unemployment, sickness, old age and disability. It also creates employment opportunities by providing stress on village and small scale industries, irrigation, afforestation etc.

Thus, we may conclude that the importance and role of public administration in a modern democratic polity cannot be undermined. It provides the best possible assistance to bridge the critical gap between the stated objectives of the society and their fulfillment.

PUBLIC ADMINISTRATION—SCIENCE OR ART?

The concept Public Administration is such a vast and numerous concept that it has different meanings in different situations. It can be considered as a process, it may be an approach, it may be a subject. A student is very often confused as to the real nature of Public Administration. Whether it is an art or it can termed as a Science? The question is very much debatable and requires proper attention.

Public Administration as an Art

What is an Art ? An art is a technique –a technique to shape and reshape the ideas, a technique which fines the mind, bring excellent derivatives to the user. Therefore, art is a technique to manage the affairs smoothly, gently and effectively. Viewed from this angle, public administration is an art because it inducts into the minds of an administrator a technique to man the affairs of people effectively, efficiently and smoothly by their cooperative efforts. Thus, it teaches the administrator about the technique to develop leadership qualities to able him to adopt to the changing environment. Public administration shapes and reshapes the human mind, brings derivative excellence, develops leadership traits, manages the affairs of the people through planning, coordination, guidance and effective supervision and control. Thus Public administration is an art, quite an art that teaches not only the administrators how to behave but also equally teach the people how to work coordinately to achieve the desired objective.

Public Administration as a Science

Although there is unanimity among the scholars that Public administration is an art, yet the same degree of diversified opinion is there on the subject when it is treated as a Science. There are some scholars like Charlesworth and Charles Beard who considered Public administration as exact science. But the scholars like Merson, L.D. White, Huxley and Herbert Simon were very much reluctant to ascribe it the position of real science and considered it to be a social science like that of economics, sociology and politics. Besides that, the scholars like L. Urwick, Henri Fayol and Luther Gullick considered that although it is an art, yet its principles can be studied scientifically.

Before examining the concept as a science, we must know what actually is a 'Science'. A Science is a body of systematic knowledge which gets shaped and reshaped by laboratory experiments. Thus, science is one where laboratory experiments can be possible.

If we analyze the concept given by **Charlesworth** and **Charles Beard**, they held that Science is not a conceptual vocabulary represented by mathematical values. Rather science is a systematic body of knowledge, derived from experience and observations and supported by a body of rules or axioms. These rules are practically applicable to practice and thereby lead to formulation of generalizations.

Viewed in this sense, **Beard** held that public administration fulfills all the conditions laid by science. For instance, the rule by bureaucracy is universally applicable to all states whether developed or developing, capitalist or communist or totalitarian. Thus, public administration is an exact science.

However, this view of treating public administration as a natural science was rejected by other scholars. Merson held that "Science is investigation and observation, followed by tabulation, classification and correlation. The subject matter of exact sciences is measurable and consisted of facts which have a relative uniformity. But these condition do not exist in the science of public administration.

The votaries of this school held that public administration can at best be a social science and not an exact science. They put forward certain arguments in their favour as such:

(1) Like Social Science, Public administration deals with human behaviour which is far more complex and intrinsic. On the other hand, exact science does not take into human behavior into consideration.

(2) Unlike Science, the generalizations of public administration do not have universal application. However, it does not mean that the generalizations in public administration are totally invalid. But like social sciences, the generalizations have limited applicability and it differs from one political system to another political system and even within the same political system under different circumstances.

(3) Like other social science, public administration deals not only with the rational behavior but also takes into account the irrational behaviour of the people. But science, never takes into account the irrational elements.

(4) Unlike science, public administration cannot be studied objectively. So like other social sciences, public administration has to apply its rational value judgements to make its principles more valid and situation oriented. However, value free approach is highlighted by exact sciences.

Therefore, Huxley has rightly observed that "the difference between the social sciences and the so called exact sciences does not depend on any fundamental distinctions between the sciences themselves, but on the accidents of their subject matter, of their relations, complexities and consequent relative perfection". Therefore, Public administration is only a social science.

The third group of scholars held that though at present public administration is an art, in due course of time it will become a science. In other words, the administrative phenomena can be studied scientifically in due course of time through a systematized body of knowledge. The scientific study of administrative phenomena is highly desirable because it may throw light on the tools and techniques of administration and its organisational pattern. **Ordway Tead** recommended the scientific study of administration on the ground that it would lead to a much more widespread professional self consciousness and convinced sense of direction and social justification among executives. This would increase the influence of administration and administrators in the social life.

Therefore, we may conclude that public administration is neither pure science nor an art, rather it is a curious combination of both art and science.

APPROACHES TO THE STUDY OF PUBLIC ADMINISTRATION

Public administration, as a scientific study of administrative phenomena, can be studied from different angles. Ever since its birth in 1887, it has been approached by various scholars in different ways by taking recourse to various methods. These methods of study have showed an insight to the subject. Each method has its relative advantages. Basically, there are two approaches to the study of public administration. Such as:

(1) Non-Political or Traditional Approach, and

(2) Political or Behavioural Approach.

1. Traditional Approach

The traditional approach to the study of Public administration was in vogue during the period when behavioral revolution did not open its account in the field of social sciences. This does not mean that the traditional approach is altogether absent now days. It is still holding its and way in the present society. This approach highlights only the non-political aspects of administration. The following methods are used in this approach:

(a) Scientific Methods

Public administration, in order to achieve the status of

Science, adopted this scientific method from natural sciences, Like that of science, this method laid stress on the collection of data, quantification, analysis, classification, observation, verification and prediction. This method is followed by the scholars. Because they believe that generalizations could be formulated in public administration which could help in solving the various administrative problems in the society in all future times to come. This method was highly followed in the writings of F.W. Taylor who developed effective techniques of management, accounting, budgeting, Work-Flow charts etc. Although today the behavioral approach dominates the politico-administrative scene, still this scientific method is used as a effective instrument to check the administrative problems.

(b) Legal Method

Another method for the study of Public administration is from juridical point of view. This method laid much emphasis on devising a variety of laws and principles on the basis of which administrative structures could be organized, evaluated and function. This method is in operation in mostly European countries like France, Belgium, Germany etc., where stress is laid on administrative law. The politico-administrative dichotomy is clearly observed in these countries where political institutions function on constitutional laws and administrative organisations follows the administrative law. Such method determines the procedure of organisation and functions of department, local bodies, public corporations etc., their correlations, powers and responsibilities.

However, this method neglects the sociological background of administrative structures which exerts a deep impact on the styles of functioning of these institutions. The study based on legalistic method would lend the subject too much formal and legalistic missing the behavioral aspect of administration.

(c) Historical Method

This method is used to study the historical growth of administrative institutions, their structures and functions. As the name suggests, it tries to explain the present administrative institutions in the light of past experiments. Such method is, therefore, very much descriptive, analytical and evaluative in nature. Here the administrative decisions, phenomena and processes are made the focal point of historical exposition. It investigates in to socio-economic and politico-cultural factors that influence the decision-making.

(d) Case Study Method

It is an American contribution to the methodology of public administration. Case means a particular problem. Therefore, as the name suggests, case study method laid stress on studying at depth the particular problem, the procedure adopted to solve the problem and the decision making at the authority level and to evaluate the decisions in the light of the results which followed. The followers of case study method believe that generalisations would help the administrator in providing solution to the problem in the light of those case studies.

The case study method helped the students of public administration to know in details the relationship between political and permanent executives, between generalists and specialists, between legislature and executive as well as to know the management process.

This method was followed not only in USA, but also in U.K. and India.

(e) Comparative Method

This method is used to study the administrative institutions of various political societies and thereby to formulate generalizations on the basis of comparison. Although this method is even followed nowadays, yet there is a change in the technique of study. In earlier days, the comparative study prescribes the ideals of administrative structures and functions. But nowadays, emphasis is laid on descriptive and analytical information. Thus, the new trend in comparative study laid stress on the study of environmental factors. Which influence the administrative institutions.

2. Political Approach

The political approach to the study of public administration developed only as a reaction against the traditional or non-political approach. The traditional or non-political approach laid stress on politics—administration dichotomy i.e. both of them are separate subjects and can be studied independent of each other. The political approach on the other hand rejected this politico-administrative dichotomy' view of traditional school. This approach held that administration cannot be an end in itself, rather it is a means to an end. It cannot isolate itself from its social and political background which exerts a deep influence. On the study of administrative behaviour.

Political approach is represented by the behavioral method and Human relations method.

(a) Behavioural Method

The behavioral method passed its way in public administration during the forties i.e. 1940's. It established its credential as a reaction to the institutional and historical method of traditional approach. It laid stress on the study of individual and collective human behaviour in administrative problems. Administrative problems are looked upon from an inter-disciplinary view point and stress was laid on solution of those problems by taking into account the socio-political background.

According to **Smithburg**, the behavioral method of study of public administration has the following four main characteristics:

(i) It gives increased attention to the individual and his relationship to the administrative organisation.

(ii) It studies the administrative organisation as a social system and gives equal attention to both formal and informal behaviour and relationship of man;

(iii) It gives more attention to the informal means of communication than to the formal ones; and

(iv) It laid emphasis on administrative leadership and motivation.

Mary Parker Follet, Elton Mayo, Herbert Simon and Douglas McGregor were the chief exponents of behavioral methods.

Besides these, the political approach is also supported by the Human-Relations Method.

(b) Human Relations Method

The political approach to the study of public administration also is approached the administrative organisation from human relations point of view. This human relations method is the direct offshoot of the behavioural analysis. Elton Mayo is considered as the chief votary of this human relations method. It considered the human factor as the most important element that shapes the functioning of administrative machinery.

This method held that a good administrative organisation must recognize the creativeness in its employees and the employees must not be considered to be more cog in the administrative machine. Thus, it laid stress on leadership quality as an instrument for success of the organisation. It also laid stress that administration must be accountable to the employees and it must come up to the expectations of the employees. This method strongly advocates good working conditions, reasonable wages, equal payment, assistance in case of disability etc., for success of organisation.

Although all the above methods used for the study of public administration, yet none of them is complete by itself. The various approaches and methods complement and supplement each other and provide a real insight into the complex nature of public administration.

Chapter III

PHYSIOLOGY OF ADMINISTRATION

INTRODUCTION

After conceptualizing the concept of public administration, a student is somewhat satisfied that public administration is really an instrument for the service of the people. Instead of looking into their profit, administration always leans towards the general public, although it is not profitable on the part of the administration. Caring for the people and managing their affairs with cooperation and planning is the element in administration which elevate it to the position of 'Public' in contrast to 'Private' administration. Any reader can satisfy himself that the purpose of a welfare state could definitely be chalked out only with and through public administration.

When public administration cares so much for the people, it generally interests a person to know the A, B, C, of the administration and that of the administrative phenomena. The administration itself and the phenomena on which it operates can best be understood when one does deeply into the physiology of administration.

As we know that administration deals with getting things done, it gives us an idea that administration generally operates on two basic principles such as:

(a) there is a goal or purpose; and

(h) there is a technique to achieve the goal.

It is well known to a student of public administration that goal or purpose of administration is service to the people. As the goal is already set, so all eyes concentrate on the 'technique' to achieve the goal. The 'technique' to achieve the goal is first to devise a 'structure' with the help of man and available material through which the purpose can easily be achieved. This or creation of 'administrative structure' for the accomplishment of the purpose is called "Organisation". Therefore, every administration revolves round the 'Organisation' only and exclusively through which the goals can be accomplished.

WHAT IS ORGANISATION?

As administration involves the cooperative efforts by a number of individuals to achieve the goal set by administration itself, it therefore starts with devising an administrative structure called 'organisation'. Thus, organisation is a means to an end, but not an end itself. It is the administrative structure set up for the attainment of goals. An insight into the organisation would definitely throw light on the physiology of administration.

Organisation, in common usage, means the act of putting things in proper places with working order. But in the terminology of public administration, organisation is used in three different senses:

(a) It denotes to the structure. For example: the organisation of Education department.

(b) It denotes to the technique of designing an administrative structure. For example: Nehru is the architect of modern India. This approach definitely laid stress on 'planning' as organisation.

(c) It denotes the planning and building up of the administrative structure. This approach, thus includes both men and material as the essential elements of organisation.

Among the three views, we held the third view as the most

appropriate view of organisation because it highlights the essential components of an organisation, the combined efforts of which make the attainment of goal easy.

Although the above views represent the general angle of approach to an organisation, yet some particular angle of approach is also designed to define organisation in its broadest sense. Some of the definitions of organisation are compiled below:

Definitions

1. **J.D. Mooney** – "Organisation is the form of every human association for the attainment of a common purpose."
2. **L.D. White** – "Organisation is the arrangement of personnel for facilitating the accomplishment of some agreed purpose through allocation of functions and responsibilities.
3. **Milward** – "Organisation structure is a pattern of inter-related posts connected by line of delegated authority."
4. **Pfiffner** – "Organisation consists of the relationship of individual to individuals and of groups which are so related as to bring about an orderly division of labour."
5. **Herbert Simon** – "Organisation means a planned system of cooperative efforts in which each participant has a recognized role to play and duties and tasks to perform."

An analysis of the above definitions leads us to conclude that although to a layman, organisation mean only the structure, yet to an expert as well as to a student of public administration, organisation refers to the timely combination of men, and materials and utilization of their services through supervision, coordination, planning and control to achieve the desired objectives.

ASPECTS OF ORGANISATION – FORMAL AND INFORMAL

Organisation, as we know, involves two elements – the element of mechanisation and the element of humanisation. These two elements are really named after the two theories forwarded about organisation i.e. the mechanistic theory and the humanistic theories about organisational structure. On the basis of these theories, there are two aspects of organisation—the formal organisation and the informal organisation.

Formal Organisation

The people who believe in mechanistic theory believes that organisation is only a machine consists of different elements of parts. Each part of the machine has to perform a specific function. The machine can function effectively if the various parts can be arranged in systematic manner and put to use. As such, these people held that as the machine and its parts can very well neatly be diagrammed on the basis of which the machine can build up, similar is the case of administrative organisation. The mechanistic theory of organisation, therefore, held that organisation is a machine which consists of different elements and it can function effectively when all the elements starts functioning. The structure of organisation can very well be diagramed by the organisational engineers which can be known from the organisational chart, work flow etc.

This mechanistic view of organisation thus, highlight only the formal aspect of organisational structure and as such is known by the name formal organisation.

By formal organisation, thus we mean the organisation which is formally and deliberately planned, designed and duly sanctioned by the competent authority. It approached organisation from the mechanical angle and held that the structure and function of organisation could be known from organisational chart, work flow, manuals and rules etc. Therefore, formal organisation depicts the view of organisation as observed from outside by a lay man.

Informal Organisation

The informal organisation is based on the humanistic theory of administrative organisation. The humanistic theory of organisation stands in sharp contrast to the mechanistic theory of organisation. While the mechanistic theory did not give any emphasis to the individual elements of an organisation, the humanistic theory, on the other hand, is very keen and particular about this aspect. This theory rejects the mechanistic approach on the ground that it completely ignored the human elements in administration. The mechanistic theory wrongly assumed that organisation is a machine, which can be understood by nearing the diagram of organisation with the help of organisational chart, workflow, manuals and rules.

On the other hand, the people who advocates humanistic theory held that organisation consists, not of lifeless elements, but of human beings who are guided more by their emotions, sentiments and ethos. They have their rational value judgement which they apply in their relation with other human beings. Thus, to the humanists, administrative organisation consists of a complex web of social relationship. The proper functioning of organisation depends not upon arranging the various elements into different positions but upon tactfully using the emotional human values in their organisational dealings with each other. Thus, it laid stress on informal human values instead of rigorous rigid principles based on formal organisation. This humanistic view of organisation is also known as the informal view of administrative organisation.

The **informal organisation**, thus views the functioning of organisation in terms of patterns of actual human behaviour who compose it. Therefore, if there is a good deal of coordination and cooperation among the employees on the one hand and between the employees and authority on the other hand, resulting in smooth exercise of supervision, direction and control then only the organisation can achieve its goal effectively. As behaviour of a person is situational, so we cannot predetermine the behaviour of personnels in an organisation as expected by formal organisation.

The informal organisation, therefore strategically emphasise on the cultivation of informal relationship such as inter-personal trust, cooperation, coordination, supervision, control, planning etc. in any organisation. It therefore advocates that leadership, in an organisation can function effectively through consent of the employees and not based on authority. It, thus highlights the inter-personal behaviour in the superior-subordinate relationship as an effective instrument to determine the efficiency of any administrative organisation.

Thus, to sum up, while formal organisation views organisation as a layman from outside, the informal organisation, on the other hand, is more practical and thorough in its outlook which views organisation as an export from within the organisation itself.

Distinction between Formal and Informal Organisation

Both the formal and informal organisations are contrary to each other. While the formal organisation deals with the organisational structures, informal organisation deals with the proper functioning of the organisational structure with the help of informal communication process.

The distinction between the formal and informal organisation are of general importance which strengthen the idea of both the concepts in the mind of the student of public administration.

Pfiffner and **Sherwood** have depicted the following distinctions between formal and informal organisations.

Formal Organisation	*Informal Organisation*
1. It is traditional in nature	1. It is dynamic in nature
2. It is concerned with structures.	2. It is concerned with the functions.
3. It lais stress on Hierarchy.	3. It lais stress on Coordination.

4. It views Organisation at a bureaucratic structure.	4. It views Organisation as a social institutition
5. It consider Organisation as a mechanical process.	5. It consider Organisation as a human process.
6. It held that efficiency increases by putting the various elements in proper places.	6. It held that efficiency increases by proper coordination and cooperation between the elements.
7. It wants to control the Organisation through command.	7. It wants to Control the Organisation through communication.
8. Leadership is based on authority.	8. Leadership is based on consent.
9. It believes in politics-administration dichotomy.	9. It believes in politics-administration continuum.
10. It is incomplete and leads to delay in information flow.	10. It is complete and leads to free flow of Information.

However, to conclude, a general question may arise in mind as to which is the best between the formal and informal organisations? While the formal structure emphasises the importance of forms, structures, methods and procedures, the informal organisation emphasises the importance of informal communication, coordination and cooperation. Actually none of these can be considered as mutually exclusive alternative. **Dimock and Dimock** has rightly opined that formal organisation is likely to be inaccurate and incomplete. It is not connected to informal organisation. Therefore, an effective organisation is one which blends successfully the elements of both 'formal and 'informal' organisation. For instance, while we must have a well defined system of positions, functions and relationships, we should also have the unity of command, the citizen's participation in management.

BASES OF ORGANISATION

From the above discussion, we come to know that to build up an organisational structure is the first and foremost task before public administration in order to achieve its goal which it has set for itself. Now question arises as to what are the basis on which administrative organisations could be developed. The 'base' of an Organisation, therefore, refers to the 'edifice' on which the whole structure stands. An efficient organisation need to have a strong base i.e. there must be sufficient ground for constructing the organisational structure. By convention, we have only 4 bases of organisation that deals with 4 P's—purpose, process, persons and place.

1. Purpose or Function

The first base on which the Organisation develops is related to the purpose or functions. Every organisation has a goal or purpose and in order to fulfill those goal, it has to perform certain functions. Thus, on the basis of functions, sometimes the organisations are developed. For example: The Human Resource Development Ministry is organized to promote education among the people. Besides this, certain other ministries in India are organized on functional basis. Some of them are the Ministries of Defence, Railway, Post and Telegraph, Health, Home, Food Processing, Industries, Agriculture etc.

2. Process

Another base on which administrative organisations are developed is called 'Process'. The term 'Process' in ordinary sense refers to continuity. But in administrative vocabulary, the term 'Process' refers to a specialized skills in vogue such as Engineering, Doctors, Typist, Stenography, Carpentry, Accounting etc. Among these specialized professions some are considered to be more important like the engineering, accounting, doctor etc. At the same time there are certain non-important or minor skills are also there like stenography, typing, carpentry etc. Among all these specialized techniques, importance is given only to major skills and the organisational structure is always constructed on the basis of that major skill. The administrative organisations are never constructed on the edifice of minor skills like typing, stenography etc. For instance, there is a Public works department which consists only of Engineers. But there is no such department consisting of typists only.

Sometimes one may ask question why Organisations are not based on 'Minor' process. The answer lies with the distinction between the 'Major' and 'Minor' processes. A major process is one which requires specialized knowledge and technical ability to grasp the technique. All are not endowed with this technique. So anybody cannot be a Engineer if he want. But any body can be a 'typist' if he wants. Therefore, while organizing the structures on the basis of process or technical skill, importance is given only on 'Major' skills.

However, the number of organisations based on process is very few. The examples of process-based organisations are the Ministry of Law and Justice, Urban Development, Electronics Space Research etc.

3. Persons or Clientele

Another base of administrative organisation is 'Clientele' or persons to be served. In such type of Organisation emphasis is laid on the category of persons and stress is also there to include more and more persons in the scope of operation of the Organisation. The all-round development of the 'Clientele' is the chief aim of the organisations. For example: The Welfare Ministry is organized to serve the interest of the Scheduled Castes and Scheduled Tribes people.

4. Place or Area

Again , sometimes, area or territory serves as the base of administrative organisation. The organisation is constructed to include a wide range of area and it took up for consideration the variety of problems in these areas. The operation of these organisations thus very wide and vast and as such it requires special attention of the administrator in charge of the organisation. For example, the Ministry of External Affairs is based on territory consideration. It deals with relation of India with other foreign states. The proper functioning of the organisations based on 'area' principle depends on decentralization of powers. Therefore, India have 'Embassies' in almost all the states with which India has a relation and these 'Embassies' functions under the direct control and supervision of the Ministry of External Affairs.

Although in overall view, the administrative organisations are based on the above four principles yet, a keen study reveals that none of the organisations base entirely on any one principle. In actuality, every governmental organisation make use of several, if not all, of the four bases at different level and in different times because sticking to any particular principle would cause numerous difficulties that would act as a stumbling block in the successful working of governmental organisations.

PRINCIPLES OF ORGANISATION

Every organisation requires proper base in order to be constructed. After the organisation is organized successfully, it starts functioning in order to achieve the goal. Every organisation—government or private, have their own style of functioning. However, there are also certain broad principles which are universally valid and found to have been the corner stone of these administrative organisation. Whether private or government, large or small. Thus 'principles' are the basic idea on the basis of which the organisation runs. The various universal principles which have their ways not only in private enterprises but also in governmental organisations are as follows: the principle of hierarchy, the principle of span of control, unity of command, delegation, centralisation, Decentralization and Coordination.

1. Principle of Hierarchy

The effective functioning of any organisation depends upon communication. Communication means keeping both the superior and subordinate informed. The successful flow of communication in any organisation is based on the principle of Hierarchy.

Although, literally the term 'hierarchy' means the line of control, yet in administrative sense, hierarchy means the control of the higher over the lower. As I told you that hierarchy is basically a system through which all communications flows in the organisation, so hierarchy can be defined as the 'process of communication' through which both superior and subordinate are kept informed about what is going on in the organisation."

Hierarchy, in any system of organisation, involves two types of communication—the upward communication and the downward communication. Upward communication means the flow of information and other relevant facts from the subordinate, in a ascending order, to the superior. Thus, hierarchy in one sense, means keeping the superior informed about what is going on in the organisation. Downward communication means the flow of orders and administrative decisions, in a descending order, from the superior to the inferiors. Thus, considering from the other angle, the principle of hierarchy refers to the actual line of control by the superior to the inferiors. The basic purpose of downward communication is to achieve coordination among the subordinates and to integrate the whole system of administration into a single unit so that the organisation achieves its goal.

In actuality, every organisation, for administrative conveniences, division into a number of divisions. Each division is again subdivided into a number of sub-divisions. This process continues till each base has to perform only one function. This division of responsibility and division of work, thus resulted in specialization of functions and thereby help in the speedy disposal of the function which they have to perform. The superior, in such a case, keeps only an supervision over the functioning of his immediate base and if necessary, gives direction and thereby controls the subordinate base. Besides, he also communicates the performance of the bases under his supervision, to this immediate authority and this process continues, till the information reaches the chief executive. Similarly the administrative decisions and orders of the chief executive are communicated to the bases through the intermediary superiors. This process of communication of information and command travels either in a ascending order or in a descending order is called the principle of hierarchy.

This flow of orders and direction, in an organisation can be chaled out in the diagram as follows:

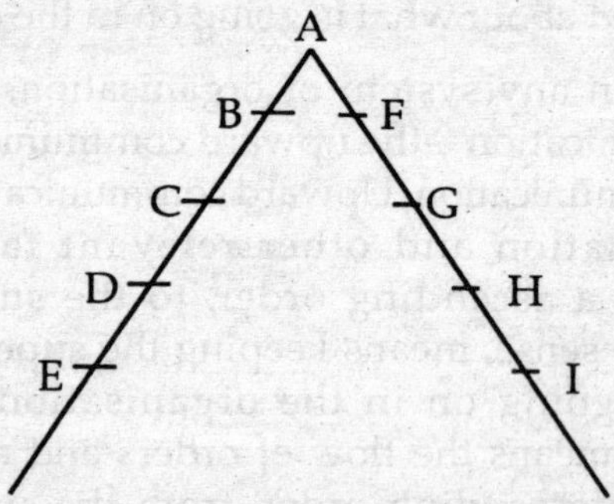

Principle of Hierarchy

As the information and command flows in a step by step method, the process is also known as the **scalar system**. From the above diagram, it is obvious that orders and decisions flows in a descending order i.e. from a (the Chief Executive) to E (base subordinate) through the channels of B, C and D, who are considered as immediate subordinates of A, B, and C respectively. The flow of information in a similar way moves upward travelling from E through D, C, and B to A the chief executive. The flow of communication from A to I and vice-versa refers to the various divisions of an organisation.

The basic purpose of those scalar process or the hierarchical system is to keep both the superior and subordinate informed. It, therefore, wants to strengthen the superior-subordinate relationship. As the process moves from one channel to another without skipping the intermediary channel, it is also called the "**system through proper channel**."

Advantages of Hierarchy

The principle of hierarchy or the scalar process has the following merits or advantages:

(1) It helps in the free flow of information and orders along the line through proper channel.

(2) It helps in integrating the activities of various units and sub-units of an organisation into a concrete whole.

(3) It leads to functional specialization. Each base is devoted to its own function and is not at all concerned with the activities of other base.

(4) It makes both the superior and subordinate conscious about what is going on in the organisation.

(5) The system of proper channel serves as a basis of superior-subordinate relationship and thereby it teaches the subordinate about the principle of discipline which is highly essential for any administration.

(6) It inducts into the subordinates the sense of duty and responsibility the effective discharge of which leads the organisation to success.

(7) It helps in decentralization of powers and authority in a downward direction. This definitely boost up the morale of the subordinate staffs who felt satisfied that at least, their views have also weightage in the organisation.

(8) It simplifies the process of administration through the simple and easy method of file movement.

Disadvantages of Hierarchy

Although the principle of hierarchy has several merits, yet it is not altogether free from flaws. It has the following demerits also:

(1) It causes unnecessary delay in the disposal of work because every work has to pass through proper channel.

(2) It may lead to superiority complex among the superiors and inferiority complex among the inferiors which is detrimental to the successful working of organisation.

(3) It also leads to red-tapism in file disbursement thereby it causes unnecessary inconveniences to the ordinary people for the sake of whom the administration exists.

(4) The scalar process do not allow communication in a horizontal line i.e. from one division to another division and allows only vertical communication.

Alternatives

However, in order to avoid the several disadvantages of scalar process, **Henri Fayol** suggested that there must be shortcut in the information flow. His views, when represented diagrammatically looks like a pyramid which is shown below:

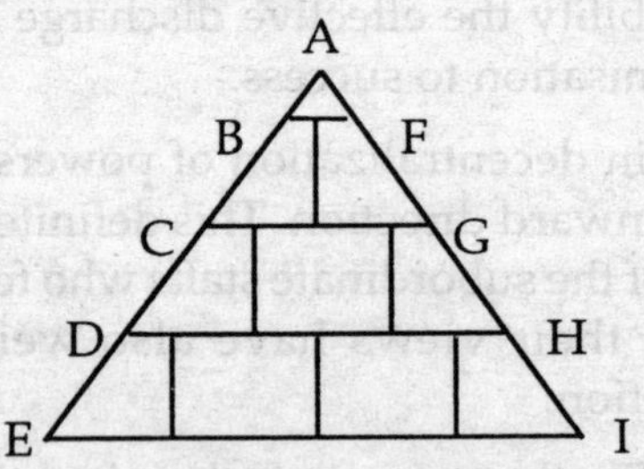

An analysis of the pyramidical structure of Henri Fayol reveals two short-cuts in the flow of communication. They are as follows:

(a) that E can have direct contact with c and vice versa provided D is kept informed about the activities and the content of discussion between C and E.

(b) that E can contact I directly instead of travelling along the vertical upward mobility provided their immediate superiors i.e. D and H respectively are kept informed about their intention and the content of discussion between them i.e. between E and I.

However, in spite of the several defects and shortcomings, the scalar process has long remained as the unbeaten principle along which every administrative organisation revolves.

Span of Control

As the organisation is based on the superior-subordinate relationship, the efficiency of organisation depends upon the integration of activities of both the superiors and the inferiors. Actually the function of subordinate is to carry out the direction and orders given by the superior. Similarly, the function of superior is not only to give orders but also to see that those orders are being carried on by the subordinates effectively. Thus, the superior has to perform a heterogeneous function. As the superior is entrusted with the task of getting things done, he has to perform it with the help of leadership traits such as supervision, control and coordination.

In every organisation, importance is always given in the function of the superiors because the efficiency of organisation depend on them. It is the superiors to decide over whom supervision is to be exercised. However, the number of subordinates over whom the superior has to exercise control is one of the most intrinsic problem of organisation. This is called the span of control.

Thus, span of control is a principle which relates only to the superiors. It has nothing to do with the subordinates or their functions. 'Span' necessarily mean the 'areas' or ' number '. In administrative usages, the term 'span of control' refers to the number of persons to be controlled and supervised effectively by a superior. 'Span of control' is therefore, essentially a process involving the superior-subordinate relationship through supervision, command, control and direction.

However, there is no unanimity among the scholars as to what is the exact number of Subordinates that are effectively supervised, controlled and directed by the superior without any hindrances. While **Hamilton** fixes the number of subordinates between 3 to 4, **Haldane** and **Graham Wallace** considers that span of control varies from 8 to 12 number of subordinates depending upon the situation. However, Urwick gave a dynamic view on span of control when he says that at the higher level of Organisation the span of control should be between 5 to 6 and at the lower level of organisation, it should be raised to 8 to 10.

However, the span of control in any administrative organisation is not static rather it is dynamic. It depends on the following factors:

(a) Functions

Span of control in any organisation depends on the nature of work to be performed. If the organisation has to perform similar functions of homogeneous nature, then the span of control is definitely more. For example, an Engineer can supervise the activities of engineers effectively than the activities of the doctors. Similarly when the experior has to supervise a heterogeneous activities, then the number of controlled subordinates would tend to decrease. For instance if the executive has to supervise not only over the engineers, but also over the doctors and teachers as well as general employees, then the span of control is less. Therefore, the nature of function determines the extent of span of control.

(b) Efficiency

The extent of span of control is also, to a large extent, shaped by the efficiency of superior as well as subordinates. If the superior is a man of farsightedness and enthusiastic, he can supervise over more number of subordinates. But at the same time, the subordinates too, equally have to be energetic and enduring. If, on the contrary, the subordinates are lethargic and idle, then the superior has to devote his whole time in providing them with enthusiasm and direction. This greatly affects the organisation and reduces span of control.

(c) Size of the Organisation

The size of the organisation also determines, to a great extent the span of control. If the organisation is too large in size, then the nature of works to be supervised also increases and this reduces the number of subordinates to be supervised effectively without hindrances. On the other hand, if the organisation is small in size, then the nature of functions to be performed are small. This increases the ability of the supervisor to control and direct more number of subordinates. In a medium organisation, the span of control varies accordingly.

(d) Age of the Organisation or Experience

The age of organisation also determines the span of control. If the organisation is quite old and is acquainted itself with the customary and conventional rules, then span of control increase. This is because the superior have acquired the traits of controlling more and more number of subordinates from his experience. Similarly if the organisation is born recently, then its superior has not yet gained sufficient experience and therefore, his span of control stands very small.

(e) Place

The span of control is also determined by the place or area where the organisation operates and the supervisor exercises control. If the supervisor has to control the subordinates under the same roof or under a compact and continuous area, then definitely he is able to supervise and control the activities of more number of subordinates. At the same time, if the superior has to travel a long distance to exercise supervision over the subordinates and where there is no direct link between the subordinates themselves due to geographical factors, the span of control, reduces significantly.

(f) Nature of Organisation

Finally, the span of control is also determined by the nature of organisation. If the organisation is highly a centralized one, like that of military organisation, it requires a close and more vigilant eye over the activities of the subordinates. This decreases the number of subordinates to be supervised. On the other hand, if the organisation is highly decentralized are, then the span of control is essentially more.

Difference between Hierarchy and Span of Control

The difference between the principle of hierarchy and span of control lies with the following point.

HIERARCHY	*SPAN OF CONTROL*
1. It is a principle on the basis of which the administrative structures organized.	1. It is a process through which the administrative organizations operate.
2. It refers to communication – both command and information.	2. It refers to supervision and control.
3. It is concurred with the structures only – both superior and subordinates.	3. It is concerned with the functions of the superiors only.
4. It determines the course of action in an organization.	4. It is being determined by the course of action in an organization.
5. It decides the functions of subordinates	5. It decides the extent of subordinates i.e. their numbers.

UNITY OF COMMAND

Another principle that is in vogue in administrative organisations is the principle of "Unity of command". However, this term is quite dynamic and have different interpretations in administrative organisation.

The term 'unity of command' is derived from military vocabulary where it means that 'command should flow along the line of authority'. Therefore, from a layman's point of view, unity of command resembles the principle of hierarchy where also command flows in the chains in a descending order. But actually there is a difference between them and the difference is only of degree, not of kind.

The dynamic meaning of unity of command, in administrative usages have arisen due to the peculiar problems face by administrative organisations. Actually every organisation has to perform a duality of functions such as administrative function and technical functions. As technical functions cannot be done by a layman, so every organisation has to secure the service of various technical staffs. However, problem arise as to whom the technical staffs should obey. Actually the technical staffs have their technical superior to whom they are responsible and also answerable. At the same time, they are also under the control of administrative superior to whom they have to obey and whose order they have to carry out. For example: an Engineer, when employed in the Block Level, have two superiors. Administratively, he is under the control of the block development officer (BDO) and technically he is under the control of the Chief Engineer of his dept. who does not necessarily employed in the block. Thus, confusion lies here and the problem arise when there is more than one superior, to whom the subordinate bow down?

No doubt all are agree that a subordinate is to obey one superior only at a time, yet confusion arise as to who is the superior to whom one must obey? This gives rise to various meaning of unity of command.

The general view held among the scholars is that by 'unity of command', we mean, 'that no individual employee is subject to the orders of more than one immediate superior'.

J.D. Millet held that in administrative organisation, unity of command means two things:

(a) it is an arrangement whereby all administrative authority flows from one responsible head i.e. the president or governor etc.;

(b) it means that there should be only one person and not a body of persons at the apex of the organisation, and all line of authority should concentrate on his hand.

Thus, Millet stressed the merit of a single-headed organisation in comparison with the board or commission system of organisation.

However, although the existence of dual heads i.e. technical head and administrative head creates confusion in the mind about the authority to whom the subordinate should be responsible, yet the matter is not out of solution. In reality, the 'technical superiors' are only technical advisors who render advice to the head of the organisation i.e. the administrative heads. Thus, they are not in the chain of command. Therefore, the technical staffs should obey the administrative heads only and carry out their direction.

Again, an employee should not receive orders from more than one superior in respect of the same subject does not mean that an employee cannot receive orders and guidance from different superiors in different matters and also in different times.

However, one thing should always be kept in mind that one superior, who gives direction and orders should not give conflicting and contradictory orders to the same subordinate at the same time. It means there should be consistency and unity in the orders given by the superior to the subordinate.

DELEGATION

Division of Work

Every administrative organisation is based on superior-subordinate relationship, each having a specified area of operation. The efficiency of administrative organisation always depends upon the honest and timely performance of their respective duties. However, a question may arise in mind that whether, in an organisation, the tasks are equally divided between the superiors and the subordinates or not? The reality is that although there is a division of work and responsibility between the superior and subordinates, yet the division is not of the same degree. While the superiors are assigned with more supervisory and less manual functions, the subordinates, on the other hand are assigned with more manual and less supervisory work. The concentration of more supervisory function make the officer superior and the aggregation of more manual and clerical function make the incumbent a subordinate. This is the normal division of work between the superior and subordinates in any organisation.

Although division of work is a feature of administration, yet it cannot be equated with the concept of 'delegation'. Division of work involves a thorough and systematic separation of functions based on legal and formal method. But delegation always and very often leads to giving away of functions through informal means.

The term 'delegation' means 'to give away' or ' to assign with'. It is always an interpersonal activity that involves a thorough and systematic separation of functions based on legal and formal method. But delegation always and very often leads to giving away of functions through informal means.

The term 'delegation' means 'to give away' or ' to assign with'. It is always an interpersonal activity that involves the superior-subordinate relationship. I have already told earlier that the supervising power. However, the superior has to perform two functions. Firstly, it has to supervise the activities of the subordinates and secondly, it has to get the things done at an earliest possible time. There is always the concentration of power and authority at the superior. But the superior cannot exercise those authority by himself. For the purpose of getting the things done, he delegates some of his powers and authority to his subordinates, but having the ultimate power of supervising their functions. This is called delegation.

Delegation of power and authority does not mean the delegation of responsibility. Responsibility is inalienable. Thus, an administrator has the responsibility of accomplishing the total activities assigned to him, though he assigns some of the activities of him to the subordinates.

Delegation necessarily involves the assignment of the power of decision making upon the subordinates. Although decisions are made by the administrator, yet the moment he delegates his powers to the subordinate, he assigns with the subordinate the power of making decision according to situation. Delegation of power without the power of decision making is always futile.

Thus, to sum up, although all authority, legally belongs to the head of the organisation, he cannot perform them all by himself. For successful performance of those authority, he delegates some of his authority and powers to his subordinates. However, he retains a general supervision over the activities of these subordinates. Thus he transfers the powers and duties to his assistants without losing the ultimate power of revision, supervision and control, himself. This is called delegation.

Delegation involves dual authority. Firstly, that the subordinates to do the job and secondly, that the superior to get the job done through supervision.

Delegation arises from two factors: – a) because no heads can actually exercise all powers vested in him; and b) because without delegation, the subordinates would not be able to do their work.

Sometimes, the superiors, being very efficient and hard

working, are reluctant to delegate powers because they thought that no one can do the job so well than themselves. On the contrary, sometimes, the superiors, being reluctant to take responsibility, delegates all his powers to the subordinates. Actually both these extremes are bad. The true and efficient authority, always pursues a middle course i.e. he is neither reluctant nor eager to delegate, but he is ready to do so when needed.

The best example of delegation in India is that of the delegation of powers by the president to his council of ministers, though, theoretically all powers belong to him.

Types of Delegation

Delegation may be full or partial. Full delegation means complete renunciation of power by the superior and its thorough confirmation upon the subordinates. Partial delegation means conferment of only few powers upon the subordinates depending upon the situation.

Delegation may be **conditional** or **unconditional**. Conditional delegation means although the power are conferred upon the subordinate, yet the superior has the power to revise it depending upon the performance of subordinate. Unconditional delegation means the superior cannot interfere with the powers delegated, although it can revoke or annul it.

Delegation may be **formal** or **informal**. When the delegation of powers and authority takes a formal shape through embodiment in some written laws and rules, it is called formal delegation. Informal delegation, on the other hand, based on customs, understanding and conversation. It does not have any written element.

Delegation may be direct or indirect. In a direct delegation no third party come to play any role. But in indirect delegation, the delegation is made through an intermediate like. Example:- delegation of ruling power to the US president through the electoral college.

Plus Points in Delegation

Delegation has the following advantages to its credits:

(1) delegation creates a systematic division of work between the superior and subordinates. While more important functions are done by superior, less important functions are carried on by the subordinates.

(2) It develops an increased sense of responsibility among the subordinates and thereby enhance their work capabilities.

(3) It develops a cordial and trustworthy relationship between the superior and subordinates.

(4) It leads to efficiency in the administrative organisation.

(5) It eliminates unnecessary delay and red tapism in the organisation.

(6) It ensures smooth running of administrative organisation.

To conclude, delegation is successful instrument used by the superior to maximize the efficiency of organisation and to get the work done by the subordinates effectively by supervising and controlling their activities in the organisation.

CENTRALIZATION AND DECENTRALIZATION

Every organisation involves, to a greater extent, power, rule and authority. There is a simple relationship between these factors i.e. the authority rules the organisation through power. Thus importance is laid always on power. Power is a relative concept which is always situational, interpersonal and behavioural. The concept of "power" always rules supreme in the interpersonal activity between superior and subordinate. As the effective functioning of organisation depends on prompt decisions making, question arises as to who is competent to make a decisions and to what extent? No doubt, it is the superior who takes decisions and subordinates who carry out them .But it is also a fact that the superior cannot take all the decisions by himself because it overburdens him.

To solve this question, it is suggested that the superior should decide only in case of important matters and power of decisions making should be delegated to the subordinate agencies in case of non-important matters .When there is the concentration of power of decision-making at the superior or center, it is called centralization. On the contrary, the disbursement of the power decision making at the subordinate or field level, is called decentralization.

What is Centralisation?

In its broadest sense, centralization refers to the concentration of power of decision making at the hands of center. Thus, in a centralized system of organisation, the subordinates or the field unit have to refer to the center for all problems and ask its help for its solution. They cannot make independent decisions of their own. There is the delegation of power to the unit only in limited area. At the same time , the center or superior has the power to reverse or withdraw these powers.

Merit of Centralisation

The scholars, who advocated the centralization system, put forth the following plus points in favour of centralization. They are as follows:

(a) Centralization leads to effective functioning of administration as communication flows downwards. As such it leads to efficiency in administration.

(b) Centralization acts as a check against inefficiency, waste and nepotism because the persons involved in decision making are usually of high calibre, more experienced and dynamic in their outlook.

(c) Centralization helps in stabilizing financial administration in the organisation.

(d) Centralization leads to security of the century more tight and economic planning more rigorous, thereby leading the organisation towards success.

Demerits of Centralisation

Centralization has also the following several flows for which it is criticized by scholars.

(a) Centralization leads to bottleneckness and causes delay in decision-making.

(b) It kills the incentive to work by the field units as they cannot take any independent decision.

(c) Centralization is highly defective because the local problems can be easily solved by local units. But centralization wants to solve the local problems directly by directing from the centre.

(d) Centralization reduces the opportunities for popular initiative to participate in administration directly. This definitely weaken democracy at its base.

What is Decentralisation?

Decentralization is just opposite centralization. It gives more power to the field units in matters of decision making. Only matter of high importance is required to be referred to the centre. Therefore, the local units enjoy a good deal of autonomy in administration, subject to final supervision by the centre. Only essential powers are concerted at the centre, leaving more powers to the fields. It laid stress on popular participation in decision making process by giving autonomy to local elective bodies to solve their local problems through local resources. Decentralization emphasizes coordination and cooperation at the fields as an essential element of organisational structure.

Merits of Decentralisation

(a) Decentralization helps in solving the problems of organisation more effectively as it provides solution after a thorough understanding of the local situation.

(b) It provides the field units with incentive to work by allowing greater autonomy for them.

(c) It helps in prompt decision making and taking quick action to check the problem before it spreads.

(d) It is an instrument of popular participation in administration.

(f) It increases organisational autonomy and thus relieves the burden of centralization.

Demerits of Decentralisation

In spite of several merits, decentralization has also its drawbacks. They are as follows:

(a) Too much decentralization may lead to anarchy because it makes coordination and integration of administration activities difficult.

(b) It may lead to inefficiency, waste and nepotism in organisation.

(c) It kills the superior-subordinate relationship and try to tilt the balance in later's favour.

(d) It reduces the importance of centre in comparison to the fields.

(e) It cannot effectively control the financial administration which requires a more centralized process.

The Balance

To conclude, centralization or decentralization involves the problem of relationship between the higher and lower levels of an organisation in matters of decision making. Neither of the principle can be accepted as the sole criteria to judge a good organisation. Each has its relative merits. A good organisation always strucks to the balance between these two extreme principles in order to flourish. It is based on the centralized, its administration should be decentralized.

However, whether the organisation should be centralised or decentralized depends on a variety of factors. If the organisation has to perform a task of responsibility and national importance, it requires to be centralized. If it has to deal with administrative functions, it requires to be decentralized. While decentralization is a regular feature in an old organisation, centralization becomes the governing factor, for the same reason, in a young organisation.

Similarly, while centralization is the principle of organisation involving insatiable policy, decentralization is preferred in such organisations where policy is somewhat stable and concrete. If the subordinates or field staffs are competent enough, it requires the organisation to be decentralized. But inefficiency among field staffs leads to centralized organisation.

Again, if the organisation involves technical function requires centralization, organisations having multifarious functions leads to decentralization. Last, but not the least, while popular participation leads to decentralization, popular neutralization, for the same reason, requires the organisation to be highly centralized.

TYPOLOGY OF ORGANISATION: LINE, STAFF AND AUXILIARY

Every administrative organisation operates to fulfill the goal – the goal to serve the people. The functions of administrative organisation thus commensurate with the goal. On the basis of functions which an organisation performs, there can be three broad classifications of administrative organisation—the line, the staff and the auxiliary one.

Willoughby was the first person who divided the governmental activities into two parts—the primary or functional activities and the secondary or institutional activities. The primary activities are those which an organisation performs in order to accomplish the purpose for which it exists. For example, the purpose of ministry of railway is to connect different places through rail-roads. For the accomplishment of this purpose the ministry is divided into various wings and divisions i.e. South-eastern Railway, Central Railway etc. the arrangement of organisation in a hierarchical order to fulfill the purpose is called the line organisation. The secondary or institutional activities are those which are necessary for the performance of services by the organisation. For example the ministry of railway has to take on certain activities like construction of railway station, rail tracks, purpose of rolling stocks etc. in order to connect the different places through rail-roads. Therefore, the secondary functions act as an aid to the first function. These functions are not an end in itself, but a means to an end. The arrangement in the organisation to help the line organisation in achieving its purpose is called the **staff organisation**.

Besides these two main types of organisation, another type of organisation can be traced out which exists to perform the manual functions of the organisation and thereby relieves the burden of both line and staff organisation. These are called **Auxiliary Organisations**.

Line Organisation

We come to know from the above discussion that line organisations are the broad division of administrative organisation which exists to promote the primary function for which the organisation exists. The term 'line' is derived from the military vocabulary which means 'command'. Thus, the hierarchy which commands the military forces in the battle field are called ' line'. In administrative usages, the term 'line' refers to those administrative agencies which are concerned with the primary function of the organisation. For example, the ministry of education, the ministry of railway etc. are primarily organized to promote education and communication through rail-roads. Thus, they are called the line organisations.

Types

The line organisations are broadly divided into three categories depending upon the nature of authority exerts upon them by the government. They are:

(a) Department;

(b) Public Corporations; and

(c) Independent Regulatory Commissions.

(a) Department

Department is the largest and the most prevalent type of line organisation. The department is directly controlled and directed by the government. It does not have any independent existence outside the government control. The command flows downward in a line from the chief executive at the top to the mere clerk at the bottom. The examples are – the department of Home Affairs , Foreign Affairs, Defence, Education, Railway, Health etc.

(b) Public Corporations

Public corporations are the new inventions by the government which is organized in the same manner as the private organisation. In a private enterprise, there are share holders, board of directors, General Manager etc. to conduct the affairs of the enterprise. Similarly, the corporation has the effective features of shareholders, board of directors as well as managing director to look into the day to day affairs of the corporation. It holds and acquires property in its own name. It can sue and be sued in the course of law. Thus, at large, the public corporations are quite different from the government department where there is excessive centralization and governmental control. But a public corporation is marked by decentralization of powers and subject to general supervision by the government. Examples – the Damodar Valley Corporation, the Life Insurance Corporation etc.

(c) Independent Regulatory Commission

A third type of line organisation is the independent Regulatory commissions which have some features of public corporation as well as some other features of governmental departments. While at the top, it has a corporate character, at the internal sphere, it has a departmental structure. Examples : Public Services Commission, Election Commission etc.

STAFF ORGANISATION

The staff organisations are the broad divisions of governmental organisation whose main function is to assist the 'line agencies' in achieving their goal. Thus, they are only the helping verbs which carry out the secondary or institutional activities of the government. The staff agencies act as a means to an end, but not an end in itself. These are the organisations which help the line organisations at large.

Like 'line' the term ' staff' has also its origin in military vocabulary. Literally, 'staff' means a stick which is carried for support. In public administration, the term ' staff' thus refers to such activities in an organisation which assist the head of the departmental organisation in the performance of his duties.

Functions

However, a general question may arise, if the staff assists or supports the line organisations, then what is the nature of function that they have to perform? Whether the 'staff' have to perform the whole body of activity that relieve the 'line' officer of his burden or it carry out only a limited number of activities which are very essential for the 'line' officer, leaving the rest to be performed by the officer himself ?

The answer is obvious. The staff organisation, as the name suggests, does not perform the whole activity as to relieve the executive of his duties and responsibilities. Rather they only confine themselves to the task of advising, planning and suggesting to the chief executive in matters of policy formulation; they never take on the manual functions which is the main function of auxiliary organisations.

According to Prof. **L.D. White**, the staff organisation has to perform the following functions:

(a) To ensure that the chief executive and other officials at the top is adequately and correctly informed.

(b) To assist him in foreseeing the problems and planning future programmes.

(c) To ensure that the matters for his decision reach his desk promptly.

(d) To protect him against hasty or ill-considered judgements.

(e) To exclude every matter that can be settled elsewhere in the system.

(f) To protect his time; and

(g) To secure means of ensuring compliance by subordinates with executive, policy and directions.

According to **Pfiffner**, the staff organisations has to perform the following broad functions:

1. Advising, teaching and consultation;
2. Coordination through plans and human contacts;
3. Fact finding and research;
4. Planning;
5. Contact and liaison;
6. Assisting the line; and
7. Sometimes, exercising delegated authority from the line commander.

J.D. Mooney, on the other hand, held that the staffs have to perform three general functions such as (i) informative; (ii) advisory; and (iii) supervisory.

The informative function of staff organisation is to collect all relevant information for the chief executive on which his decisions may be based. It includes research, study and inquiry.

The advisory function means to advise the chief executive, as to what , in its option, the decision should be.

The supervisory function means to see that the decision taken by the chief is duly communicated to, and implemented by the subordinates in the line organisation.

Features

The general knowledge about the functions of staff organisation reveals the following features of staff organisation:

1. That they have no responsibility for actual conduct of duties for which the organisation exists.
2. That they only carry on research and consultative functions and advise the chief executive in the line agency.
3. That they have no power to give orders.
4. That they do not bother whether their suggestion is accepted or not by the chief executive.

Types

The above idea about the structure and functions of staff organisation lead on to conclude that there may be two types of staff organisation s– the administrative and the technical.

The administrative or general staffs are those who advice the chief executive in general matters. They are the people of long experienced, farsightedness and vast knowledge on the basis of which they advise the executive in the line organisation.

The technical staff, on the other hand, are those who advise the chief executive in the technical matters only. These are the people who possess a deep and indepth knowledge about the technical aspect in their own sphere of specialization .

However, Pfiffner, in addition to the above two types of staffs, adds third category—the auxiliary staff . The auxiliary staffs are those who are concerned with actual conduct of functions in the organisation, and therefore, helps the line organisation in discharging its function faithfully to achieve the goal.

The examples of staff agencies in India are:—the cabinet secretariat including the prime minister's secretariat, the cabinet committees, the national development council etc.

AUXILIARY ORGANISATION

Besides the broad two categories of administrative organisation – the line and the staff, there is another organisation called the auxiliary organisation. These are the organisation which help both the line and staff organisations in performing their duties effectively.

The term 'auxiliary' as the name suggests means 'to help' or 'to aid'. Therefore, in administrative terminology, auxiliary organisations refer to those broad groups of administrative organisation exists for the sake of aiding and helping the line and staff organisations in achieving their goal. However, the peculiarity in the auxiliary agency lies in the point that it helps not to any particular line organisation but to all of them, in different situations. Their main purpose is to recruit, to train and to help the personnel in collection of data as well as to do all the major manual and clerical functions in the organisation, examples of Auxiliary organisation in India are the Planning Commission, the printing and stationary division of the government etc.

The auxiliary organisation serves the line and staff organisations instead of service the public at large. They perform functions common to all the departments.

Pfiffner did not distinguish between staff and auxiliary organisations and consider the later as a part of the former. But other scholars seem not to have agreed with them. They distinguish between them on the basis of the nature of function that each organisation performs. While staff organisations are essentially conceded with policy formulation and advising the chief executive, auxiliary organisations are concerned with the manual functions that are common to all line organisations. The activities carried on by auxiliary agencies are called the "institutional' or 'house keeping' activities by Willoughby.

Functions

The auxiliary organisations perform the following functions:

1. They render certain services of house keeping in nature i.e. essential for management to all the line organisations.
2. It relieves the 'line' officers of those duties which do not pertain to their activities. i.e. recruitment, training, data collection etc.
3. It assists the 'staff' officers in formulating policies by providing them with all the relevant information, data, fact, facts and figures etc. which are necessary for policy formulation.

Relation between Line and Staff Organisation

The line agency is concerned with the primary functions of the organisations for which it came into existence. On the other hand, the staff agency is concerned with function of planning, organisation and advise.

Although these two agencies are having different functions, yet they have a systematic relation between them. Theoretically there is a distinction between the line and staff functions. But practically, both functions may vest in one and the same person. In a small organisation, the staff and line functions are vested in the single person. In relation to his superior, a person may be a staff officer. It is also very difficult to completely separate between these functions in any organisation. No organisation is completely upon the situation.

Both the staff and line agencies coordinate each other by operating not in a hierarchical relation, but in a horizontal plane. 'The staff who does not give commands to the line is ineffectual, and a line man who does not understand the staff function is a failure."— say **Lepawsky**. Actually, the heads of "line" agencies, spend a chuck of their time in general staff work.

Thus, the relationship between the line and staff agency is one of prime importance in organisation. **Earnest Dale** held that indeed, it is the 'staffs' who exerts greater influence on 'line' at least in five ways. They are:

(a) Staff men are generally skilled in persuading others to accept their ideas.

(b) The staff specialists has technical skills and knowledge which is not possessed by line. Thus his advice is accepted by the line as legal counsel;

(c) The staffs normally consists of senior experienced specialists who have high status in the management hierarchy. This enables them to secure the acceptance of their advice;

(d) If a line executive donot agree with the staff proposal, the staff may appeal to his superior and get his proposal accepted;

(e) The line agencies may authorize the staff specialists to reach agreement in view of their knowledge and ability.

Distinction between Line and Staff

The line and staff organisations, being two separate agencies, have the following major distinctions between them:

1. Line agencies issues commands where as staff agencies issues advice to the line.
2. Line is an end in itself but staff is a means to and end.
3. Line agencies comes in direct contact with the people but the staff agencies .ies behind the screen.
4. Line agencies are executing agencies, staff agencies are advisory and consultative agencies.
5. Line agencies are issues orders down the line, but staff agencies does not enjoy that power.
6. Communication, in line agency is vertical in down ward, but communication, in staff agency is horizontal i.e. from 'staff to line' as against ' in between' the line.
7. The line agency is endowed with responsibility but the staffs donot have such responsibility.

Distinction between Line and Auxiliary

Line agencies are those who perform services in order to accomplish the purpose for which the organisation exists, auxiliary agencies are those which perform the services in order to assist the line agencies. However, the distinction between the line and auxiliary agencies are as follows:

1. While line agencies are an end in its itself, the auxiliary agencies are a means to an end.
2. Line agencies are concerned with the primary objectives of the organisation; Auxiliary agencies are concerned with the secondary objectives of the organisation.
3. Line agencies have 'functional basis'; auxiliary agencies have 'institutional' basis.
4. Line agencies comes in direct contact with the public; auxiliary agencies do not have direct access to them.
5. Line agencies implement the public policies; the auxiliary agencies do not.
6. Line agencies are primarily concerned with the functions; Auxiliary agencies are primary concerned with how economy can be maintained in the performance of those functions undertaken by the line agencies.
7. The efficiency and success of line agencies depend on the performance of proper functions by the staff and Auxiliary members; the efficiency and success of auxiliary agencies depends on the successful transaction of its responsibilities.

Distinction between Staff and Auxiliary Agencies

The distinction between staff and Auxiliary agencies are as follows:

1. Staff exists to advise the line; Auxiliary exists to assist the line in other ways except advice.

2. Staffs are planning and advising body; auxiliary agencies are the operating bodies whose main function is to purchase materials, recruitment of personnel and maintenance of accounts.
3. Staffs is concurred with policy formulation; Auxiliary agencies are not concerned with policy at all.
4. Staff laid stress on 'improvement' in the line; auxiliary agencies laid stress on 'strengthening ' the line agency.
5. Particular staff agency is linked with particular line agency and therefore, there are a number of staff agencies tending to advise the equal number of line agencies. Only one auxiliary agency is linked with many line agencies.
6. Staff agency is dealing at the top levels of the line agency, Auxiliary agency is dealing with the bottom levels of the line agency.
7. Staff agency carried on research and consultative work and therefore, are not concerned with the operational responsibilities, Auxiliary agency carried on operational work and is not concerned with research and consultative work.

To conclude, the line, staff and Auxiliary agencies are the broad nomenclatures of administrative organisation. Each has specialization of authority in their competent sphere. The efficiency of organisation depends on the successful coordination and cooperation between and among these agencies.

Chapter IV

ADMINISTRATIVE STRUCTURES

Every administrative organisation operates in environment. The environmental factors exerts a long degree of influence over the administrative process. As we know, the process of administration operates through the various line, staff and Auxiliary agencies. Among these agencies, stress is always laid on 'line agencies' which is the main unit of organisation in administration. A line agency is divided into three structural arrangement such as department, public corporation and independent Regulatory commissions

DEPARTMENT

Department is the major administrative structure on the basis of which line units are organized. Literally, the word 'department' means 'a part of'. Therefore, department refers to a part of the whole administrative organisation through which the organisation achieves its goal.

The structure of department shows that it is that type of organisation which is under the complete control and authority of the government. These structures do not enjoy any degree of independence if run by strict legal rules and administrative orders which the government determines from time to time. Discipline and regulation are the cardinal principles on the basis of which the department is structured. The government regulates the transactions of department and exercises a close and more vigilant supervision over the activities of the personnel's who compose it. The command, rules, orders and decisions flows downward in a line. The principle of hierarchy, span of control and unity of command prevails extensively in the department. In short, the department is a controlled system of administrative organisation, directed, guided, managed and runned by the government at its free will. It laid stress on formal organisational procedures instead of informal one.

Advantages

The advantages of departmental structure are as follows:

1. It simplifies the machinery of administration.
2. It gives the executive an upper hand in deciding the problems of organisation through legislation.
3. It ensures efficiency in administration because there is unity of command and principle of hierarchy.
4. It avoids the administrative fallacies like duplication of work, overlapping of functions etc. because each person has a formal sphere of work.
5. It facilitates the standardization of administrative procedures.
6. It reconciles the line of authority with responsibility and therefore, ensures an effective system of administration.

Bases of Departmental Organisation

Due to the above said advantages, most of the governmental organisations are organized into department. This arrangement of governmental organisations leads one to a pertinent question – what is the base of departmental organisation?

Actually, there is no single base of department, rather there are several bases on which departments are organized. Each base has its distinct merits and demerits. **Luther Gullick** devised the formula of AP's to represent the base of department purpose, process, persons and place.

(a) Function or Purpose

The departments are sometimes organized on the basis of broad objective or purpose. So there is a functional base of department. For instance, department of health, education, agriculture etc.

The department is further subdivided into a number of branches wings on the basis of minor purpose or functions which the department undertakes. For example, a Board of Secondary Education is only an wing of the Education department.

Again, each wing is divided into a number of divisions on the basis of nature and content of functions to be performed. For example: the text book division, the syllabus division etc. are only part of the major wing of Board of Secondary Education in the education department.

Further, each division is again subdivided into a number of sections depending upon the content of the subject. For example: the text book division may contain a section on social studies, another on English etc.

Therefore, the broad classification of a department on the basis of function may be represented diagrammatically as follows:

Department

|

Wings or Branches

|

Divisions

|

Sections

|

Individual Posts

Merits of Functional Base

The functional bases of department has the following merits –

1. It ensures efficiency because it facilitates the performance of the given task by each organs of the department.
2. It ensure economy in administration by eliminating the wastage of time and energy.
3. It reduces overlapping of functional and duplication of work.
4. It provides for functional specialization.
5. It is easy to fix up the responsibility for failure.
6. It ensures discipline in the administration because everybody will be attending to their jobs.

Demerits of Functional Base

The demerit of organisation of department on functional basis are follows:

1. It neglects the means to achieve the goal because it always laid stress on the goal or purpose itself.
2. It also tend to neglect the secondary functions which are integrated with the primary functions. For example: the education department may not give importance to the health of the student which has a direct influence on the education system itself.
3. It may lead to departmentalization of work when each will be attending to their own job. Thus, the goal as a whole is affected.

(b) Process

"Process" is also considered as a base of departmental organisation. Process means ' technique' or 'specialized knowledge'. So sometimes, departments are organized on the basis of specialized knowledge because the goal of department, being increasingly complex requires special technique to solve them. Examples: department of law, department of health, department of electronics, department of science and technology etc.

Advantages

1. It provides apprenticeship in a specialized area by utilizing the technical skill.
2. It ensures efficiency in administration by maintaining economy through the use of machines.
3. It facilitates coordination among the personnel's employed in the department because there is uniformity in their nature of work.

Disadvantages

1. It creates 'process bias' which is inimical to the development of department.
2. In its efforts to emphasize the means; it may lose the real destination i.e. the goal of the department.
3. Too much emphasis on machine instead of manual labour leads to financial extravagance instead of economy.

(c) Clientele or Persons

'Clientele' means the class or classes of people. The departments are sometimes organized on the basis of the 'classes of people it serves', such type of basis provides for an all-round development of the persons covered. For example: the welfare department is arranged on clientele basis.

Merits

It aims at the general all-around development of the persons in question, thus securing a healthy sound growth of administrative capabilities.

It generates faith of the beneficiaries upon administration that gives morale for efficient working of the department.

It helps in developing the principle of coordination not only among the beneficiaries but also between the members of a department. This gears up the momentum of administration in the department.

Demerits

The department, organized on clientele basis shows the following defects:

1. It neglects the vast majority of sections of people and concentrate only with the development of a particular section only. Therefore, it is narrow in approach.
2. The administrative authority became puzzle and therefore this retards the process of development in the society because the authority has to cater to the all-around development i.e. the heterogeneous interest of the particular people. Thereby it cannot give justice to any particular interest because a jack of all trades is a master of none .
3. It is against the principle of specialization of functions which creates apprenticeship in work.Therefore, such department cannot lead to apprenticeship.

(d) Place or Territory

The last and final base departmental organisation situation or place. The network of department based on territory is always vast and numerous. It has to coordinate the activities of its lower units in a Trans-national background. For effective and smooth functioning of these departments, the department is divided into numerous divisions, each concentrating itself on its own area of operation. However, peculiarity of these geographical base of department is that it refers only to the top level of department organisation. However , the lower unit of department still have their functional bases. For example : The Ministry of Foreign Affairs is organized on geographical base, the basic purpose of which is to conduct India's relation with foreign states. It has its numerous divisions like south-east division, far-east division, middle-east division etc.

Plus Points

1. The geographical base has a wider range of application as its covers a very long distance.
2. It facilitates the planned development of the strategic 'area' under consideration.
3. It facilitates the better adoption of policies to the needs of the area concerned.

Minus Points

1. It is difficult to maintain coordination in such a department which stretches to a vast geographical area.
2. There is no cooperation and communication between one division and another. For example: the Middle-East division do not have any idea about the problem of far-east division.
3. The delegation of power to the subordinate units may encourage hollowness and insincerity in the department organisation.

However, in spite of the above negative and positive points, the departments are organized on broad bases of functions, purpose, clientele and territory. Actually no single base is adequate for representation of department and as such more than one base is used to represent the departmental organisation.

STRUCTURAL PATTERN OF DEPARTMENT

After knowing the department from a close proximity and its base, a student of public administration would certainly take a keen interest in the pattern of structural arrangement of the department.

Headquarter

Every department is divided into two broad structures– the Headquarter and the field establishments. The headquarter and field units are arranged in a superior-subordinate relationship where each has assigned with a function. The power of headquarter is related with decision making and therefore, its function is to make all sorts of decisions with the help of staff and auxiliary agencies which it exists. On the other hand, the broad function of field units is to implement those decisions taken by the headquarter. Therefore, while headquarter is concerned with policy formulation, field establishments are concerned with policy implementation.

The headquarter is again specialized into three wings such as political wings, administrative wing and institutional wing.

(a) Political Wing

The political wing consists of the ministers popularly elected by the people, whether direct or indirect. It consists of the cabinet ministers, the minister of state and deputy ministers. The cabinet ministers outline the broad objectives of department from time to time and take all sorts of decisions for the people. However, the decision about the functions of a particular department is taken by majority of votes in the cabinet. The minister of state relieves the burden of the cabinet minister by sharing some of the responsibility in the department. But they do not play any role in decision making. The deputy ministers exists only to assist the above two ministers in discharging their functions.

(b) Administrative Wing

The administrative wing of a department includes all the bureaucrats and technocrats. These are the people who play real role of decision making by available of relevant information, data, facts and figures etc. to the concerned ministers that will be essential in decision making. These people also, through their vast experience and knowledge, suggest the ministers the ideas that is helpful for proper functioning of the department. It consists of the secretary and under secretary. They all belong either to class I or to class II or Indian Administrative Service or of state administrative service. They all arranged in a vertical division where authority and command flows in a "line" downward.

(c) Institutional Wing

The institutional wing of a department functions below the administrative wing. It refers to the broad institutional structure of a department in the headquarter. On institutional side, the department is broadly divided into a number of wing or branches. Each branch is subdivided into a number of divisions, which, further divided into a number of sections.

Normally, there are four types of sections each headed by a section officer and a number of upper division clerk, stenographer, typist and peons to assist them. They are: the diary and dispatch section, general section, field and establishment section and accounts section. Diary and dispatch section has to receive letters and dispatch papers, files etc. to other departments, to the field units as well as to the public. It also records the events of routinized transactions. General section supervises the overall activities, debate and discuss the questions affecting the department as a whole field and establishment section is concerned with the staffs and internal administration of the department. Accounts section has to prepare the estimate and reviews the expenditures of the department.

Field Establishments

The field establishments are only the implementing division of the department. Public administration exists for the people. So all the matters relating to public in a department must be implemented at the public level to accelerate the pace of development. In the field organisation while the base or bottom level unit is given with the task of implementing the decisions of the department as arrived at by the headquarter, each superior grade is assigned with the task of supervision over the lower units under its purview. The field unit is divided into regional divisions, which in turn, divided into district organisation. District organisation has to supervise the activities of the subdivisional level organisation of the department. The subdivision is the lowest unit of field establishment entrusted with the task of implementing the administrative decisions.

The diagrammatic representation of departmental structure shows the following:

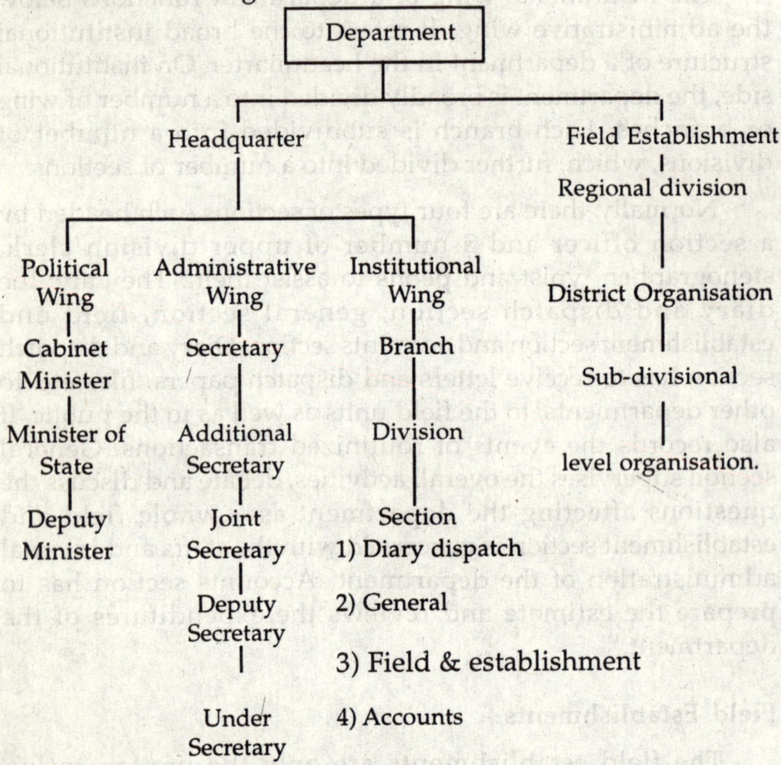

FIELD–HEADQUARTER RELATIONSHIP

One of the most pertinent question arises in mind as to what is the field-headquarter relationship in an administrative department? This question can be analyzed effectively if we go deep into the details of department administration.

What is a Headquarter?

Headquarter is the broad classification of department where all the policies are formulated. Therefore, headquarter is the nerve centre of departmental administration. It is a position where the management of department is carried on. It consists of not only the political wing, but also the administrative wing as well as the institutional wing. However, the combination of efforts of both political and administrative wing coupled with the procedure of institutional wing give headquarter its real meaning. A headquarter may be defined as "the structure of organisational hierarchy where decisions are framed". Therefore, headquarter deals with the top level management in the administration. It is concerned not only with policy formulation but also with directing, supervising and controlling the lower units of administration called the fields.

The authority in headquarter, emanates from the chief executive and run vertically along down the line of command. There is a strict adherence to the principle of superior-subordinate relationship in headquarter.

Therefore, a headquarter is that part of departmental structure where decisions are made. The decisions are reached by the chief executive on the basis of data, facts and figures provided to it by the staff and auxiliary agency.

What is a Field?

The field, stands in sharp contrast to the headquarter. It is the implementing level of department which is away from the headquarter and scattered all over the state so as to bring administration to the people at the bottom level. Therefore, the field units operate at the bottom level of administrative hierarchy. The personnels in field units have to workout with the broad outlines suggested to them by the headquarter. 'Field units', can be defined as 'those structural arrangements in administrative hierarchy which implements the authoritative decisions reached by the headquarter."

Distinction

A field is always distinguished from the headquarter on several grounds. Firstly, while headquarter is the upper division of the administrative branch, field refers to the lower division. Secondly, while headquarter consists of top level management, field consists of bottom level management of the departmental administration. Thirdly, while headquarter takes the decisions, field units carry out or execute them. Fourthly, while headquarter is assisted by staff agency, field is assisted by the Auxiliary agency. Finally, while importance is given to political and administrative wings in a headquarter, importance is given to structural and institutional arrangement in the field.

Organisation of Field Units

The legal status of field units lies in the fact that it is an elongation of administrative organisation. It facilitates to bring administration to the reach of the people. While headquarter makes the administration efficient, field makes it popular.

However, the problem of Line administration lies with the point that how field units are created? Sometimes the field units are created by an administrative order of the Executive. But in some other cases, field establishments are created by the statute of legislature. When established by legislature, it enjoys more security and freedom than established by the Executive.

Both the system leads to two extremes. Thus, usual practice is that while field units are created by Executive, their numbers, location and grades are determined by the legislature.

For smooth and efficient functioning of administration, the field units are often graded and classified according to the importance of their work. The gradation of field units into a number of stations lead to administrative conveniences.

Sometimes, due to the vastness of the departmental functions, each field station is divided into a number of substations. This facilitates the speedy disposal of functions.

Field and Headquarter — The Interface

A general study into the actual functioning of both field and headquarter reveals that while headquarter makes decisions, fields carries it out. However, this interface between the field and headquarter often invite problems. Actually the problems of department lies in their complexity of nature. The people are faced with diversified problems. The problems differ from each other both in their magnitude and intensity. At the same time, the problem of one area is not similar to the problem faced in another area. Due to the complexity of problems the headquarter has to face a lot of hardships. The decision it reaches out to solve the problems, in reality, are arrived at the headquarter without the practical knowledge of field supervisors. This creates another problem. The decisions are not found suitable to the needs of the people of the area. Even it solves the problem, yet we cannot universalize the decision i.e. those decisions cannot be applied to other areas facing identical, not similar problems. This creates resentment among the people about the functioning of the department. However, the field units became a mere cog in between the headquarter and the beneficiaries.

The problems in the field and headquarter relationship, therefore, lies in the sphere of centralization *vs.* decentralization.

Field and Headquarter — Relationship

Two group of scholars have given their views regarding field and headquarter relationship. The first view held that the relationship between the field and headquarter should be governed by the principle of centralization. It means the field stations should act only as an executive agency. They should have no power of control over their own activities even in their internal administration such as purchase of stationary, transfer of employees etc. Each and every activity of the fields should be guided and directed by and from the headquarter. The headquarters' power should extend sufficiently so as to include the internal administration of the fields also

Centralization in field-headquarter relationship is advocated on the following grounds:

(a) It ensures efficiency in administration by providing maximum control.

(b) It makes administrative abuses difficult.

(c) It achieves effective control over field units.

However, the scholars who are in favour of centralization were not aware of the shortcomings in centralization. Centralization involves the following defects:

(a) It lacks flexibility.

(b) It causes unnecessary delay in decision making;

(c) It makes the fields a cog at the hands of the headquarter.

(d) It overburdens the headquarter with work.

To rectify the defects of administrative centralization, the second group of scholars advocated that the principle of decentralization should rule the relationship between the field and headquarter.

They advocated that the field units should be left free to decide the local matters without any reference to the headquarter. Only those matters which involve major policy approaches should be decided by the headquarter. The subordinate officers should be free to initiate proposals for the solution of local problems because these staffs have direct access with the people and they have a better understanding of local problems than the headquarter. Therefore, it is the field staffs that know better how to solve the local problems with the help of local resources and utilizing the local people in administration without referring the matter to the headquarter. This relieves the headquarter of its burden and allow some degree of autonomy to fields in administrative matters. Decentralization also helps in reaching out prompt decision and taking about quick action for the redress of people's grievances.

However, a third view undertaken by the scholars reveal the real and actual relationship that should exist between the centre i.e. the headquarter and the field units.

To these scholars, neither centralization nor decentralization is necessary, yet too much decentralization may tend to reduce the importance of the headquarter. Therefore, they are in favour of "reasonable delegation" which advocates that there should be a limitation to delegation of powers at the field units from the headquarter.

They held that although delegation of power (of decision making) is necessary to revitalize the functions of fields units, the officer who delegate powers i.e. the headquarter should take into account the following factors while delegating:

(a) That delegation of authority should always follow proper channel of communication.

(b) That delegation should be made to the 'post' and not to the 'person' holding office.

(c) That delegation should always be made by a competent authority.

(d) That shifting of responsibility i.e. sub-delegation should not be allowed; and

(e) That the extent and procedure of delegation should be clearly defined in the office manual and every office in the organisation should be familiarized with them.

Besides these, the headquarter must exercise some degree of supervision and control over the field units. The control exercised by the headquarter should be in the nature of following:

1. The headquarter should receive information from the field units in the form of reports, returns, statistics etc. pertaining to the progress of field operations.
2. The headquarter is to see that the field units confirm to the budget allotments made for the purpose of enabling the fields to function properly.

3. The headquarter should carry on 'audit' of the expenditures made by the field units and to find out irregularity if any, made by the field units.

4. The headquarter should 'investigate' the matters of mal-administration and corruption done at the field units and penalize the persons responsible for them.

5. The headquarter should have ' personal inspection' from a close proximity over all the administrative activities done by the field units.

6. The headquarter should use the technique of 'promotion' and 'demotion' to reward positively or negatively to the field officers for their activity.

PUBLIC CORPORATION

The traditional unit of administration is the department whose head is responsible for all the acts of the department, to the Chief Executive. There is excessive centralization in department. As against this centralization principle, there emerged the concept of decentralization of administrative power. The advent of the 20th century marked the growth of a new type of governmental organisation – the Public Corporation. Unlike the departmental organisation, the public corporation enjoys a great deal of autonomy both in administrative and financial matters. However, they are not quite independent of the control of the Chief Executive like the Regulatory Commissions. Public Corporation, therefore exhibit both the qualities of department and regulatory commission, and yet is an advance over both the systems. Prof. **W.A. Robson** therefore remarked that 'the most important innovation in political organisation and constitutional practices in the 20th century are the Public Corporations."

Distinction Between Public Corporation and Public Undertaking

Very often public corporation is confused as public undertakings. But both of them are quite different from each other. Public undertaking or public enterprises are the broad groups of organisations where the government has a role to play. It includes three things – the departmental management type of public undertakings; the joint-stock company type of public undertakings; and the public corporation type of public undertaking. On the other hand, public corporation is only a narrow division of the various types of public undertakings.

Another point of difference between public corporation and public undertaking lies with the composition structure. The public undertaking may be of three types – (a) those completely owned by the central government, example: Life Insurance Corporation of India; (b) those completely owned by the state government, example: State Transport Corporation; and (c) Joint enterprises of both central and state governments. Example: Damodar Valley Corporation.

Public Corporation, being a part and parcel of public enterprises or public undertaking, is also of three types such as: (a) Government Corporations; (b) the mixed enterprises; and (c) Corporate enterprises.

The Government Corporations are those which are owned by the government, whether central or state, and also controlled by them. Examples:- Food Corporation of India.

The mixed enterprises are those in which the government has at least 51% shares and the rest share is vested with by private share holders. Examples :- the State Bank of India.

The Corporate enterprises are those which are established by private parties under authority of law, but are subject to some degree of supervision by the government. Examples: Indian Airlines, The Ashoka Hotel Groups etc.

Factors of Growth

Public corporation is the product of twentieth century only. Mainly three factors have contributed significantly for the growth of Public Corporations. They are as follows:

There has been an increasing realization that there are gaps in the departmental pattern of organisation. To fill up the gap, public corporation emerged.

The influence of Marxism compelled the government to think that state control in some form is highly essential in the economic activities of the state. This led to the growth of public corporation.

The impact of great world wars led to the growth of public corporation. Because the government was forced to take steps for public welfare which later on, resulted in public corporation.

Definitions

Public Corporation has been defined by Prof. **Robson** as "one of the most innovative creation in the political organisation and constitutional practices." But Prof. **L.D. White** denies Robson's statement and considered "public corporations to be only the modified version of governmental departments." Besides, various other scholars have contributed their thought on public corporation.

M.E. Dimock–"It is a publicly owned enterprise, that has been chartered under federal, state or local law for a particular business of financial purpose."

M.C. Shukla–"Public Corporation is a corporate body created by legislature, with defined powers and functions, and financially independent having a clear-cut jurisdiction over a specified area or over a particular type of commercial activity."

Herbert Morison–"It is a corporate device combining public ownership, public accountability and business management for public ends."

Pfiffner–"Corporation is a body framed for the purpose of enabling a number of persons to act as a single person."

W. Grange–"It is an artificial person authorized by law to carry on particular activities and functions."

Characteristics of a Corporation

The analysis of the above definitions revolve six characteristic features of a public corporation. These are:

(a) It is a legal person, capable of suing and being sued, entering into contracts, acquiring and owning property in its name.

(b) These are statutory in character. They are created by the legislature which also lays down their powers, purpose and functions.

(c) Their functions are essentially business like but not profit motive. They have a purpose of social service. Roosevelt remarked, "Public Corporations are clothed with the power of government but possessed of the flexibility and initiative of private enterprise."

(d) They have their own finance separated from national finance. They hold funds in their own name and enjoy complete autonomy in the management of these funds.

(e) They enjoy complete administrative autonomy from the control of Chief Executive.

(f) They have their own personnel. They do not form a part of civil service but are recruited independently.

Public Corporations *Vs.* Joint Stock Company

Very often the students are confused between Public Corporation and Joint Stock Company which resembles as the same entity. From a legalistic point of view, both public corporation and joint stock company are juridical persons acting in their own names, owning property and carrying out the various economic, industrial, agricultural and commercial activities. However, both differ from each other in the following matters:

(1) Public Corporation is created by the legislature where as Joint Stock Company is created by Executive.

(2) The separate statute created by legislature creates thc Public Corporation. Thus, each Corporation is established under a special statute. But the Joint Stock Company is established by the governmental order

of the Executive and are registered under the General Companies Act.

(3) While public corporations do not have a profit motive, the joint stock company has a profit motive, although it carry on the functions for public benefit.

(4) The public corporations has no share holder in ordinary sense of the term because there is nothing like share holder's meeting in it. No doubt private investments are allowed, but the investors are allowed interest on their investment. The joint stock company, on the other hand, have a system of shareholders participate in the management of the company. They receive share, not interest, for their investment in the company.

(5) The joint stock company is subject to state control either entirely or on majority of matters owning to the Government's investment. In other words, the joint stock company acts under the control of the government. Public corporations, on the other hand, enjoys immunity from governmental control and as such considered as autonomous bodies to some extent.

(6) The functions of public corporation covers a wide range of areas from public to private sectors and as such it has universal application. The joint stock company, on the other hand, have only a limited application covering private enterprise only.

Besides the above differences, the public corporation and joint stock company resembles each other on the ground that both are opposed to the departmental structure of government and advocated for flexibility in transactions.

Distinction between Public Corporation and Private Enterprise

Public corporations and private enterprises differs from each other on the following grounds:

(1) Public corporation, as the name suggests is managed by the government. Private enterprises, on the other hand, is established and managed by private entrepreneurs.

(2) Public corporation has a service motive. But private enterprises have a profit motive business.

(3) Public corporation, sometimes, issue share certificate in the form of bonds, debentures etc., under government guarantee. Private enterprises, being essentially a purely business company, do not enjoy any freedom to issue share certificates to the public.

Besides these differences, the only similarity that exists between public corporations and private enterprises is that both of them operate on business line.

Public Corporation Vs. Government Departments

Similarities

Both public corporation and government departments, though have significant distinctions, yet exhibit some sort of similarities. They are follows:

(a) Both of them are controlled by the government.

(b) Both of them are identical in their internal structures.

Differences

Besides the similarities, the public corporation and government department differ from each other in the following ways:

(1) While departmental system is applied for state regulated activities, the corporation system is applied for business enterprises.

(2) Department is headed by a single person called the Secretary. But corporation is headed by a group of persons called the Board of Directors.

(3) Departmental personnel are recruited through Public

Service Commission whereas the corporation has its own personnel recruited independently by its own method of examination.

(4) In corporation, the promotion is made on the basis of merit whereas in a department promotion is guided on the basis of seniority.

(5) In department, there are formal set of rules regarding recruitment, promotion and removal of personnel, which are strictly adhered to. But in corporation although these rules have their presence, they are not at all strictly adhered to.

(6) There is flexibility of policy and procedures in the working of public corporations where as the working of department is highly complex characterized by red-tapism, routine, formalism and rigidity.

(7) Public corporations are subjected to less political pressures but the departments are constantly under the pressure of the government.

(8) The corporations enjoy both administrative and financial autonomy and as such is free from the clutches of Chief Executive. The departments, on the other hand, works under the complex control of Chief Executive.

(9) Corporations are generally meant to produce revenue whereas departments are mostly spending units of government.

(10) The financial status, methods and procedures of the corporation differs from those of the departments. Corporations are usually given grants once at the initial period when it is created. After this initial grant the Corporation is authorized to raise its own capital funds, earn income, accumulate savings, build up reserves, borrow and make its budget and spend the money as it thinks best. But the departments cannot have their separate capital. It functions on the basis of annual grants made available to it by the government.

(11) The corporations are subjected to commercial audit i.e. it takes into account the profit, loss, wasteful expenditures and financial soundness. On the other hand, departments are subjected to government audit i.e. it takes into account the legality and honesty of expenditures.

(12) The corporation do not enjoy immunity from action in torts. But the department, as a participant in the sovereign powers of the state enjoys so.

(13) Corporation is a juridical entity insofar as it can sue and be sued in the court of law. The departments do not enjoy such status.

(14) Corporation is created by an Act of legislature where as the department can be created by an order of the Chief Executive.

(15) The corporation operates in a small area whereas the department extend to different corners of the state and spreads throughout.

Role of Public Corporations in Modern States

Public corporations have come to play a dominating role in modern states. The modern states are welfare States which carries on its activities for the benefits of the people at large. The public corporation gears up momentum by adding hands to the state. However, the role played by public corporation can be well understood in the context of process in public corporation.

The Process in Corporations

The public corporation runs purely on business and technical services of the government. They maximize their activities due to their independence from the Executive. Their function is based on merit representing the talent and intelligence of the employees.

Unlike the legislature, public corporation does its duties

constantly and continuously which adds flexibility to the working process and helps in prompt decision making and instant action taking.

Being granted with financial and administrative autonomy, the corporation works on its own administrative structure which is devised to suit its fundamental needs.

The simple business procedure, prompt decisions and quick actions of the public corporation also provides the employees with incentive to work efficiently and economically.

The above process of public corporations provides the basis for a constructive role in the interest of the people to be played by the corporations in modern states. Normally the following positive role is played by public corporations:

1. It leads to efficiency and economy in administrative procedures because the day to day transactions of the corporation are determined, unlike the departments, by a body of Board of Directors selected on the basis of their merit, not of seniority.
2. It provides the basis for administrative operations outside the domain of politics because the corporations are not subjected to a stringent governmental control.
3. It relieves the burden of the legislature by managing its own activities constantly by itself. Thus it helps the legislature to concentration on other matters of national importance.
4. Public corporation works for the welfare of the people and not with profit motive like private enterprises. Therefore it shares the activities of government for providing general welfare measures.

However, although the public corporations run on public interest and provide the basis for a good and operational governmental structure, yet its style of functioning have poses certain fundamental problems in the government. There are mainly three problems:

(a) the problem of responsibility towards the legislature;

(b) the problem of responsibility towards the Executive.

(c) the problem of safeguarding the consumers interest, and

(d) the problem of labour welfare.

(a) Problem of Responsibility towards Legislature

Responsibility is the corner stone of democratic government. It provides a check on the arbitrary use of power and therefore, laid the foundation of a good government amenable and accountable to the people at large. The Public Corporations seem to have violated this principle. Although they are created by the statute passed by the legislature, but they are not at all amenable and accountable to it for its activities and procedures. Once created the public corporation draws its own plans and execute them in a manner decided by itself. The legislature do not possess the power to go through the transactions of business of a public corporation. So there always remain the possibility of danger of being arbitrary and monographic by a public corporation.

(b) Problem of Responsibility towards Executive

The administrative autonomy enjoyed by the public corporations also created the problem of responsibility and relation towards the executive. Normally, the executive has to determine the broad policy outline of the corporation only. Here ends the executive control. But the details of day to day administration are filled in by the corporation itself. This reveals that there is no convenient line of congruence between the activities of both executive and corporation. This leads to clash of interests where each party may transgress the others area. This really is a problematic situation witnessed in the style of functioning of the public corporations.

(c) Problem of Safeguarding Consumer's Interest

The functioning style of public corporation also arose the

problem of safeguarding the consumer's interest. As the corporation works on business line, there is the possibility of unrepresentation of consumer's right. The consumers have a right to be provided with better quality goods at low prices. But while producing the good or fixing up the prices of those products, the corporation seems to have totally neglected the interests of the consumers. This resulted in hardships faced by the consumers who has to buy the product at a very high price but with a relative poor quality.

(e) Problem of Safeguarding Labourer's Interest

Another problem in the functioning of the public corporations is how to reconcile the autonomy of the corporation with the interests of the labourers who compose it. The interest of labourer lies with their right to participate in the management of the corporation. But in a public corporation, the labourers are deprived of this right. They are only a means to achieve the end of the corporation.

On the view of the above role played by the public corporation, it is held that public corporations have solved many problems and have created some others.

Control Over Public Corporations

Public corporations enjoy a great deal of autonomy not only in administrative matters, but also in financial matters. However, they are not so independent as that of the Regulatory Commission which runs exclusively on its own procedures and rules. Attempts have always been made to reconcile the autonomy with the accountability. It means some sort of government control is always exercised over the public corporations.

Normally, control over public corporations in India, is exercised in two ways:

(a) Executive control; and

(b) Legislative control.

1. Executive Control over Public Corporations

The government of India exercises the following executive controls over public corporations:

1. The government has the power of appointment and removal of the members of Board of Directors of the public corporations.
2. The government issues general policy directions to the corporations for effective functioning. However, in some public corporations like the DVC, not only the broad policy outlines but also the details of administrative procedures are directed by the government.
3. The capital investments and borrowings by the corporation requires the government's approval.
4. The accounts of the corporations have to be finalized in consultation with the Comptroller and Auditor General of India.
5. The government's approval is necessary for some corporations to implement its schemes and programmes. For example: In DVC, the construction of canals and its distributaries are subject to the approval of Provincial government.
6. The government has the power to obtain necessary information from the corporations to facilitate the preparation of reports and estimates.

These are the normal executive control exercised over public corporations in India.

2. Parliamentary Control over Public Corporations

Besides the Executive control, certain Legislative control is also exercised over public corporations in India. The general form of Parliamentary control over corporations are as follows:

1. The Parliament enacts the Statute for the establishment of public corporation.

2. The members of parliament can move questions, Adjournment motions and Call Attention motions to discuss into the matters relating to any public corporation.
3. The Parliament can exercise control over corporations by asking questions to the Minister, in charge of that corporation. However, the ministerial responsibility is limited only to the general policy matters of the corporation, not to the details of their administration.
4. The financial estimates and statement as well as the annual reports and account statements of the public corporations are submitted before each House of the Parliament and provides an occasion for debate and discussion in the affairs of corporation.
5. The Estimates Committee and Public Accounts Committee of Parliament can go deep into the details of financial administration of the corporations and can make appropriate report to the Parliament on any matter falls under their purview.
6. Besides the Committee on Public Undertaking also exercises control over public corporations in India.

Besides the above, the Parliament can exercise control over the public corporations on all matters which falls within the purview of executive control also.

Working of Public Corporations in India

Contradictory views have been expressed by scholars on the actual working of public corporations in India. Some critics says that public corporations are put to excessive executive and legislative control in India so as to destroy their autonomous character. On the other hand, those who advocate greater control over corporations held that working of public corporations is not satisfactory. Rather greater control is necessary to make them function effectively as a unit of the government administration.

Paul Appleby held that there is a satisfactory control over public corporations but the officers are burdened with too much duty. Work is slowed down because of lack of delegation of power. Thus, he recommended that "public corporations must not be thrown into the arms of a ministerial father unless a fond parliamentary mother is available to restrain excessive application of paternal discipline."

Ashok Chand feels that parliamentary control is excessive. **A.D. Gorwal** also held that public corporations are subjected to too much executive interferences. Such type of parliamentary and executive control retards the growth of public corporations in India.

Prof. **J.K. Galbraith** while commenting on the functioning of public corporations, held that:

(i) there is shortage of managerial skill in the management of public corporations; and

(ii) there is too much centralization of authority and red-tapism.

Justice **M.C. Chagla,** on his recommendation for efficient administration of public corporations said that:

(i) The government should not interfere in the autonomous working of public corporations.

(ii) The chairman of the corporation should be appointed from persons who have business and financial experience.

The Administrative Reforms Commission (ARC) has made a large number of recommendations for better management of public corporations. Some of those recommendations are as follows:

(a) The nature of executive and legislative control sometimes remains weigh. So there should proper definition of the extent of control by the Executive and the Legislature.

(b) The Directors of the Board should be full time and functional directors with business and financial experiences in place of part-time and dysfunctional one.

(c) There should be improvement of employer-employee relationships in public corporation.

In short, we can say that the working of public corporations in India is far from satisfactory.

COMMITTEE ON PUBLIC UNDERTAKINGS (CPU)

In spite of the two standing committees of Parliament – Estimates Committee and Public Accounts Committee, the Parliamentary control over Public Undertakings in India are chaotic, inadequate, lack of control and intermittent. Thus, demand was made first in 1953 for the creation of a separate Committee on Public Undertakings to look into the details of their functioning and to report its findings, from time to time to the Parliament. The demand was made in late 1953 by Lanka Sundaram.

The demand for CPU was strongly advocated by L. Sundaram on the following grounds:

(a) That public corporation in India are impervious to public control and criticism.

(b) The Comptroller and Auditor General of India (CAG) is having only limited control over public enterprises. He has no power to report to the Parliament on the financial activities of corporation.

(c) The already existing two committees are over loaded with their normal work. So they do not have enough time for detailed scrutiny of budget and report of public undertakings.

(d) The absence of competition made the corporations essentially monopolistic. This creates difficulty in price fixation of the commodity.

(e) Such a CPU will strengthen the hands of the minister

and will affirm and enforce the authority of the Parliament over public enterprises.

However, the finance minister T.T. Krishnamachari did not agree with L. Sundaram and turned down his demands on the plea that it would amount to throw the baby with the bath water.

The issue for the establishment of CPU was again cropped up in 1956 when Ashok Mehta Committee recommended in favour of need of such a Committee to have a proper control over Public Undertakings. The finance minister, agreed with the report of Mehta Committee this time. As such the Krishna Menon Committee was appointed to make recommendations for the establishment of a Standing Committee of Parliament on Public Undertakings. The matter gathered momentum from many quarters. The Planning Commission has also too, visualized the need for the establishment of CPU.

In 1963 the Indian Parliament resolved in favour of creation of such a Committee on Public Undertakings. However, deadlock arise as to the representation in CPU. The Lok Sabha did not agree to give full fledged representation to Rajya Sabha members. But it is in favour of taking these elderly members of Rajya Sabha as associate members only. The Rajya Sabha objected to this suggestion of Lok Sabha. However, the constitutional deadlock was finally resolved by the constitution of Joint Committee.

Composition

The Committee on Public Undertakings (CPU) consists of 15 members –10 from Lok Sabha and 5 from Rajya Sabha. The members are elected on the basis of proportional representation by means of single transferable votes.

Tenureship

The tenureship of the members of the committee on public undertakings is fixed at 5 years, one fifth of the members, retire in every year by rotation. However, the members are eligible for reappointment.

Jurisdiction

The jurisdiction of committee is restricted to a set of public undertakings only. However, all the public undertakings do not come under the purview of jurisdiction of CPU. The jurisdiction of CPU extends to the following: (a) Damodar Valley Corporation (DVC), (b) Industrial Finance Corporation (IFC), (c) Indian Airlines Corporation (IAC), (d) Air India International (AII), (e) Life Insurance Corporation of India (LIC), (f) Central Warehousing Corporation (CWHC), (g) The Oil and Natural Gas Commission (ONGC), (h) Hindustan Aeronautics Limited (HAL), (i) Bharat Electronics & Bharat Heavy Electricals Limited (BHEL), (j) Steel Authority of India Limited (SAIL). It also includes certain other governmental companies.

Functions of CPU

The functions of the Committee on Public Undertakings are as follows:

(a) To examine the reports and accounts of public undertakings.

(b) To refer to the Comptroller and Auditor General of India (CAG), if the committee feels that something should be referred to him for his recommendations.

(c) In the context of efficiency and autonomy, the committee examines the business and commercial practices of public undertakings.

(d) To consider such other functions vested in the Public Accounts Committee and Estimates Committee relating to public undertakings, if the speaker allots the committee specifically.

Limitations of CPU

(i) The committee is precluded from discussing the governmental policy relating to public undertakings.

(ii) It cannot interfere in the day to day administration of the public undertakings.

(iii) Those Companies in which the government is the largest shareholder, the jurisdiction of the committee is limited to maximum extent.

(iv) The size of the committee is a limitation of the authority of it.

(v) It cannot deal with all those powers which the PAC and EC deals with.

Evaluation of the CPU

By evaluating the powers and functions of the committee as public undertakings, the critics held the following views:

"that one does not really understand why the committee is debarred from scrutinizing the government policy."

However, the committee submitted its first report on 1st April 1965 to the Parliament. It shows that it is not, of course, a limited body. The CPU plays a fact finding role. It assists the Parliament for effective debates.

In spite of several steps, the performance of public corporations are far from satisfactory. The public corporations spend too much on guest entertainment, on training programme. Besides due to low level of production, wasteful expenditures, overstaffing, groupism , unionism , consultancy programmes, and widespread corruption, the public undertakings, are often, run at loss.

INDEPENDENT REGULATORY COMMISSIONS

Meaning

Another administrative structure in the governmental organisation is called the Independent Regulatory Commission. These are the Organisations which are peculiar to the system of USA and therefore, this system owes its origin to USA.

These are the commissions or Boards which enjoys complete independence from the Executive control. Thus, they are named as "Independent". At the same time, they are called

'Regulatory' because they are devised in such a way as to 'regulate' certain activities of national importance.

Definition

Therefore, independent regulatory commission is defined as *"those commissions established to regulate certain activities of national importance, independently of the Executive control"*. His definition raised a question as to who establishes such commissions. The answer is that normally these regulatory commissions are established by a statute passed by the legislature. However, there are certain instances in India, where these commissions are created by the statutory provisions of the constitutions.

Characteristic Features

The Independent Regulatory Commissions, as the name suggests, have the following distinguishing features. They are follows:

(a) This is a body of authority created either by the statutory provisions of the constitution or by the statutes passed to that effect by the legislature.

(b) It is always collegial in nature and consists of a number of persons as the chairman and members of the commission who are entrusted with the task of decision making.

(c) The commission is relatively small and works as a unit to achieve the broad outlines for which it is being created. It is staffed not only by the generalists but also by expect technocrats.

(d) The commission is relatively independent from Chief Executive and as such resembles to that of the corporation. Although the members of the commission are appointed by the Chief Executive i.e. President, they are neither responsible to him nor do they report him. The Chief Executive also cannot remove them from their office at his sweet discretion. Therefore, the commissions stand outside the framework of departmental organisation.

(e) Their independence is not absolute. It means although they are independent of the Executive, yet they are not independent of the clutches of the Legislature which created them. The members of the commission can be removed only by the legislature in a way specified in the statute which created the office. At the same time, the commission is not independent of the judiciary also. The judiciary has a power to examine the legality of proceedings of these commissions and declare them void if it transgresses its authority.

(f) The commission exhibits the features of both department and public corporation and yet represent a step ahead of both. Although it has a corporate structure at the head, yet there is departmental pattern at the bottom level. i.e. the staffs are under the control of the Board or Commission. There is also excessive centralization, principle of hierarchy, span of control, unity of command etc. in these organisations which resembles at once the departmental structure. But at the same time, the collegial executive, financial and administrative autonomy resembles the public corporation. Therefore, the Independent Regulatory Commissions are departmental in form but corporate in their spirit.

(g) The Regulatory Commission is marked by administrative autonomy. The top level management decides the structure and functions of each part to have administrative efficiency. They are free to choose their internal administration.

(h) It is also marked by financial autonomy. The commission can raise funds, hold and acquire property, prepare its budget, authorize expenditure to itself, build up reserves and also to carry on internal audit over the accounts.

(i) The regulatory commission is a juridical person i.e. it is a legal entity capable of suing and being sued in the court of law.

(j) Last, but not the least, they do not have any business like operation and as such profit motive is not their motto. At the same time, they do not function on strict centralized principles of a department to carry on social service motto. Rather they carry out those functions and regulate those activities of the government which stands preeminent and fundamental in the governance of the state.

Functions of Independent Regulatory Commissions

The functions of independent regulatory commission are as follows:

1. It carry on administrative function. The commission enjoys wide range of power in rule making as well as rule application and also enjoys the power of rule adjudication. However, the administrative function refers to the power of the commission to implement the rules.
2. It carry on quasi-legislative function. It means the members of the commission enjoys enormous powers in making rules and framing its own policies for proper functioning. The policies are framed by the 'Board of Directors' of the commission known as the 'chairman and members." They are the men of enduring ability, knowledge, farsightedness and technical know-how. The rules framed by the commission is quasi legislative because it is binding on the members and staffs although like ordinary legislation, it is not sent to the Chief Executive for his approval.

3. It carry on quasi-judicial functions. It means the commission has the power of rule adjudication. They can review their own decisions either from their own initiative by the complaints from others. This 'initiative' element in the independent regulatory commission that distinguishes it from administrative tribunals. A tribunal never take initiative to decide cases.
4. Another function of independent regulatory commission is to formulate policies relating to technical matters free from political influence.
5. It reconciles the controversies between the 'generalists' and 'specialists' by necessarily including both as the members of the commission.
6. It relieves the burden of legislature and executive from formulating and implementing certain general policies which are necessary for the success of the democratic government. For example: The Election Commission conducts the general elections thereby relieving the legislature and executive from utilizing their time and resources for the same.

Independent Regulatory Commissions in India

In India, we come across two types of independent regulatory commissions such as Constitutional Commissions and Statutory Commissions. The statutory commissions are those which are established by a statute passed by the legislature to that effect. Examples: University Grants Commission, Atomic Energy Commission etc.

Constitutional Commissions are those which are established in accordance with the provisions of the constitution. Examples: Finance Commission, Planning Commission, Union Public Service Commission, Election Commission, Official Language Commission etc.

Chapter V

ADMINISTRATION AT WORK: CHIEF EXECUTIVE

WHO IS THE CHIEF EXECUTIVE?

Administration has to do with getting things done. It thus implies both the structure and functions. The primary function of administration is to devise or build up the organisational structure through which the goal is to be achieved. After the structure is organized, stress is laid on the goal. It is the administrative process which emphasizes this aspect of administration. The process of 'getting things done' implies the arrangement of personnels in a hierarchical order in which the orders and directions flows from top to bottom and information and report flows in a reverse direction. As such the administrative organisation consists of the superior, the subordinate and their relationship.

The administrative structure resembles a pyramidal structure i.e. broad at the base and tappering towards the top, till it ends at a single point—the apex. The superior-subordinates are arranged in the similar way. The superior remaining at the apex of the administrative hierarchy is called the Chief Executive.

The Chief Executive, is essentially a predominant feature found in the governmental departments. However, it does not mean that there is no apex level superior in private enterprises which is organized in business or profit motive. But the term 'General Manager' is preferred to Chief Executive in a private concern. The Chief Executive in a departmental concern is a single person. But in case of public corporation, it is called the "Board of Directors." Therefore, Chief Executive is only the predominant feature of a governmental department.

Chief Executive may be regarded as that person in the apex of the administrative hierarchy who is responsible for carrying out the functions successfully for which the organisation is created. In India, the President is the Chief Executive whereas in Britain, it is the Queen who acts as the Chief Executive.

TYPES OF CHIEF EXECUTIVE

The Chief Executive may be of two types depending upon the nature of government i.e. whether Parliamentary or Presidential. In a parliamentary form of Chief Executive all the powers are vested in the Parliament or Legislature. The Parliament, in turn, appoints a person or group of persons to act, on its behalf, as the Chief Executive. As such there are two subdivisions may be witnessed in the parliamentary government—the nominal and the real. The nominal Chief Executive is one who wields all the powers in theory only. He is merely a rubber stamp. The Real Chief Executive on the other hand is one who exercises all the powers in reality. Example: The Prime Minister and Council of Ministers.

In a Presidential form of government, the President wields all the powers in toto. He acts not only as the Head of the State but also as Head of Government. Example: the President of USA.

Besides these two broad types of Chief Executive, another collegial system of Chief Executive is also found. Here the executive powers are vested in a body of persons consisting of Seven persons as in case of Switzerland, all the members equally exercising the powers.

'Chief Executive' as the term means, implies the highest executive officials who executes the administrative decisions and orders in the organisation. This implies that there must be another system which takes the decisions and issues the administrative orders. This is the Legislature, in fact, which formulates the executive decisions.

From the above analysis, we may define *"Chief Executive"* as "that person or body of persons in the top level of administrative hierarchy who is responsible for enforcing public policy as decided by the legislature."

FUNCTIONS OF THE CHIEF EXECUTIVE

The Chief Executive, as the head of the administrative hierarchy has to perform the following functions:

(1) It executes the administrative decisions as arrived at and decided by the legislature.

(2) It exercises general supervision over the activities of the administrative organisation.

(3) It appoints and removes the staffs of the organisation.

(4) It gives directions to the subordinates through administrative orders, rules and regulations for the enforcement of Public Policy.

(5) It coordinates the activities of various parts of the organisation to achieve the object fulfilled.

(6) It implement the budget of the organisation.

(7) It investigates into and collect information on any irregularity in the administrative organisation and punishes the convict.

(8) It maintains public relations in the organisation and as such acts as the chief liaison officer between the organisation and the legislature.

DYSFUNCTIONS OF THE CHIEF EXECUTIVE

The dysfunctions of the Chief Executive refers to those functions which the Chief Executive do not perform. The Chief Executive do not perform the following functions:

(a) It do not formulate the executive policy which is the function of the legislature. It only executes the formulated policy.

(b) It do not make planning for the creating of new administrative structures. It can be done only with legislature's approval.

(c) It cannot change the functions of the organisation. It can only supervise the functions as determined by the legislature.

(d) It cannot formulate the budget and authorize expenditures unless it is sanctioned by the legislature.

(e) It cannot act independently of the legislature. It is responsible to the legislature either directly or indirectly for each and every activity of his own, as well as in his collective capacity.

WHO IS A GENERAL MANAGER?

General Manager refers to that person in the private enterprises who is responsible for all round development of the enterprise. He is a man of enduring capacity possessing leadership qualities like farsightedness, dignity, endurance, technical know how, wisdom, intelligence, enthusiasm and affability. He is a person who is very much influential in the organisation and is capable of tackling any situation through his sound knowledge. He is a person who keeps a close and direct contact with his employees and by using the quality of persuasiveness, extracts the best out of them. It is through his able guidance that the private enterprise achieves success with a minimum use of coercion and maximum use of man power.

Functions of General Manager

The General Manager of a private enterprise perform the following functions:

(1) He determines the purpose of the enterprise and for the realization of this goal he frames plans and policies and executes them through.

(2) If necessary, he may revise the goal of the enterprise to achieve maximum profit.

(3) He exercises influence over subordinates through persuation, not coercion.

(4) He controls and coordinates the subordinates to revitalize the enterprise.

(5) It not only prepares the budget but also executes the plan on the basis of budgetary provision.

(6) It is not responsible to any body else for the activities he performs.

(7) He takes all those actions which are necessary to make the enterprise run smoothly and efficiently.

Chief Executive and General Manager – A Comparison

A comparative analysis of the powers and functions of both the Chief Executive and General Manager of a private enterprise reveals that while the Chief Executive is subject to manifold limitations in performance of his duties, the General Manager is quite free and independent. He can tackle the situation more easily than the Chief Executive. The decision is promptly carried on by the General Manger than the Chief Executive and as such he can take instant actions to reinforce the lost vigour in the enterprise. The Chief Executive on the other hand, though takes a decision, cannot implement them instantly without the authorization of legislature. This causes delay in the implementation of policies and as such retards the development of departmental organisation. The General Manager, being independent can take up rational action as he thinks best for his enterprise. But the Chief Executive being responsible to the legislature, requires to satisfy his points through legal norms, rules and procedures and then to carry out the authoritative power as authorized by the legislature.

This comparison reveals that the General Manager is more practical than the Chief Executive.

Chief Executive as General Manager—Role

Borrowing the idea from business management that the General Manager performs more viable and stable role in the life of the enterprise, some people argued in USA that the Chief Executive should be raised to the position of General Manager. In other words, they are in favour of granting more powers and authority to the Chief Executive in order to make the departmental organisation more strong and efficient.

The movement gained support from many quarters of the society. As such, according to **Willoughby**, a number of legislations were enacted in USA conferring several administrative powers upon the President. The President is given an upper hand in the formulation of budget. Besides, the administrative system is organized into the departmental type.

Besides the above steps, the administrative officers are made subordinate to the Chief Executive and they are directed to act in accordance with the direction given to them by the Chief Executive. The Chief Executive got an upper hand in the control of internal administration of the department.

As such the functions of Chief Executive got multiplied. It has become not only an implementing agency but also an initiating agency. The roles played by the Chief Executive as General Manager are as follows:

(a) He not only formulates administrative policies but also implement the same.

(b) He authorizes the details of the organisation to be filled in by subordinate officials according to the changing situation.

(c) He not only appoints and removes the staffs of the organisation but also determines their conditions of service, promotion, etc.

(d) He directs the subordinates on any matter relating to organisation.

(f) He exercises the general supervision and control over the internal administration and staffs.

(g) He ensures coordination, control and cooperation among and between the units of organisation and the staffs.

(h) He not only prepares the budget but also manages the funds of the organisation.

(i) He is responsible for overall development of the organisation.

LEGISLATURE AS BOARD OF DIRECTORS

What is a Legislature?

"Legislature", in modern usage refers to the policy formulating body of the democratic government. Legislature may be defined as "the representative body of the people whose main function is direction, supervision and control of administration.'

The Legislature is essentially different from the Executive on the ground that while Legislature frames the policies and programmes, the Executive executes those plans and programmes as passed by the Legislature. However, people are very often confused between Executive functions and administrative functions and use them interchangeably. The Executive function relates only to the supervision and general guidance to the administrative branch. Its function is to see that the laws passed by the legislature are successfully translated into action. The administrative function on the other hand, refers to the successful implementation of laws passed by legislature. Therefore, Legislature is supreme in its power in comparison with the Executive and administrative branch.

Functions of Legislature

The Legislature performs the following functions:

(1) It enacts all laws necessary for governmental

administration through drafting the bill and passing it.

(2) It carries on deliberations extensively before passing the legislation and thereby evaluate the pros and cons of administrative law.

(3) It helps in amendment of the constitution.

(4) It helps in representation of people and their will.

(5) It exercises control over Executives through question hour, interpellations, call attention motions, no-confidence motion, adjournment motions etc.

(6) It define and determine the public policy.

(7) It prescribes the rule of conduct for administrative activities.

(8) It helps in passing the appropriation bill.

What is Board of Directors?

"Board of Directors" refers to those body of men or group of people organized to decide the policy matters and day to day administration of public enterprises. Therefore, Board of Directors presupposes the existence of a public enterprise. They guide the corporation to achieve its goal through their expert knowledge and timely action.

Functions of Board of Directors

The Board of Directors, perform the following functions in a public enterprise:

(1) They fill in the details of day to day administration of the public enterprise.

(2) They carry out the general administration in accordance with the broad policy outlines as determined by the legislature.

(3) They prepares, enacts and passes the budget, raise funds, build reserves, own and acquire property and

carry on such other financial activities as may be necessary for the enterprise.

(4) They coordinate the activities of various parts of public enterprise and also enquire into and carry on investigation about the misuses and irregularities, if any, in the public enterprise.

Legislature as Board of Directors—Role

An analysis of the functions of both Legislature and Board Directors of a public enterprise reveals that the Legislature performs the same role in administrative organisation as played by the Board of Directors in a public enterprise. Therefore, Legislature is considered as the Board of Directors.

The role played by Legislature as Board of Directors are as follows:

(1) It determines the activities to be undertaken by the Government to fulfil its social objectives.

(2) It determines the administrative agencies and organs through which the goal to be released.

(3) It determines the personnel to be recruited to the organisation and also decides their conditions of service, promotion, pension etc.

(4) It determines the rules and procedure through which the organisation has to be managed.

(5) It determines the funds of the organisation and try to improve the funds through its budget, share certificates etc.

(6) It also determines the forms of legislative supervision over the administrative organisation to make them accountable to popular demands.

Chapter VI

ADMINISTRATIVE PROCEDURE

Administration, in general sense, involves the most intrinsic problem of rule application. It exists for the benefit of the people and therefore, is considered as an indices of social development. However, the growth of industrialization and urbanization, the unprecedented development of science and technology and the expansion of man's idea and knowledge have altogether contributed for the complexity of administration and its procedures. Nowadays, administration has to cater to the diversified multi-faceted needs of the people. For successful implementation of its programmes, it has to rely heavily upon certain procedures, rules and regulations. Among those, the concept of administrative law stands pre-eminent.

ADMINISTRATIVE LAW

Meaning

Administrative law, viewed in the above sense refers to one of the procedures through which the administration reaches its goal of social development. The students of Public Administration sometimes confused by this new term 'Administrative Law'. To comprehend their knowledge in a simple way, I must say that law is something which is binding upon the people; administrative law is something which is binding on the administrative organ of the Government. Administrative organ must not be confused with the Executive organ because there is a relative difference between those two organs. While the Executive organ consists of the Political Executive, charged with the over all responsibility of seeing the enforcement of public policy, the administrative organ consists of the non-political or Professional Executives who are entrusted with the real charge of implementing the legislation i.e. public policy.

Definitions

Administrative law has been defined variously by the scholars. Some of them are follows:

1. **Ivor Jennings**–"Administrative law is the law relating to administration. It determines the organisation, powers and duties of administrative authorities."
2. **Kenneth C. Davis**– "It is a law concerning the powers and procedures of administrative agencies, including even the law governing review of administrative actions."
3. **F.G. Goodnow**–"It is that part of public law which fixes the organisation and determines the competence of administrative authorities and indicate to the individual, remedies for violation of his rights."
4. **W.B. Munro**–"It is a system of jurisprudence which on the one hand relieves public officials from amenability to ordinary courts for acts performed in their official capacity and on the other hand, sets up a special jurisdiction to hold them accountable."

Nature

The above definitions reveal the real nature of Administrative Law. It is something which determines and necessarily involves the public officials who are engaged with implementing public policy. It can be viewed in two general senses—from broad sense as well as from narrow sense.

Viewed from broad angles, administrative law would mean

the whole body of law relating to public administration and as such it constitutes a part of public law. It covers all statutes, charters, resolutions, rules, regulations, judicial decisions and orders which have a bearing upon the administrative authorities.

From a narrow angle, administrative law, refers only to that part of public law which determines the amount of discretion permitted to administrative agencies and officers, the legal basis of administration and the various types of administrative responsibilities.

Origin of the Concept

The concept of administrative law is not of recent origin. It is emerged ever since French Revolution in 1789. It is typically a phenomena in the administrative structure of France. Therefore, a general understanding of administrative law should always be preceded by the peculiarities found in French administrative system.

In France, there exists a dual administration called *"Droit Administratif."* It means two types of laws have their existence in France. The first type of law governs the relations between and among the citizens and French people. This is called the ordinary law. The civil and criminal justice is always administered on the basis of this ordinary law of land.

Another type of law that exists in France is called the administrative law. This law governs the relationship between the citizens and the officials of the state. A special type of administrative court is established in France under this system of law which try cases that involves the activities of the public officials in their official capacities.

These two types of courts – the civil and criminal courts on one hand and the administrative courts on the other hand act independently of each other. However, this does not mean that the officials of Executive authority in France are free from any legal liability. Rather this system imposes a more effective liability upon the officials. The Executive official are liable and accountable before the civil and criminal courts for their personal actions and at the same time, they are accountable to the Administrative courts for all actions they perform in their official capacity. Thus, in France there exists a dual control over the administrative officials. While they are subject to ordinary law for all of their personal activities, they are subject to the administrative law for all of their official activities. This is called "Droit Administratif" in France.

However, such type of dual law is not found in any other states except France. In India, England and USA, the administrative officials are subject to accountability to the Ordinary law of the land not only for their personal actions but also for their official actions. In other words, no such system like administrative court do exist in any other State except France and as such the ordinary civil courts also try cases involving administrative responsibility.

DICEY'S HYPOTHESIS ON ADMINISTRATIVE LAW

A.V. Dicey, the famous English Jurist, have given the most controversial definition of Administrative Law. He considered Administrative Law as a part of Droit Administratif. To him, "Administrative Law is a part of Droit Administratif according to which the actions by the citizens against the officials for wrongful acts committed in their official capacity are tried, not by ordinary court, but by special administrative courts manned by civil servants'.

Dicey distinguishes the 'Droit Administratif' from the Ordinary Law of the land called the 'Rule of Law' prevalent in England. To Dicey, Droit Administratif has three features:

(a) The rights of State officials are determined by a body of law and rules which is not applicable to ordinary citizens.

(b) That the ordinary courts do not have jurisdiction in the cases where administrative officials, in their official capacity, is a party.

(c) That it gives a special protection to its officials for wrongful acts done in the course of their duties.

As against the 'Droit Administratif' in France, there is 'Rule of Law' in England which has also three features:

(a) That there is absolute supremacy of ordinary law of the land and as such the administrative officials cannot use arbitrary powers at its own wish. Every activity of the officials should confirm to the law of the land.

(b) That all are equal in the eyes of law and as such whether official or non-officials, all are subject to the ordinary law of the land.

(c) That there is primacy of individual rights over the State rights and as such constitutional rights are derived from individual rights.

Comparing the nature of law prevalent in France and England, Dicey concluded that there is no Rule of Law in France and no Administrative Law in England.

Disprovement

However, the view on Administrative Law held by Dicey fails to have universal application. Prof. **Robson** negated Dicey's hypothesis of Administrative law on the following grounds:

(1) Dicey's concept that the Droit Administratif' gives special protection to officials in their dealings with the citizens in their official capacity, is wrong. Because instances shows that 'Droit Administratif' is only due to French Revolution which gives effect to the theory of separation of powers. In reality, this has proved to be a boon to the private citizens whose liberty is hampered and interest is aggrieved upon by the officials. Thus, it is only a means to give protection to individual rights and liberties against the possible encroachment by administrative officials.

(2) Dicey's concept that 'Rule of Law' governs both the activities of state and citizens is also incorrect. Rather, there has always been a special body of law applicable to the activities of administrative authorities. Example: The Income Tax Act places the inland revenue authority in totally different position from the ordinary citizens.

(3) Dicey's contention that both officials and non-officials are equally subjected to the ordinary law of the land is also fallacious. The Crown in general and the Executive in particular enjoys much privileges than ordinary citizens.

(4) Dicey's observation that individual rights determines the basis of constitutional law is also wrong. Because, a vast part of constitutional law is formed on customs, conventions and parliamentary enactment's.

Thus, Dicey's hypothesis proved to be wrong by Prof. Robson.

Salient Features

The above discussion reveals the following characteristic features of administrative law:

(1) It relieves the public officials from the jurisdiction of ordinary courts for their official acts.

(2) The Administrative Tribunal deals with the wrongful official acts of administrative officials.

(3) It deals with rules relating to validity of administrative decrees.

(4) It distinguishes official acts from personal acts.

(5) It regulates the relationship of administrative authorities with private citizens.

Importance of Administrative Law

Administrative law plays a very important role in modern

state. Its importance and role cannot be undermined in a welfare state. The importance of administrative law can be summed up as follows:

(1) It upholds the primacy of common good over the personal interest and personal freedom as well as over private property.

(2) It stands for the promotion of social good.

(3) It places public authorities in a superior position to the private individuals.

In short, it guides the society towards social progress. It not only formulates policy but also develop new techniques and methods to work out the plans.

DELEGATED LEGISLATION

The most important innovation in the history of Public Administration and Constitutional Practices has been "Delegated Legislation". The concept is the product of twentieth century phenomena only. It refers to the law making power exercised by the executive on behalf of the legislature.

What is Delegated Legislation?

The term delegated legislation is the combination of two concepts–"delegation" and 'legislation.' Delegation means to 'give away' or to 'part with'. Legislation means 'rule making' or 'policy formulation'. Delegated legislation thus means to give away the power of rule making to somebody else.

This involves two questions–who frames rules and whom it delegates? The answer is obvious. The Legislature in modern states are entrusted with the task of policy formulation or rule making. The answer to the second question is a direct offshoot of the first one. It delegates the power to somebody who is responsible for policy implementation i.e. the Executive. Thus, the term 'delegated legislation' means 'the power of the legislature' to transfer the responsibility of policy formulation to the Executive organ of the government which acts in consonance with the directives of the legislature itself.

What Delegated Legislation is not?

Thus, we may say that when the 'rule making' power is given by the legislature to the Executive, the Executive naturally became more powerful. This may pose a threat to the independence and autonomy of legislature for which it exists. However, the apprehension is fallacious. Because delegated legislation does not mean to give away the whole power of law making to the Executive and observing the Executive activity simply as a silent spectator from a distance. Rather it only mean passing the policy only in a skeletal form and then delegating the power of detailed legislation to the Executive, at the same time exercising supervisory control over the Executive authority.

Definition

Delegated legislation, is a process of administration and as such it lacks any precise definition. We may consider that "delegated legislation is an administrative process through which the legislature entrust upon the Executive the task of filling the details of legislation as passed by herself in a skeleton form and authorize it for implementing the same through administrative orders and decrees."

The Donoughmore Committee defined delegated legislation as follows: " it means two things–either exercise by a subordinate authority such as a minister, of the legislative power delegated to him by the Parliament, or the subsidiary law themselves passed by the ministers in the shape of departmental regulations and other statutory rules and orders."

Fundamental Principles in Delegated Legislation

(a) Role of Executive

Delegated legislation, as an important device or as an administrative tool gives an upper hand to the Executive. However, one thing must be kept in mind that the power of rule making delegated to the Executive, does not end the role of policy formulation of Legislature. The Legislature only formulates the general policy outlines and left the details to be filled in by the Executive. By Executive, here we refer not the Executive in real sense of the term i.e. the political executives but it implies to the large body of administrative executives who are endowed with general knowledge, technical know-how, mental ability and administrative excellence. These are the persons who really mixes with the people at large and understand their basis problems. They filled in the very details of administrative law through governmental orders, decrees, rules and regulations. The political executive always exercises a supervisory role in delegated legislation. They have to see that the detailed legislation do not contradict the basic values underlined in the general policy as passed by the legislature.

(b) Role of Legislature

Besides these, the legislature itself, exercises a clear vigilance over the activities of the executives on the one hand, and over the administrators on the other hand.

(c) Role of Judiciary

Besides them, the judiciary also possess the power to review the administrative decrees and governmental orders from time to time on the basis of the general guidelines framed out by the legislature. If the detailed legislation stands in unavoidable conflict with the general legislation, the judiciary has the power of interpretation of the administrative order and may turn down the governmental decrees as unconstitutional, thus null and void.

(d) Delegated Legislation Vs. Subordinate Legislation

Delegated legislation is also known as subordinate legislation. However, these two terms are differing from each other in degree only although both the terms are frequently interchanged with each other. Subordinate legislation means the legislative action done by the subordinate i.e., the Executive. Therefore, while delegated legislation refers to the activity of legislature, subordinate legislation refers to the activity of Executive. While delegated legislation informs one about the general policy outlines of the law, subordinate legislation informs one about the details of the particular policy. Thus, we can say while delegated legislation is a 'prefix', subordinate legislation is only a 'suffix' added to legislation. We may thus conclude that subordinate legislation is only the supplementary to delegated legislation but it cannot be its substitute.

(e) Extent of Subordinate Legislation

As subordinate legislation involves the governmental orders and official decrees to give effect to the general policy of the government, it plays a significant role in administrative structures. However, all the governmental decrees, orders, rules and regulations cannot be considered as subordinate legislation. Only those decrees, order, rules and regulations which are issued to give effect to the policy framed by the legislature, are called subordinate legislation. The instruction of the government to its officials for the conduct of the business of the organisation does not mean subordinate legislation.

Limitations

Although the legislature can delegate the power of rule making to the Executive, yet it cannot delegate all powers. It means that some sort of limitation is also exercised upon the legislature while delegating its power of policy formulation. It cannot delegate the following powers to the executive what ever matter may be:

(a) to legislate on matters of principle

(b) to impose taxation

(c) to impose penalties

(d) to amend the Acts of Parliament

(e) to extend the duration of the Act.

(f) to extend the application of the Act

(g) to suspend or dispense with the Act.

Causes of Growth of Delegated Legislation

Delegation of legislative powers to the Executives have not emerged by accident. It is the product of a number of factors which occurred gradually and made the legislature think in terms of delegating the rule making power. The different reasons for the growth of the concept of delegated legislation are as follows:

(1) The concept of Welfare State unusually extended the frontiers of governmental power. It required more time and more knowledge on part of the administrators to go deep into the details of socio-economic and political problems. This requires the flexibility in the operation of government and resulted in the growth of delegated legislation.

(2) The growth of administrative law in the field of Public Administration have created new standards of administrative legislation. Thus, more emphasis was needed on Executives. This helped in delegated legislation.

(3) The growth of science and technology multiplied the role of modern states. It requires technical capability to manage the administration. The technical emphasis on administrative officials paved the way for delegated legislation.

(4) The general nature of legislature itself has also contributed significantly for the growth of delegated legislation. The average legislators, being layman, find it difficult to go details into the technicalities of the complex laws. They think it better to left the matter to the Executive and this led to the growth of the concept.

(5) Flexibility is the need of hour. Laws needed to be flexible in order to cope up the situation. The lack of time at the hands of legislators to go deep into the details of law and made it flexible also caused for the growth of delegated legislation.

(6) The role of administrators in the society also provided the basis for delegated legislation. The administrators are the liaison officer between the legislature and the public. Therefore, they are better aware of the requirements of the situation than the legislature. If they are provided with the powers of filling into the details of legislation, it would not only made the law flexible but also relieve the legislature of the burden of passing the cumbersome legislation in details. This also is responsible for delegated legislation.

Positive Impact of Delegated Legislation

Delegated legislation has the following plus points to its credit:

(1) It saves the times of the legislature.

(2) It provides for the flexibility of rules in day to day administration.

(3) It helps in utilizing the expert knowledge of administrators who happens to be the man of farsightedness, in social legislation.

(4) It saves the state from poor legislation by laymen who happens to be the representatives of the people.

(5) It helps in achieving prompt decision and instant action in times of exigencies.

(6) It avoids all sorts of litigation regarding the sphere of legislative action.

(7) It facilitates proper drafting of rules by the expert administrators.

(8) Delegated legislation guides the state towards progress at a rapid rate because the administrators need not waste their times in debate and discussion.

(9) It is suitable for meeting the emergencies which requires immediate action.

(10) It gives new direction to Public Administration by expanding the administrative horizons.

Negative Implications of Delegated Legislation

Every moon has its dark side. Similarly delegated legislation is not free from drawbacks. The negative points of delegated legislation can be summed up as follows:

(1) It poses a threat to individual freedom and as such may jeopardize the liberty and rights of the individuals.

(2) It may lead to too much delegation of law making power and as such undermines the role of legislature.

(3) In case of limited delegation the inability of the legislature to have a thorough scrutiny of the administrative rules and orders may give excessive power at the hands of the Executive.

(4) It may lead to deprivation of the rights of the individuals because the courts cannot interfere in this matter.

(5) It undermines the principle of democracy which favour separation of powers.

(6) It gives too much emphasis on Executive and therefore give privileged position to the State in the control of public.

(7) It overburdens the Executive organ in general and the administrative branch in particular with work and creates 'work mania'.

(8) The superiority complex developed among the administrators may lead to the destruction of the very purpose for which legislative power has been delegated.

(9) Too much flexibility in the administrative rules may lead to frequent changes too. This results in chaos and uncertainty.

(10) The average persons are ignorant about the nature and contents of delegated legislation because no strict emphasis is given on popular publicity of the rules and regulation. This negates the principle of democracy which says that people are supreme in democracy.

Looking at the above dangers of delegated legislation, scholars have apprehended that too much of delegated legislation would turn the legislature with only a registering body and the Executive with excessive burden on its shoulder which it can neither perform satisfactorily nor delegate to somebody else. The judiciary would be a silent spectator observing at a distance this hide and seek game between the Executive and Legislature. It cannot interfere in the game even if it wishes to be. All this may lead to mockery giving way for administrative despotism. **Hewart** considered it as a "triumph of bureaucracy" whereas **Dicey** apprehended that "Rule of law is exposed to New Peril" due to delegated legislation.

Safeguards in Delegated Legislation

Although delegated legislation may lead to administrative despotism, yet hopes cannot be altogether given out to guard successfully against the arbitrary nature of delegated legislation. The following steps may be considered as a safeguard against delegated legislation's absolutism:

(1) A well-defined limit should be prescribed to legislation by administrative branch so that they may not violate the fundamental principle on which delegated legislation is based. This will also lead to retention of power of supervision by the legislature.

(2) Delegated legislation should be made only for normal purpose. The abnormality should not be delegated. Only those powers which involves odious responsibility and complexity of administrative procedures should be delegated. The other important and superior powers like imposition of taxes, passing

of Parliamentary legislation etc. should be retained by the legislature herself.

(3) Another safeguard against absolutism in delegated legislation is that before delegation, a proper consultation should be made with the people whose interest is affected. This may be possible by eliciting public opinion on a bill to be passed by the legislature. This gives a picture of general and detailed legislations to be done by the Executive.

(4) The details of administrative legislation should be subject to strict scrutiny by the legislature. There should be the establishment of a separate Committee of Parliament on delegated legislation who will devote all its times in going through the details of legislation on the broad outlines passed by the legislature and to report there on, to the Parliament if the main purpose is destructed for which delegation is made.

(5) The details of administrative legislation should always be made public by giving sufficient and widespread publicity to the administrative rules and orders. This may give the people an ample scope to understand and comprehend the administrative legislation easily. As such public vigilance would definitely keep the administrative legislation within its proper bounds.

(6) Last, but not the least, all the administrative legislation's should be subjected to judicial review. This may give upperhand to the judiciary to supervise administrative legislation and declare them null and void, if they violate the fundamental principles of the Constitution.

PARLIAMENTARY CONTROL

In India, a Committee on Subordinate Legislation, established in December, 1953 provides a basis for Parliamentary control over subordinate legislation.

The Committee on Subordinate Legislation consisted of 15 members who are appointed by the speaker annually. The chairman of the Committee happens to be an important member of the Opposition party. The Committee has been entrusted to evolve a uniform pattern of terms of delegation and to scrutinize the details of administrative legislation. The functions of the Committee are follows:

(1) To examine the details of administrative legislation in the light of general policy outlines as laid down by the legislature and to report there on to.

(2) To report to the Parliament about the progress and stability of administrative legislation i.e. whether it is in consonance with the broad objectives of the policy and does not violate the constitutional rules.

(3) To suggest, if any, to the Parliament, on delegated legislation if it thinks to improve up the procedure of administrative legislation and other things related with delegated legislation.

Administrative Adjudication

Administration, in present society, involves a stupendous task of policy formulation as well as policy implementation. However, another distinctive feature of administration lies in the fact that it takes the enormous task of resolving the numerous controversies between the citizens themselves or the citizens and the organs of the government. To quote **Wade** and **Phillips**, "modern government gives rise to many disputes which cannot appropriately be solved by applying objective legal principles or standards and depends ultimately on what is desirable in public interest as a matter of social policy." Therefore, in some cases, the actions of the government is truly administrative, while in some other cases it is judicial.

In other words, we can say that administration do exists for the people. It wants to promote people's interest by way of policy formulation and policy implementation. However, sometimes the policy formulated by the administrative body, as a part of delegated legislation, may, in fact, encroach upon the interest of the particular individual or group of individuals. The party whose interest is aggrieved upon, therefore, appeals to the government or to the judiciary. When the administrative branch of government take due notice of the interest of the individual and general public and decides the case judiciously without the help of judiciary, it is said that administration has decided the case. This power of administrative authority to decide the dispute or cases in their official capacity is called Administrative Adjudication.

What is Administrative Adjudication?

Administrative adjudication is a process at the hands of the Executive branch of government. It gives some sort of judicial power, not to the full extent, to the administrative authority through which the controversial policies of the government are simplified and cases are dispensed with.

Administrative adjudication is combination of both 'administrative' and 'adjudication'. 'Administrative' means the 'authority who administers or decides". At the same time 'adjudication' means to decide judiciously'. Therefore, Administrative Adjudication means the authority of the government who judiciously decide the cases or policies.

Administrative adjudication, therefore, have two implications–firstly, it refers to the adjudication of administrative affairs. Viewed in this sense, administrative adjudication means deciding the legality of administrative decisions and administrative laws in a societal context. Secondly, it refers to administratively adjudicate the affairs. Viewed from this angle, administrative adjudication means the settlement of the case by the administrative authority only. As such it negates the interference of judiciary in matters involving administrative law and decisions. In both the implications, the administrative authority is provided with the task of interpretation of administrative decisions. Therefore, administrative adjudication, is essentially a quasi-judicial process.

The quasi-judicial character of administrative authority, sometimes, confronted a student with the question: What it decides? Actually decision making is a legislative process and interpretation of those decisions is a judicial process. Then what is left for the administrative authority to decide? The answer involves a technical knowledge. The power of judiciary extends to the interpretation of the legislative procedures only and as such all laws passed by legislature is subject to review by the judiciary.

However, we know from the previous chapter that the legislature passes only the general form of the law and leaves the details of legislation to be filled in by the Executive. But the judiciary cannot interfere in the subordinate legislation made by the Executive in general and the administrative branch in particular unless the same contradicts the provisions of the constitutions or distort the general policy outline of the law.

The subordinate legislation, as filled in by the Executive, may sometimes, got ambiguous and may encroach upon the individual liberty and rights. This ambiguities cannot be decided by the judiciary. On the contrary, it is the administrative Tribunal, set up by the administrative authority, looks into the matter and gives the exact interpretation of the 'policy' filled in by the administrative branch and thereby helps in deciding the ambiguity. This power of Administrative Tribunals to interpret the details of subordinate legislation is called Administrative Adjudication.

It is thus obvious that the administrative authority have close relationship with the public. In their dealing with the public, the authorities may adopt two ways. Firstly, there may be personal dealings and secondly there may be official dealings. In their personal dealings with the people, the officials are accountable to the judiciary and the judiciary interferes in deciding the personal cases i.e. either civil or criminal. However, the dealing with the people by the authority in their official capacity and the ambiguities thereof, is the special prerogative of Administrative Tribunals.

Therefore, we may conclude that while administrative adjudication is a process. Administrative Tribunal is the agent to that process. In other words, it is the Administrative Tribunals which adjudicates the administrative decision, orders and policies and decides the ambiguities thereof.

The whole concept of administrative adjudication necessarily involves and reveals that there always exists a 'dispute' between the public and authority in his dealing with them in official capacity. However, this concept is not always true. As such the existence of 'dispute' is not a universal phenomena having universal application. There are certain instances where administrative adjudication does not involve 'dispute'. Rather there is generalization of 'ambiguities' i.e. it is the presence of 'ambiguities' not 'dispute' which provides for a case of administrative adjudication. For example: the granting of license by the authority does not involve dispute rather ambiguities–whom to give license and whom to not. Here the concept of 'rights' came to play a significant role. Thus, when the rights of the individuals or private parties are aggrieved upon by the administrative authority in his official capacity, there comes the role of administrative adjudication by the Administrative Tribunal.

Definitions

After conceptualizing 'administrative adjudication'. We are left with the choice of examining the various interpretations of the term given by various scholars. The definitions are follows:

L.D. White–"Administrative adjudication means the investigation and setting of a dispute involving a private party on the basis of a law and fact by an administrative agency."

M.E. Dimock–"Administrative Adjudication is a process by which administrative agencies settle issues arising in course of their work when legal rights are in question."

Encyclopaedia of Social Sciences–"Administrative adjudication is a process upheld by the Administrative Tribunal—an authority outside the ordinary court system which interpret and apply the laws when the acts of public administration is attacked in formal suits or by established methods."

Sadan & Sharma–"Administrative adjudication means determination by the administrative agencies of issues or cases involving the rights and obligations of private parties."

The above definitions reveals that administrative adjudication involves the establishment of a special administrative organisation called Administrative Tribunal which is outside the authority of both the Legislature and Executive and settles the 'case' according the established 'policy'.

Features

Administrative adjudication exhibits the following characteristic features:

(1) There is an Administrative Tribunal to decide the case.

(2) There is 'ambiguity' in the interpretation of government policy.

(3) It involve the cases where the 'right' of the private individuals are at stake.

(4) It is quasi-judicial process i.e. it can settle the dispute.

(5) It is a process done at the administrative level.

(6) It is quite different from judiciary and follow its own methods.

Administrative Adjudication *Vs.* Judicial Adjudication

A distinction can be made between administrative adjudication and judicial adjudication. While administrative adjudication is done by the administrative branch, i.e. the Executive, the judicial adjudication is carried on by the Judiciary. The following can be considered as the point of differences between them:

(1) Judicial adjudication is administered by 'settled

principles of law', but administrative adjudication is guided not by any legal precepts but by 'common good' or 'public interest'.

(2) Judiciary exists to interpret legislative policy of Legislature; Administrative Tribunals exists to interpret the legislative plans of the Executive and as such, its aim is not the administration of justice but the execution of legislative plans.

(3) The Judges in judiciary courts are independent of the Executive control; the judges in the Administrative Tribunals are officers from the Executive branch.

(4) While Judiciary is free from any personal biasness, Administrative Tribunals are ordained with administrative biasness.

(5) The judicial functions cannot be delegated to the subordinates; but in administrative adjudication, the delegation of power is possible.

(6) Judicial adjudication involves a dispute between the parties; but in administrative adjudication such dispute may be absent. It takes into account the 'rights' of the parties.

(7) Evidence and witness is necessary for judicial adjudication; but administrative adjudication do not necessarily depend on witness.

(8) The judicial procedure is rigid in judicial adjudication; but judicial procedure is flexible in administrative adjudication.

(9) The authorities in judicial adjudication are expert in law; but the authorities in administrative adjudication are expert in administration.

Advantages of Administrative Adjudication

Administrative Adjudication, as an administrative process, has the following merits to its credit:

(1) It provides a basis for protection of individual freedom and rights against the authoritative abuse of administrators.

(2) It helps in speedy disposal of justice to the people in administrative matters.

(3) It lessens significantly, the burden of judiciary by sharing its judicial power in administrative cases.

(4) It makes the administration of justice cheaper and therefore, reposes the faith of the people in Executive.

(5) There is flexibility of operation of administrative tribunals than the law courts.

Disadvantages of Administrative Adjudication

Administrative Adjudication has also the following defects:

(1) It gives undue importance to Executive and as such violates the principle of rule of law.

(2) The right to appeal from the decisions of Administrative Tribunals is limited or even non-existent.

(3) There is no uniformity of procedures which Administrative Tribunal follows.

(4) Administrative Tribunals are manned by administrators and technical heads who do not have the acumen for judicial work.

(5) Administrative adjudication lacks publicity of its proceedings and as such it cannot predict the trends of future decisions.

How to Improve up Administrative Adjudication?

Although administrative adjudication is an important element of democratic process, yet people are more confused with it and as such they look down the concept of administrative adjudication. Actually, if sufficient safeguards can be organized administrative adjudication would be more viable, strong and fasten the process of democratic administration. The following safeguards can be considered as elements to improve up administrative adjudication:

(1) The Administrative Tribunal should consists of more than one person.

(2) The Chairman and Members of the Tribunal should be appointed not on political grounds by the ministers, rather they are to be appointed by a Council on Tribunals.

(3) A person who is involved in dispute, should not be the adjudicator of disputes.

(4) Neutrality should be observed by the administrative adjudicators i.e. they cannot be both judge and prosecutor at the same time.

(5) Every body should be given an opportunity to represent his case either by himself or through a legal expert.

(6) Party concerned should know the reasons for the decision.

(7) All the evidence and documents on the basis of which a decision is taken should be disclosed publicly.

(8) The accused should have the right to cross-examine the evidence and challenge the evidence produced against him.

(9) Every person should be allowed to have right to appeal for higher judgement against the decision of the Administrative Tribunal.

(10) There should be a judicial review of all the judicious and semi-judicious actions of the administrators.

If these safeguards can be utilized, administrative adjudication will definitely tend to improve up.

Chapter VII

NEW ASPECTS OF ADMINISTRATION

DEVELOPMENT ADMINISTRATION

Every modern Welfare State is characterized by its institutions which serves the purpose of growth. The administrative structures of any political system is wielded to change — a change from traditional social structure to a more comprehensive modern one; a change from essentially normative outlook to a more dynamic and rational outlook; a change from efficiency and economy to growth; a change from centralized structure of administrative hierarchy to a flexible participatory one; a change from status quo to modernity and so on. Such type of positive and dynamic orientation on part of the administration is often represented by development administration.

Historical Legacy

The term 'development administration' is a combination of both 'development' and 'administration'. Development, in common parlance refers to growth or extension. "Administration", similarly mean power by an authority'. Development administration, therefore, mean to a common man as the extension of the powers of an authority. Normally, in a traditional society, the authority is only entrusted with ruling i.e. imposing reasonable restrictions on the enjoyment of liberties by the people for the higher societal order. Therefore, the authority in a traditional society performs only a negative function. However, with the growth of the concept of Welfare State, science and technology, invention of modern means of transport and communication, expansion of man's knowledge beyond the family and so on, the functions of authority got enhanced and enlarged. The authority, now started not only exercising negative functions but also undertake certain positive functions. i.e. it started giving positive amenities to the people. This positive or growth oriented activity undertaken by the administrative authorities give rise to the concept 'development administration'.

Development administration therefore, is a concept which got its origin due to the extension of administrative functions. The term was first coined by **U.L. Goswami** in 1955. However, credit goes to **Edward W. Weidner** who first introduced the concept development administration in Public Administration. After that the concept got popularized by the scholars like Fred. W. Riggs, Joseph La Palombora, Albert Waterson, Merle Fainsod, Lucian Pye and a host of others.

Definitions

The meaning of the term development administration cannot be understood simply by its historical legacy unless we go deep into the definitions. The various definitions of development administration are as follows:

Edward W. Weidner—"Development administration is a process of guiding an organisation towards the achievement of progressive social, economic and political objectives that are authoritatively determined in one manner or the other."

Merle Fainsod—"Development administration ordinarily involves the establishment of machinery for planning, economic growth and mobilizing and allocating resources to expand national income."

Montgomery– "Development administration connotes

carrying planned changes in the economy or capital infrastructure and to a lesser extent in the social services especially health and education."

Ramesh K. Arora—"In the literature of public administration the term development administration has been used in two inter-related senses. First, it refers to the administration of development programmes. Second, it involves the strengthening administrative capabilities."

Donald C. Stone—"Development administration is concerned primarily with the tasks and processes of formulating and implementing 4P's–plans, policies, programmes and projects."

Meaning

An analysis of the above definitions gives an apparent meaning to the concept development administration. Generally speaking, there are two meanings of development administration. Viewed from narrow angle, development administration means merely a programme oriented approach to administration. It is concerned with the mobilization of resources and cultivation of appropriate skills to achieve the developmental goals of administration.

But viewed from a broad base, development administration includes the entire process of nation building. The narrow meaning of development administration was advocated by Montgomery and Fainsod, while the wider meaning was highlighted by Fred. W. Riggs, E.W. Weidner and Lucian Pye. The narrow meaning of development administration is conceived only by taking into the administration of developing societies. But the wider meaning includes the study of administrative structures and their functions of developed societies in relation to the developing societies.

However, the real meaning of development administration can be understood by sticking to the middle path, thereby leaving both the extremes. As **Fred W. Riggs** have rightly observed that "Administration cannot normally be improved very much without changes in the environmental constraints (the infrastructures) that hampers its effectiveness, and the environment itself cannot be changed unless the administration of development programmes is strengthened."

Therefore, development administration is essentially a concept of administration which is action-oriented rather than structure oriented. It involves not only the study of traditional administrative systems but is more directed towards the dynamics of administrative systems.

Development administration, is therefore, mean two things–the administration of development programmes and the development of administrative structures to raise its capabilities for development. It is not only action-oriented but also structure oriented. It try to sought a proportional balance between the administrative structures and developmental programmes. A growth in administrative structures would proportionately lead to a growth in development programmes. Development programmes, is essentially determined and shaped by the structures.

However, one thing should always be kept in mind that only quantitative growth is not the criteria for development administration. Rather development administration emphasises on both quantity and quality as an index of development. For example: a rise in the number of educational institutions does not mean development. Development also includes the quality of teaching in these educational institutions. The poor quality of teaching, the lack of strict discipline, irregularity in teachers and students attendance etc. would definitely point to 'negative development' in spite of the rise in the number of schools. Development administration, on the other hand, wants to develop the quality of teaching simultaneously along with the growth of schools. This certainly is 'positive development.' Therefore, development administration only takes into account 'positive development' i.e. both quality and quantitative growth and certainly negates the "negative development."

Nature

Development administration is such a vast concept that after analysing the multi-faceted and multi-dimensional aspects of the concept, one is left with the impression that he has not mastered adequately the concept itself. The nature of development administration could be analysed from the basic assumption on which the edifice of development stands.

One of the assumptions of development administration is that it stressed on institution building in order to achieve nation building. The growth of a number of administrative structures would facilitate specialization of function. Development administration thus diverted more power, more energy and more initiative in building up a variety of administrative institutions.

Another assumption of development administration is that is stressed on modernization in order to achieve Development. Modernization is viewed as a means to achieve development goals. This necessarily helped in institutional transfer i.e. from tradition to rationality, from ascriptive to achievement orientation.

It helps in economic growth. Economy being the foundation stone of every political system, is successfully increased gradually and steadily with planning and setting up of goals.

Besides economic issues, development of social structures and social institutions has also been a regular feature of development. It helps in creating a variety of societal structures to combat the social problems like hunger, poverty, unemployment, diseases, illiteracy, population explosions etc.

Development administration is characterized also, by a commitment for socio-political and economic growth. The commitment to change made bureaucracy deeply involved and emotionally attached to the goal itself.

It is always oriented for achievement of the goals. The setting of goals is always held prime importance in any society, whether development and developing without the goal, the administration would be a nulity.

Planning is yet another distinguishing feature of development administration. The target is always followed by a plan to achieve it. It may include long-term planning as well as short-term planning. It also determines the amount of money to be invested for development.

Development administration, in order to achieve rapid and all round development also sometimes, emphasized on 'project packages.' A number of projects have been undertaken not only by the governmental agency but also by the private voluntary organisations whose role cannot be denied in development administration. Each 'package' aims at development.

It is also client oriented. Every developmental programme, in order to be successful, require the help of the personnels. It stresses on small sector of clients and clings onto their development which in turn, would facilitate nation-building process. For example: women's development, children development, development of socially and educationally backward classes, development of scheduled castes and scheduled tribes etc. are certain instances of client oriented approach of development administration.

Last, but not the least, development administration is time-bound. It always seeks after people's development within a time span. Within the specified time set in the goal, it aims at changing the status quo. However, this time bound approach, even sometimes, made development impossible in practice. Because the goal is fixed and within the stipulated period the target is to be achieved. In their attempt to achieve the target, the administrators sometimes lost the content and helps in poor quality development i.e. negative development only. For example: if 500 people are to be provided with IRDP loans within a year, the target is fulfilled in time. But whether real development of the beneficiaries have taken place and raise their standards of life or not, is totally ignored. This certainly is not development, rather growth only.

Characteristics

The above nature of development administration reveals the following characteristic features of it. They are as follows:

(1) It is an administrative process.

(2) It stressed on the growth of administrative institutions.

(3) It also stressed on increasing the personnels involved in administration.

(4) It emphasized the extension of administration to the fields i.e. the real area of development.

(5) It called for bringing about a socio-economic change in the society.

(6) It strategically emphasized on planning for development.

(7) It is goal oriented.

(8) It is time oriented.

(9) It is client oriented.

(10) It stressed on popular involvement in developmental process.

From the above discussion, we must say that 'development administration' is not a feature of developing countries. It is also equally a part of public administration in developed and highly industrialized society. To equate development administration only with the functioning of administration in developing countries would certainly provide a narrow view of development administration.

Role of Bureaucracy in Development Administration

As I told you that development administration is not only a part of public administration of developing societies only but it is also contained in the administration of developed societies. The role of bureaucracy would mean its role both in developed and developing societies.

Development administration is a part of public administration. It is an instrument for rapid change in the socio-economic conditions of the people on the one hand and guiding the society as a whole towards progressive nation-building. Therefore, it is a policy which need to be transplanted into action. This policy got its direction and orientation only by the bureaucratic officials. The bureaucracy means all those administrative officials who not only take authoritative decisions but also implement them successfully to achieve the desired goals. The bureaucracy in the government has been the principal planner, energizer, promoter, director and initiator to accelerate the developmental efforts of the society.

Issues before the Administrators

In their role as 'the agent of change' the first task before the bureaucracy is to identify the various socio-economic and politico-administrative issues present in the society which acts as the main stumbling block in the path of development. However, the issues differs from one state to another in particular and from developing societies to developed societies in general.

In the developed countries, although the basic eight necessities of life—air, water, employment, food, cloth, housing, medical care and education have been provided by an large, yet many a other socio-economic and cultural issues are still dominating. A number of problems like the high rate of spending on defence, the trade relations with the developing countries, the extent of state control over economic activities, the threat of ecology and environment, of pollution, energy crisis, the heightening divorce rate, the high rate of mental cases, the high rate of suicide cases, the epidemic of population explosions and number of others are still creating headache for the administrators and stands on the way of achieving total development.

The issues confronted by the bureaucrats in developing societies are quite different from those of developed countries.

The problems of widespread poverty, heightening economic inequality, irrational wage structure, economic injustices, casteism, untouchability, superstitions, dowry, ignorance, illiteracy, malnutrition, insanitary environment, dirty drinking water, corruption, moral bankruptcy and a host of others have really checked the growth of socio-economic development of developing countries. The solution of these problems has become almost a tough and challenging job for the administrators.

What the Bureaucracy Ought to Do?

Bureaucracy in both the developed and developing societies must come up heavily to crush down the evils of socio-economic and politico-administrative issues confronted by the societies in order to achieve development administration. Its aim should always be, to achieve the desired results by faithfully executing the public policy in the interest of common welfare of the people. As Prof. **L.D. White** observes, "the aim of civil servants, in its broader context, should be the maintenance of peace and order, the instruction of the young, equalization of opportunities, protection of the people against disease and insecurities, adjustment and compromise of the conflicting interest groups; in short, the achievement, insofar as possible, of a good life."

Role of Bureaucracy—The Reality

The bureaucracy really have to provide the incentive for social change and also have to remove the bottlenecks and correct the imbalances which affect the system's functioning. Administrator's role as an agent of institutional, social and economic change has to be realized as the development process has to push ahead in a climate of uncertainty.

But the reality is far from satisfactory. The role of bureaucracy is strangely not upto the satisfaction. Bureaucracy is known for its red-tapism, division of work, hierarchical arrangement of offices, formalism etc. It is considered as a misfit in the developing countries where speedy change is needed to bring about socio-economic transformation. Its capacity for adaptation to change is considered low.

According to **Dwivedi** and **Jain**, the bureaucracy in the developing countries are western oriented and as such they have a bourgeoisie tendency. This substituted for popular mobilization and mass politics and tend to maintain the status quo.

However, it is indeed, illogical to blame the bureaucracy wholly for non-development. Our social structure is largely feudalistic in nature and as such the law, its agencies, the administration, and its machinery none of them is oriented towards the common man. The society is vertical and hierarchical society and not horizontal and egalitarian in nature. People are weighed down by superstitions. So the rate of social change is frustratingly low.

Besides that, there is some thing wrong with our plans. Our planners, policy makers and intellectual aristocrats have imitated some of the worst features of the west which are quite unrelated to the realities of home and the needs of the people.

Actually, there is no basic conflict between bureaucratic structure and development scale. But there is a sharply negative relationship between the bureaucratic behaviour and development scale. The structural weaknesses in bureaucracy consequently determines and influences their behaviour.

Remedies

The dysfunctionalities in the bureaucratic behaviour is due to its organisational hierarchy. If the bureaucracy is to play a significant role in development administration, then the dysfunctionalities are to be identified and corrected properly. The following changes may be helpful to fit bureaucracy into developmental tasks:

(1) The hierarchical organisation structure of bureaucracy should be changed in a horizontal direction.

(2) Steps should be taken for cooperative decision making and collaborative problem solving.

(3) There must be decentralization of authority in order to enable the field units to take decisions on the spot for speedy disposal of problems.

(4) There should be free flow of information in the bureaucratic organisation to ensure effective and efficient decision making.

(5) Bureaucracy must secure the cooperation and participation of the people in development work.

(6) There should be a change in the attitude of the bureaucrats to achieve people's cooperation in development administration.

(7) There should be a sense of service and a spirit of dedication on part of the administrators.

(8) New techniques are to be acquired by the bureaucracy in order to achieve development on the basis of modern science and technology.

People's Participation in Administration

No plan for development administration can be successful without the basic cooperation of the people in the implementation of the schemes. In fact, every developmental schemes, invented and implemented by the government, aims at the general development of the people at large.

The Reality

"What touches all must be decided by all"—is the famous slogan of democratic government. As such, increasing steps have been taken by the government to include the cooperation of the general mass of the society by providing them necessary support for participating in the administrative process in order to fasten the rate of development.

However, the approach taken by the government is not an approach of whole-heartedness and sincerity. Still more viable media can be developed to seek people's participation in development administration.

Suggestions

I would like to suggest that the government should take steps not only to seek people's participation in external area, but also an intensive thrust must be there in the internal participation of the people. As such, the generic form of people's participation can be done in two ways—internal participation and external participation.

Internal Participation

Internal participation of the people in development administration refers to the development of a good employer-employee relationship within the administrative system. Therefore, it means the participation of the employees in administrative process.

The following steps can be ensured to accelerate the pace of internal participation of people in administration:

(1) The employees should be taken into confidence while framing policies for development.

(2) There should be a direct contact between the superior and subordinates to facilitate the growth of development.

(3) The bureaucracy should come out of its household drudgery of maintaining strict discipline, formality, hierarchy and superior complexity.

(4) The employees should be encouraged to give constructive suggestions for development.

(5) Reward must be given to the employees for acceptable suggestions for development. This would encourage people's (employees) participation in administration.

(6) A general meeting between the employer and the employees should be convened regularly to exchange

their views on development schemes and their problems.

(7) Small groups of generous employees should be set up to guide the development schemes in the fields.

(8) There should be a regular review of the various developmental schemes, and their implementations in the society and to verify its implications—whether good or bad and to suggest how improvements can be made in the schemes to adapt them to the changing scenario.

(9) An 'Advisory Body' consisting of employees who have a 'direct bearing on developmental schemes should be there to assist the bureaucrats in solving the problems faced by them in implementing the schemes at the spot.

External Participation

External participation of the people in development administration refers to the role of citizens in administrative process. As a conscious citizen of the state, each individual should not only have a knowledge about the variety of development schemes but also involve himself actively in implementing these policies for general development.

The following steps can be ensured to accelerate the rate of external participation i.e., the citizen's participation in administration:

(1) There must be sufficient and adequate publicity of various development schemes undertaken by the government in order to popularize them among the people for whom administration really meant.

(2) A regular meeting in the form of seminars, symposiums and discussions should be there between the government and the citizens to clear up their difficulties.

(3) Citizen's participation should be encouraged through

election to local bodies like Panchayats, Panchayat Samities, Zilla Parishads, NAC's, Municipalities, Corporations etc.

(4) Small civic groups of citizens should be formed in the area where development schemes are implemented in order to review their functioning from time to time.

(5) The "citizen's forum" should be encouraged to give suggestions to government regarding various developmental measures to be undertaken.

(6) A 'Consultation Group' should be formed which will consists of the elderly, experienced and learned persons. They are to be consulted by the government before planning for any development.

(7) Some measure of autonomy should also be given to the voluntary organisations in order to fasten the process of development.

(8) Every governmental proposal for development should be guided by the advice of citizen's forum for development.

(9) Freedom should be given to private citizens, citizen forums and voluntary organisations to initiate proposal for development and the government should take a keen interest in these proposals and accept them by considering their viability.

If these steps can be categorically adhered to while framing policies, then only development administration will be a grand success.

Development Administration in India—A Critical Review

Development administration in India is considered to be a British legacy. Since the last fifty years of Indian Independence, right from the village level worker (VLW) in the village to the cabinet minister of Rural Development in Government of India, and millions of public servants are engaged in development administration. Since 80% of the people live in villages, the development administration has primarily concentrated on rural development.

In the late seventies, to help the poor directly, two schemes were started by the government–the Self Employment Scheme and the Wage Employment Schemes. These two schemes aims at removing the two greatest obstacles in development—unemployment and poverty respectively.

The first scheme i.e. the Self Employment Scheme was named as Integrated Rural Development Programme (IRDP). This scheme is conceptually faulty. Faulty because it aims to make an entrepreneur out of the poorest of the poor in the society. An entrepreneur is one who can take risks before starting any enterprise. Even where, the educated, affluent youth fears to start an enterprise, it was too much to expect the poorest of the poor to start one. He has to plan for the inputs, run the enterprise and market the output, all by himself. But the first task before a poor is to fulfil his basic needs like hunger. So any productive asset given to him under the scheme gets disposed off at the earliest possible opportunity. Therefore, despite all checks and balances, the success story of IRDP is even less than 15%.

Besides the loan waiver scheme has played havoc with commercial banking. Now people expect the government to waive loans every year. Even now also, the government fixes the targets, the nationalized banks are forced to fulfil the same within the financial year. Due to pressure, the bankers have also become smarter. They only loan out the subsidy component while they force the beneficiary to keep the loan component in a savings bank account. As a result, the IRDP has become some sort of a dole.

The second scheme was named under various names. Until 1989, it termed as Jawahar Rozgar Yojana (JRY). Since 1993, another two or three schemes like Intensified JRY, Employment Assurance Scheme (EAS) and Innovative JRY have been drawn up with the same guideline as that of JRY. Besides, there are certain other schemes which are location specific such as Desert

Development Programme (DDP), Drought Prone Area Programme (DPAP), Integrated Water-Shed Development Programme (IWDP), Integrated Tribal Development Programme (ITDP) etc. The main aim of all these schemes is to assure wage employment to unskilled people, reduce migration, ensure minimum wage and equal pay for equal work irrespective of sex. The other aim of the schemes is to create community assets which will benefit the whole community or a segment thereof. Funds are sent directly to the Panchayats or Panchayat Samities and other executing agencies to execute the projects.

The availability of funds is so huge that the allocation for Ministry of Rural Development is next only to Defence Ministry at Government of India level. The availability of funds per district can be gauged from the example of Kandhamal district of Orissa. For a population of over 5 lakhs, the total availability of funds in DRDA i.e. District Rural Development Agency is to the tune of 40 crores per year. i.e. Rs. 800/- per person. When we take the wage component and the available work force, it works out to over Rs. 4000/- per worker per year.

However, allocation of so much money creates problem of inadequate technical supervision, unavailability of labour and poor quality of works. At the same time, none of the schemes have any provision of maintenance of assets except that of Gram Panchayat JRY schemes. Any community asset, unless maintained may become dysfunctional and non-functional over the years because the concept of "Govt.'s property is no body's property."

The stress is always on the achievement of targets i.e. both financial and physical. One who can spend more money is a better administrator of development programmes. So everyone tries to show that he is capable of spending more and more amount.

But there have never been any inbuilt review of the quality of the work or whether the money spent has made any difference to the people or not. For example, if we take the plantation programmes alone under various schemes for Horticulture to Forestry, and if we go by paper works, we would have planted the whole land surface of India several times over. So we should be more practical and quality oriented so as to achieve long-term benefits. After all, the money that is being spent is either coming from the tax-payer or from borrowings or from currency press. Therefore, expenditure alone should not be the sole criteria of success of any development administrator.

I feel that development and administration should compliment each other. The job of the administration is not only to build school buildings but also to ensure teachers attendance and students attendance. Similarly, it is not enough to help the farmer to increase the productivity but also to ensure that he gets a fair price for his produce.

The Last Word

Community participation for any community project seem to be the order of the day. If we can awaken the hidden force of this community participation, the development can be sustainable. Since there is no contribution or participation by the public in either selecting or funding or executing any development project, the public apathy is increasing towards the government funded projects. Therefore, the problem before the development administrator is to get the general mass participate in the process of development.

Chapter VIII

FINANCIAL ADMINISTRATION IN INDIA

Finance is the heart and soul of every society, be it social, economic or political. The efficiency of administration, in a political society like state, depends certainly wholly on finance. Finance, in common usage refers to money. It is the basic determining factor in administration. It provides the fuel to the administration. As such it keeps the machinery of administration on wheels. The success of administration, actually depends on the successful management of finance. Management of finance means keeping proper account of the expenditures and income and to supervise that the expenditure is compatible with the income i.e. it is actually utilized for public service. This administration of financial management by the government is usually done through budget. Therefore, budget is the instrument through which the government manages its finance in a effective and efficient way.

WHAT IS A BUDGET?

The Budget is the principal instrument of action. It is an instrument at the hands of the government in order to successfully utilize the public money. As I told you earlier that the utilization of public money or finance can be secured by maintaining a strict account of income and expenditures, so the term budget also come to mean the financial statement of the government showing income and expenditures.

Etymologically, the term 'Budget' is derived from the French word "*Bougette*" which means a leather bag. The word 'Budget' was first time used in England in 1733. There is an interesting story behind the coming into being of the budget. During those period, the Chancellor of Exchequer of England used to bring to the House of Commons the papers dealing with financial matters in a leather bag secretly. When he presented those papers before the house, he opened the bag, keep out the papers and present before the House of Commons. Till that, nobody knows what is actually there in those financial statements when he brings out the papers from the bag, the Commoners satirically used the term "opened the Budget". In course of time, the budget came to be identified with the financial statements inside the bag, instead of the leather bag itself.

However, the need of a 'Budgetary System' was actually realized in 1803 in England, when there was a tremendous increase in the activities of the state. Since then the budget is laid before the House of Commons annually and as such Budget is came to be known as the '*Annual Financial Statement*' of the government. It is prepared by the Chancellor of Exchequer in secret and contains the sources and heads of income and expenditure of the government in a particular year.

Therefore, a 'Budget' is nothing but the Annual Financial Statement of the government which contains the income and expenditures of the government from various sources and on various plans, projects, programmes and policies to be carried on at an earliest opportunity in the ensuing financial year.

A budget is always laid before the popular House of the Legislature in order to let the Hon'ble members know the financial transactions carried on by the Executive organ of the government. The amount stated in the budget is always sanctioned by the Legislature in order to give the Executive an upperhand in administration. Without the prior approval of the Legislature, the Executive cannot spend a single pie at its discretion. Therefore, budget is an important instrument of legislative control over the Executive.

WHY IS A BUDGET?

Very often a student of Public Administration may ask to himself why there is the need of a budget? Can a state run without a budget? The answer to this question is quite obvious. The activities of state, in modern days have become so complex and comprehensive that a layman cannot understand them effectively. He usually interpret the activities of state in economic terms i.e. balance of payment, trade balance, monetary and credit policies, tax system, price level, interest rates and so on. A budget is a comprehensive document dealing with all these aspects of economy in a lucid manner. Therefore, by understanding the budget of a state, a person can generally get an insight into the economy. Therefore, budget is very important to comprehend man's knowledge about the state and its economy.

Besides that Budget also acts as an instrument of socio-economic changes in the policy of the state. The modern states are welfare states and as such Budget is used as a means for the promotion of welfare objectives.

Budget, also acts as the tools of financial administration in the state. It brings together the estimates of anticipated revenues and proposed expenditures implying the whole body of activities to be undertaken and the means of financing these activities.

At the same time, the budget also acts as a measure for implementing the various plans and policies of the government. It provides the basis for the formation of every policies in response to the current economic trends as well as the long-term requirements of the economy.

Last, but not the least, budget is indeed, the most important instrument for legislative control over administration. Through this budget, the legislature exercise wide powers of control, direction and supervision over the varied activities of administration.

Therefore, the importance of a budget in a democratic state cannot be undermined. Due to its growing importance, every democratic government used to have and insisted upon having a sound budgetary system to suit the changing requirements of the situation. A state, without a budget is unthinkable and even inconceivable as a baby without a heart.

REQUIREMENTS OF A GOOD BUDGET

Although Budget is most important for a state administration, yet poor quality of budget may lead the state into financial bankruptcy. Therefore, what is needed, is a good budget, a budget that serves the needs of the people to the maximum extent. The following can be considered as the criteria required for a good budget:

(1) That the budget should always be a balanced one neither surplus, nor deficit, a system where the income and expenditures are of the same.

(2) There should be proper planning before devising the budget. It should be prepared in the context of the current financial position of the state.

(3) There should be a 'group of specialists' to assists the Chief Executive in the formulation of budget. In India, The Finance Ministry consisting of experts, assists the President in this task.

(4) That the budget should be laid for one year only and there should be continuity in the annual financial statement.

(5) That all the income and expenditures stated in the budget should be realized within the same financial year without resorting to the practice in France where they are to be realized in the next financial year.

(6) That the money left unspent at the end of the financial year must lapse to the government Treasury.

(7) That the estimates made in the budget, should be, as far as practicable, exact because excess estimate may burden the people with tax while under-estimated one

may throw the whole of the budgetary process out of gear when it comes into execution.

(8) That, a clear cut picture of gross receipts and expenditures should be fully shown in the budget.

IS DEFICIT BUDGET UNTENABLE?

In a general sense, a budget may be of three types–a surplus budget, a deficit budget and a balanced budget. A surplus budget is one in which the income is more than the expenditure; in a deficit budget, the expenditure always exceeds the income. On the other hand, a balanced budget is one in which both the income and expenditure are matching.

As we know the regular feature of a good budgetary system is to have a balanced budget, every government tends to have that system. But in reality, most of the states have a deficit budget. This gives a question as to if deficit budget is a liability on the good budgetary system? Or we can say, is deficit budget untenable? But the answer is reverse. There is nothing to worry about the deficit budget. A deficit budget is always regarded as a means of fighting trade depression. It is also resorted to, to meet the huge expenditures of war and development plans.

A 'deficit budget' is also considered as an instrument of 'compensatory fiscal policy' which alone can cure the ills from which the modern capitalism suffers. The free competitive enterprise in capitalism leads to slump and under-employment due to over-production. This reduces the purchasing power of the people and make the depression progressively deeper and more widespread. To fight such depression, what is needed is to create more work and income for the people. The state can do so by increasing governmental expenditures on public works and finance such expenditure through deficit budget. A balanced budget gives back to people which it takes from them in the shape of taxation of borrowing. Its effect on private economy, is therefore, nil. A deficit budget, on the other hand, provides for more expenditure than the anticipated revenue. In other words, it puts into the hands of the people more money than it takes from them and thus increases their purchasing power which in turn, stimulates the prices and production and counteracts depression.

Therefore, a deficit budget is not untenable. However, deficit budget should not be an instrument of financial administration beyond a certain period. Because its effect is inflation which if left unchecked, results in soaring prices and serious depreciation of the currency system of the country.

BUDGETARY PROCESS IN INDIA

In India, the first budget was prepared by Sir James Wilson, the Finance Member of Governor General of India in the year 1860. In those days the financial year started from May 1st and ended in April 30th. However, only since 1866, the financial year of India began from 1st April and ends in 31st March.

According to article 112 of the Indian Constitution, the President shall cause to laid before the Parliament the Annual Financial Statement showing the income and expenditures. As such, the annual financial statement i.e. Budget is laid before the Parliament by the Finance Minister of India on behalf of the President. As a general convention, the budget is placed before the Parliament on 28th February every year. However, there is no hard and fast rule regarding this introduction on that particular date.

The budgetary process in India deals with the following things:

(1) Preparation of the budget;

(2) The budget itself;

(3) The enactment of budget in Parliament;

(4) The execution of the budget; and

(5) Control over budget.

Each process requires the elaboration in details in order to understand the budgetary process in India.

PROCEDURE OF PREPARATION OF BUDGET

The procedure of preparation of Budget is very extensive and complicated. The budget is prepared under the direct supervision of the *'Budget Division'* of Finance Ministry. The Finance Ministry, the various Administrative Ministries, the Planning Commission and the Comptroller and Auditor General of India provide the basic coordination in the preparation of budget.

The Finance Ministry has the over all responsibility of framing the budget, but it is the administrative ministries which have the detailed knowledge of administrative requirements. For incorporating the plan priorities in the Budget, the Finance Ministry has to be in close touch with the Planning Commission. The Comptroller and Auditor General provides the basic accounting skills necessary for the preparation of the estimates.

The work of budget preparation is done through the following steps:

(a) Preparation of preliminary estimates by Heads of Offices.

(b) Scrutiny and review of these estimates by Controlling Officer.

(c) Scrutiny and review of the revised estimates by the Accountant General and the Administrative Departments.

(d) Scrutiny and review of these revised estimates by the Finance Ministry.

(e) The final consideration of the consolidated estimates by the Cabinet.

(a) The preparation of Budget started 7 to 8 months earlier than the commencement of the next financial year. i.e. in the month of August-September. The Accountant General first sends the prescribed forms to the various administrative departments and heads of offices in order to prepare their estimates of revenue and expenditures separately. The heads of departments send those forms to the heads of local offices who prepare the preliminary estimates.

The forms which are supplied to the local offices contains the followings which are to be filled in by the heads of offices:

(i) actuals of the previous year.

(ii) sanctioned estimates of the current year.

(iii) revised estimates for the current year.

(iv) budget estimates for the next year.

(v) actuals of the current year available at the time of preparation of budget estimates and the actuals for the corresponding periods in the previous year.

The estimates prepared by the heads of offices contains three parts–Part-I, Part-IIA, Part-IIB. Part-I relates to revenue and standing charges like permanent establishment, travelling allowances etc. Part-IIA relates to continuing schemes like purchase of raw materials etc. Part-IIB relates to entirely new scheme of expenditures.

(b) The estimates prepared by the Heads of Offices is sent to the Controlling Office. Here the Heads of departments makes a thorough review of these estimates and scrutinizes them entirely. However, the scrutiny is purely an administrative type. If he wants, he can modify the estimates by his own judgement. By the beginning of October, this task is completed by the Heads of the departments and the estimate is sent to the Accountant General and General Administration Department.

(c) The General Administration Department exists only in the State Governments. Here the estimates are again subjected to thorough scrutiny by the department. The department may change the estimates in a desired direction and inform the Accountant General of the changes made in the estimates. The revised estimate is then being sent to the Budget Division of Finance Ministry.

(d) By the middle of November, the estimates of various Heads of Departments, after scrutinized by Accountant General and

General Administration Department, goes to the Finance Ministry's Budget Division. Besides, between November and December, the Planning Commission, after consulting various administrative ministries, government enterprises and the Chief Ministers of various states, prepares the plan estimates of the future financial year and send them to the Finance Ministry.

Thus, by the end of December, the preliminary stage of Budget formulation is over. By the end of December, the Budget Division prepares a Budget forecast by consolidating all incomes and expenditures.

The Finance Ministry, while scrutinizing the estimates prepared by various administrative Ministries is mainly concerned with economy and as such it reviews all fresh proposals on the basis of availability of funds.

Besides that, the estimates prepared by the individual administrative Ministries and Departments are placed before the Estimates Committee of the Parliament. The Committee, after examining the estimates, prepares the report on the basis of which the Finance Ministry revise the budget estimates.

By the end of December also, the Tax Research Unit (TRU) of Finance Ministry's Budget Division make recommendations to the Finance Minister about the nature of taxes to be levied upon the people or not in order to raise the tax revenues of the government. The recommendation of the TRU is based on the analysis of the current tax system.

(e) By taking into account the various recommendations of TRU and the various estimates prepared by the Finance Ministry the Finance Minister examines the budget estimates and in consultation with the Prime Minister, prepares his financial policy with regard to taxation etc. This, however, is kept a very close secret.

By the middle of February, the prepared budget is submitted before the Cabinet for approval. After it is finally approved by the Cabinet, the budget is ready for submission to the Parliament. The budget is normally laid before parliament on 28th February every year.

Before the budget is laid in the Parliament, the Finance Minister gives a comprehensive statement on the Economic Survey of India. This survey deals extensively with agriculture, industry, trade and commerce, currency, foreign exchange, import, export policy, etc. of the government and gives a general idea about the economic situation of India.

THE BUDGET ITSELF

The Budget of India consists of seven documents. They are:

(a) Finance Minister's Budgetary Speech.

(b) Annual Financial Statement;

(c) Budget at a Glance;

(d) Receipt Budget;

(e) Expenditure Budget;

(f) Finance Bill; and

(g) A Demand for Grants.

Besides these above seven documents a Key to Budget Document is also attached in the Budget.

(a) *Budgetary Speech*–The Finance Minister's Budgetary speech is of high importance in a Budget. In his speech, the minister gives a first hand information about the general economic condition of the country, the financial policy to be followed by the government, the explanation for the difference between the budget estimates and the revised estimates of current year and the explanatory memoranda which explains the reasons for variations in the current year's original estimates and for new demands. The speech always aims at providing new base to economic progress and prosperity.

(b) *Annual Financial Statement*–The Annual Financial Statement refers to the budget estimates. It shows separate estimates for expenditures charged on the Consolidated Fund of India, Contingency Fund of India and Public Accounts.

Article 266(1) says "The Consolidated Fund of India is

composed of all the revenues raised by the Government of India, all loans raised by the issue of Treasury Bills, and all money received by the Government in repayment of loans."

Among these moneys, the emoluments and allowances of the President of India, salaries and emoluments of the Chairman and Deputy Chairman of the Council of States, the Speaker and Deputy Speaker of House of People, Judges and Chief Justice of Supreme Court, Comptroller and Auditor General, their pensions and other relating official matters etc. are charged on the Consolidated Fund of India.

These items are non-votable, although the Parliament can discuss on them. All other expenditures which are paid out of the Consolidated Fund are voted by the Parliament.

The Contingency Fund of India is composed of certain amount of money sanctioned by the Parliament to the Executive to meet any unforeseen situation pending the sanction by the legislature. This fund is placed under the President of India. A Secretary in the Finance department is in charge of the Contingency Fund on behalf of the President. The amount sanctioned by the President in meeting with the natural calamities are discussed and finally voted by the Parliament when the budget session begins.

The Public Accounts includes all the funds collected by the Government from the masses like that of State Provident Funds, Depreciation and other Reserve Funds of Government departments, Postal Savings Bank, Post Office cash and other savings certificates, Postal Life Insurance refunds, adhoc funds created by the Government, miscellaneous deposits and remittances etc. The money laying in the Public Account do not belong to the Government because they are paid back to the people. However, one thing must be cleared that the payment out of Public Accounts are not presented before the Parliament for approval. The Parliament has only the power to pass the Appropriation Act charged from the Consolidated Fund of India.

The difference between charged on the Consolidated Fund

of India and charged from the Consolidated Fund of India is that in case of former the amount is non-votable although it can be discussed in the Parliament but in case of the later, the amount is votable by the Parliament.

(c) *Budget at a Glance*–It provides a clear picture of the budget in brief. It deals with the tables and statistics showing in brief from which sources how much money will be collected and on which heads those money will be invested by the Government. This document reveals the nature of the budget i.e. whether surplus, deficit or balanced one. It also gives a brief statistics about the sources from which the Government will bring money to compensate the deficit budget.

(d) *Receipt Budget*–This document deals comprehensively with the revenue received by the Government both from tax and non-tax revenue sources. The non-tax revenue deals with the loans, borrowings, grant-in-aids received from other agencies and so on.

(e) *Expenditure Budget*–This document also comprehensively deals with the heads on which the money to be disbursed by the Government. It shows the government expenditures not only in terms of the employee's salaries and other financial matters but also depicts a very extensive picture of the various interests and loans to be repaid by the Government which it has incurred from various sources. This document also gives a clear idea about the money to be spent by the Government on various developmental schemes.

(f) *Financial Bill*–This document deals comprehensively with the various proposed taxes to be levied upon the people during the next financial year in order to raise the financial position of the Government.

(g) *A Demand for Grants*–This document gives a clear picture of budget estimates of various Administrative Ministries and Departments and urge upon the Parliament to pass those grants to the various departments in order to allow them to function properly.

All the above documents constitute the Budget in toto.

THE ENACTMENT OF BUDGET

The enactment of the budget refers to the procedure of passage of budget in the Legislature. We know that all and any bill, drafted by the Executive, must get the approval of the Legislature in order to become a law. So the procedure of legislation of budget is also an important element in financial administration.

The budget is a money bill and as such it is naturally distinct from the ordinary bill. As a matter of fact, the procedure of enactment of money bill is different from the ordinary bill. The ordinary bill, in order to become a law passes through the following stages: Introduction & First Reading, Second Reading, Committee Stage, Reporting Stage and Third Reading. The procedure is just a little bit of fluctuation in case of the Budget i.e. the money bill.

The budget, involving the Annual Financial Statement may be of two types–General Budget and the Railway Budget. In India, we have separate budget for Railways. But for our purpose of study we will discuss the passage of general Budget only here.

The General Budget in India consists of two volumes–the Appropriation Bill and the Finance Bill. The passage of both these Bills constitutes the passage of the budget as a whole. The Appropriation Bill covers the whole expenditure part of the government for the ensuing financial year; whereas the Financial Bill involves the income sources of the Government for the ensuing financial year. Both the Bills are simultaneously introduced in the Parliament usually, by convention, on 28th February every year at 5 p.m. in the evening.

APPROPRIATION BILL

The Appropriation Bill passes through the following phases in the Parliament:

(a) Presentation

(b) General discussion

(c) Passage of Vote on Account

(d) Passage of Voting on Demand for Grants

(e) Passage of Appropriation Bill.

(a) Presentation

The Budget as a whole i.e. both Appropriation Bill and Finance Bill are introduced in the Parliament on the date fixed by the Speaker in the Budget Session of Parliament. In a general or ordinary bill, the first reading only mean the reading out of the 'Title' of the bill. But in a 'budget; the first reading means the thorough reading out of the details of the budget. Therefore, soon after the permission of the Speaker, the Finance Minister reads out the whole budget in details before the august body of Lok Sabha. This ends the presentation of the budget.

After the budget is read out by the Finance Minister, generally no discussion took place on the same day. However, two interesting things happen. Firstly, the Finance Bill is sent to the Select Committee of the Parliament for clause by clause analysis. Secondly, another date is fixed by the Speaker for general discussion on the Appropriation Bill.

Thus, only after the presentation of the budget at the Lok Sabha, both the Appropriation Bill and Finance Bill are dealt with differently. The budget as a whole, is presented before the Rajya Sabha on the same day after it is being presented to Lok Sabha.

(b) General Discussion

Normally, after a week of the presentation to the House, the general discussion on Appropriation Bill takes place. Four days are allotted by the Speaker of Lok Sabha for general discussion on the budget i.e. the Appropriation Bill. It is important to know here that as the Finance Bill goes to the scrutiny of Select Committee, so general discussion on the budget mean only discussion on appropriation bill.

The general discussion is a matter from political

consideration and not from financial point of view. The discussion covers all items of the expenditure including those that are *charged on* the Consolidated Fund of India and non-votable by the Parliament. The discussion relates to the general principles and policies of the Government. A major time has been allotted to the Opposition members to review the work of the Government for the whole year and ventilate the grievances of the people. At this stage no motion is moved nor the budget is submitted to the vote of Parliament. Actually the general discussion takes place simultaneously in both the Houses of Parliament. At the end of the discussion, the Finance Minister makes a general reply rebucking the attack of the opposition members.

(c) Passage of Vote on Account

The general discussion of the budget is immediately followed by the passage of the Vote on Account. The term 'Vote on Account' means the Parliament members vote in advance pending the passage of the Appropriation Bill whereby it authorizes the Government to spend money in advance to meet the various situations till the budget is passed by the Parliament as a whole.

Normally, the financial year ends on March 31st every year. The budget is introduced on 28th February. But as the legislative procedure is much complicated one, it required about more than two months to be passed in the Parliament. Therefore, it is needless to mention that the new financial year begins without a provision of money. This will cause grave situation. So in order to avoid such unseen circumstances, the Parliament passes the vote on account in advance and thereby grants money to the Government to man the situation even if the Appropriation Bill is not passed.

Normally the Vote on Account is an advance granted to the Government in respect of estimated expenditures for a part of the financial year. The Vote on Account broadly represents 1/12th of the whole year's gross expenditure.

(d) Voting on Demand for Grants

Soon after the Vote on Account is passed by the Parliament, another date has been fixed by the Speaker, in consultation with the leader of the House for Voting on Demand for Grants. Generally, 26 days have been allotted by the Speaker for the passage of voting on demand for grants.

On the said day, the Lok Sabha sits as a House to discuss the Demands for Grants. The Demand for Grants is first considered Ministry-wise and Department-wise.

However, as the time is too scanty, the Speaker fixes up a time limit for discussion on a particular demand or group of demands for the particular Ministry or Department. As soon as the time limit is over, the demand is put to vote whether the discussion is complete or not. On the last day allotted for the voting on demands for grants, at 5 p.m. the Speaker puts all the demands to vote which remain outstanding and dispose them whether they have been discussed or not.

As I told you that the voting on demand for grants are taken up Ministry-wise, all Ministries are put down for discussion. Each Ministry circulates to the Honourabie Members a report on the working of that Ministry. During discussion, the opposition members criticize heavily on the performance of each Ministries and ventilate people's grievances to the Government.

In this stage of voting on demands for grants the opposition members may move various 'Cut Motions'. Generally there are three cut motions–the '*token-cut*', the '*economy-cut*' and the 'total cut'. The '*token cut*' is usually moved in the form that 'the demand be reduced by Re 1/- or Rs 100/-'. Its purpose is not to maintain economy but to raise discussion on the policy underlaying the demand. On the other hand, the '*Economy Cut*' is used to reduce the grant item by a specific amount. This essentially wants to secure economy in dealing with financial matters. The '*Total-cut*' is in the form of total refusal to grant money to the particular Ministry. This type of Cut Motion provides an opportunity for discussion of the alleged 'mismanagement' by the Ministry on financial matters. Actually no amendment to cut motions are allowed. The approval of any cut motion will tantamount to the non-confidence upon the Government.

During the discussion on demand for grants, the concerned Minister in charge of the Ministry replies to the criticism and defend his administration against all criticisms lebelled by the opposition members and give assurances to the Hon'ble members for the removal of the grievances pointed out. Thereafter the mover withdraw the cut motion; if he did not withdraw it, the motion is put to vote.

After the end of discussion of each demand, the demand is put to vote of the House. A demand when duly voted, becomes a grant.

In a Parliamentary form of Government like India and UK, the Parliament can only reject or reduce a demand but it cannot increase it. However, in Presidential form of Government like USA, the Congress has the power not only to reduce or reject but also to increase the demand for grants.

(e) Passage of Appropriation Bill

After the voting on demand for Grants made for each Ministry, another date is fixed by the Speaker for the passage of Appropriation Bill. The voting of grants, however, does not empower the government to withdraw money from the public fund.

Hence the next stage is the consideration and passage of the Appropriation Bill. The sum total of all the grants made by the Lok Sabha for each Ministry and the expenditure charged on the Consolidated Fund of India which are non-votable by the Parliament are put together and constitute the Appropriation Bill.

The consideration of the Appropriation Bill gives the members another opportunity for discussion on the expenditures of the various ministries altogether. However, no amendment to the grants already voted by the Parliament is allowed here. It only gives the members a chance to discuss the matters which have not been discussed during the voting on demand for grants due to shortage of time. After the consideration of the Bill, it is put to vote and after it is duly voted, it is called the Appropriation Act.

The Appropriation Act, after passed by the Lok Sabha is certified by the Speaker as the money bill and sent to the Rajya Sabha. The Rajya Sabha is required to pass the bill within 14 days. It can neither reject the bill nor amend it. Even if it did so, it makes no difference because the Rajya Sabha did not have any power over money bill.

FINANCE BILL

As already told earlier that the budget as a whole is divided into two parts—the Appropriation Bill and the Finance Bill. After the general presentation of the Budget, the Appropriation Bill is subject to general discussion while the Finance Bill is sent to the Select Committee for consideration.

Committee and Reporting Stage

The Select Committee, considers the Finance Bill Article by Article and Clause by Clause. Each article and clause are subject to thorough discussion and put to vote. The Finance Bill, is a comprehensive document consisting of the proposals for taxation and to raise the revenue of the state both by tax-revenue and non-tax revenue. Each proposal is discussed extensively, and put to vote. Amendments can be moved, accepted or rejected here. After the consideration of the Select Committee, the Committee prepares a report on the Finance Bill and make recommendations to the Parliament.

General Discussion Stage

After the Select Committee submits its report and recommendations on Finance Bill, the Lok Sabha sits as a House to discuss on the Bill in general. Here also the proposed taxation is discussed article by article and clause by clause on the line suggested by the Select Committees. A time limit has been fixed by the Speaker for discussion on each article and at the expiry of that time, the proposal is put to vote. At the end, the Finance Bill is put to vote as a whole and after duly voted it is called Finance Act.

The Finance Act, after passage by the Lok Sabha is certified by the Speaker as a money bill and sent to Rajya Sabha. The Rajya Sabha returns the bill within 14 days with or without amendments. If the suggested amendment is not acceptable to Lok Sabha, then the Finance Bill, as passed originally by the Lok Sabha, is presented before the President for his assent.

The Finance Act and the Appropriation Act as a whole is presented before the President for his assent. The President as a general convention, can not withhold his assent to the budget and after getting such Presidential assent, the Budget becomes operational.

THE EXECUTION OF THE BUDGET

After the Budget is passed by the Parliament and assented to by the President, the task of execution of budget comes into forefront. As we know, budget deals not only with revenue collection but also with revenue expenditures, so first step in this regard is how to collect the revenue.

The Collection of Revenue involves two kinds of operations–assessment and collection. Assessment means as to determine in advance how much money is to be collected from different sources. It, therefore, involves a high sense of judgement and a wide use of discretions. Collection, on the other hand, is the act of actually collecting the assessed amount and as such it requires a high degree of integrity and accuracy.

As per the provisions of Indian Constitution, generally revenue is collected through taxes. There are certain taxes which are levied, collected and appropriated by the Central Government exclusively. Example: revenue earned from railways, posts & telegraphs, wireless, foreign exchange etc.

There are also certain taxes which are though levied by the

Union, are collected and wholly appropriated by the states. Example: stamp duties, excise duty on medicine etc. There are certain taxes which are levied and collected by the Union but whose net proceeds are given wholly to the states. Examples: "Estate duties, taxes on railway fares and freights etc."

There are also certain taxes which are levied and collected by the Union, but whose net proceeds are shared between the States and the Union. Example: Income tax.

In India, the revenue department both in Centre and the States are entrusted with the responsibility of collection of revenue as well as their assessment. For the purpose of assessment and collection, the revenue department is divided into two broad categories – the Board of Revenue which makes out assessment and the Finance staffs which collect the revenue. To the purpose of collection of revenue, the various departments are engaged like land revenue, excise, sales tax, agriculture, income tax, entertainment tax, forest etc.

Most of the revenue in India is collected from land revenue. The land revenue is collected by the field staffs. In each district, the District Collector is entrusted with this task which he performs with the help of the Tehasildars and other subordinate officers.

The revenue collected are safely deposited in the Treasury and Sub-Treasuries of the Government. Where the Sub-Treasury is not available, it is deposited in the Reserve Bank or in the State Bank of India as the case may be.

The next step in the execution of budget is the disbursement of those collected revenues to various administrative departments for their effective functioning. As the various administrative departments have submitted their estimated expenditure, they are disbursed with the amount by the Government. The disbursement is generally made through cheques payable at the Reserve Bank and its branches. Each Administrative department disburses the amount to its branches in the state government which in turn disburses them to each district branches. The district branches also disburse the amount to its subordinate branches and so on. In this way the amount is disbursed to each and every branches of administrative departments right from the top to the bottom level.

The amount sanctioned to each department and its various branches are to be spent with in the same financial year. The head of the offices of each branch is responsible for keeping an accurate account of the money being spent.

At the end of each financial year, the accounts showing the expenditure on different heads are subject to a rigorous audit – an act to verify the facts mentioned and related to financial transactions in order to see that the money is actually spent on the purpose for which it was granted.

CONTROL OVER FINANCE

An effective system of control over the public finance is the order of the day. An efficient control of finance on the one hand, ensures the fidelity of public officials and on the other hand, serves to accomplish the target with minimum cost and shortest time.

Normally there are two types of control exercised over the finance or public money–the executive control and the legislative control.

Executive Control

Executive control is one of the most notable feature of a parliamentary democracy. As the Executive stands for enforcing the public policy made by the Legislature, it has to ensure that sufficient economy and honesty should be exercised in implementing these policies. As the legislature passes the budget, it is the responsibility of the executive to see and implement properly the budgetary provisions. The Executive is responsible for not only collecting the money but also for maintaining a proper account of money spent as envisaged in budget. Thus the Executive control over finance is also considered as the budgetary control.

As soon as the budget is passed by the Parliament, the Finance Ministry takes up the work of distributing the grants to various administrative ministries. The head of each administrative ministry is called the Controlling Officer to whom the grants are allocated. The Controlling Officer, on the other hand, allocate these grants to the various disbursing officers working under him and this process continues till the lowest unit of administrative organisation gets the money to spend.

The money allotted to each administrative unit has to be spent for the purpose for which it was being granted by the Parliament in the same financial year. Not a single paisa can be spent otherwise. Here the Executive control sets in. The main purpose of executive control is to see that the amount as having been disbursed are actually spent for the purpose for which it was being allotted. And secondly, to see that proper accounts of various expenditures have been maintained. This is done through the system of audit.

AUDIT

Meaning

'Audit' is a process at the hands of the Executive to control the finance. It is an instrument of action. It verifies all the financial transactions of a department on the basis of factual data.

According to **James C. Charlesworth**, "Audit is the process of ascertaining whether the administration has spent or is spending its funds in accordance with the terms of legislative proposals which appropriated the money."

An audit is an examination and verification of the accounts after transactions are completed in order to discover and report to the legislative body any unauthorized, illegal or irregular expenditures, or any other unsound financial practices, if resorted to, and whether the administration has faithfully executed its responsibility.

An audit, therefore, is the examination of accounts with a view to determine the correctness of the financial transactions.

Formerly, audit was conducted only in relation to the expenditures and its purpose was to ensure that the money has been spent in accordance with the appropriation grants made by the Legislature. However, in present days, the scope of audit is widened to a maximum extent and it includes not only the expenditures but also the receipts from various sources.

Audit, therefore, is followed to Accounting. Accounting means keeping a systematic record of all types of financial transactions be it income or expenditure. It is defined as an art of recording, classifying and summarizing the whole financial transactions into two heads–the receipt head and the expenditure head. The system of accounting will make the audit simple and effective. Thus, audit begins where accounting ends.

Purpose

The purpose of audit is very simple. The primary purpose of audit is to determine the exactness of the accounts and the transactions thereof. The secondary purpose of audit is to ensure efficiency and economy in financial transactions.

Audit, in general sense, exists for the following purposes:

(a) To see, verify and report thereupon whether any financial transaction have been made against the laws, rules and regulations made by the Legislature.

(b) To verify all the financial transactions and find out whether any transaction is made against the appropriation as voted in the budget.

(c) To ensure that the public servant exercises utmost vigilance and care to check improper and wasteful expenditures.

(d) To check that the public money has not been spent for the benefit of any individual engaged in financial transactions.

(e) To ensure that all canons of financial propriety are observed by the authority while making financial transactions.

Types of Audit

As a matter of general practice, the audit is of two types – the internal audit and the external audit.

Internal audit is a process of check and balance grown within the department itself. As I told you, the controlling officer disburses the money to the various disbursing officers who are the head of offices i.e. the head of the field units of administrative departments. They not only allocate the money to the subordinates but also exercises continuous and constant control over them. The subordinate disbursing officers are required to submit to the controlling officers a detailed account of their income and expenditure every month under each sub-heads. The controlling officer then consolidate these accounts of the whole department under each sub-head in every month. Thereby they get an accurate and uptodate picture of the overall financial position of his department. This departmental keeping of accounts and checking their accuracy is called the internal audit.

External audit is a sort of audit which is conducted by the Finance Ministry alone. It sends to each administrative departments except the Defence and Railway department, its own financial officers who carried on scrutiny of the public accounts and examine the legality, accuracy and propriety of departmental expenditures.

Both the internal and external audit provides an effective instrument to check embezzlements, irregularities and misappropriations if any, in relation to public account.

Functions of Auditor

The officer who carried on the audit is called the Auditor. He performs the audit of departmental accounts and verify the documents relating to financial transaction–both income and expenditures. He has to ensure to himself that proper economy has been maintained while spending public money. At the same time, he looks upon the honesty and integrity of the officials who are entrusted with the dealing of public money. In brief, he performs the following functions:

(1) He audits the financial transactions, both income and expenditures.

(2) He verify and examine the facts on the basis of which income and expenditures are incurred.

(3) He has to ensure that all expenditures confirm the appropriation grant.

(4) He has to examine the money shown in the accounts as having been disbursed were legally made available for, and applicable to, the purpose for which they have been appropriated.

(5) To report to the government about the overall performance of the department.

AUDIT IN INDIA: THE ROLE OF CAG

In India, audit is made by a separate department called the Accounting and Auditing Department. The head of the department is called the Comptroller and Auditor General of India.

CAG—The Historical Legacy

The office of the Comptroller and Auditor General of India came into existence in 1919 according to the Montegu-Chelmsford Reforms Act. The Auditor General (AG) was appointed by the Secretary of State for India. He heads the Audit and Accounts Department. As such he was responsible to the Secretary of State for India. However, he enjoys his position during the pleasure of His Majesty. The function of this Auditor General is to audit the accounts of the Government of India The Auditor General is independent of the latter's control. After conducting the audit, he has to submit a report to the Secretary of State for India dealing with the total expenditures in India every year.

The Government of India Act, 1935 improved the status of the Auditor General and gave him constitutional recognition. He was appointed by His Majesty. The Constitution of India, after Independence, has further raised his position and his function was made more complicated. Now he not only have to make audit but also keep on the accounts of the Government of India as well as the State Governments. Because he has to make both accounting and auditing, he is renamed in Independent India as the **Comptroller and Auditor General** of India.

Appointment

The Constitution of India provides that the Comptroller and Auditor General of India is to be appointed by the President directly or under the warrant of his hand seal for a period of 5 years.

Position

The Constitution provides that the Comptroller and Auditor General of India will have the same position as that of the judges of the Supreme Court of India.

Security

The Constitution also gives enough security to the CAG of India. It says that although he is appointed by the President, he enjoys full freedom from Executive control. He cannot be removed from his office by the Executive except when impeachment motion is passed against him to that effect in the Parliament only on grounds of proven misbehaviour or incapacity to hold office.

Salaries

The salaries and emoluments drawn by the Comptroller and Auditor General is drawn and charged on the Consolidated

Fund of India and as such it is unvotable. The salaries and conditions of his service cannot be varied to his disadvantage during his terms of office.

Limitations

There is also a limitation imposed upon the Comptroller and Auditor General of India that after his retirement, he is ineligible to hold any further office under the Government. This limitation ensures him a fully independent status.

Powers and Functions of CAG

The functions of the CAG, as prescribed in the Constitution are follows:

(1) He has to keep the accounts of both the Union Government and the States.

(2) He has to prepare the accounts of each year showing the annual receipt and disbursements for the Union and the State Governments and to submit the same to the respective Governments.

(3) It is duty of the CAG to prepare and to submit to the President a general financial statement relating to the accounts of each year, showing the balances and outstanding liabilities and such other information as may be required by the President.

(4) It is the duty of CAG to give to the Union and State Governments such information as may be necessary from time to time, in preparation of their annual financial statements.

(5) To audit all expenditures of Union and State Governments and to report whether the moneys shown in the accounts as having been disbursed were legally available and made applicable to the service or purpose for which they have been granted.

(6) To ascertain whether the expenditure conforms to the authority which governs it.

(7) To audit all transactions relating to debts, deposits, sinking funds, advances, suspense accounts and remittance business of both Union and State Governments.

(8) To audit all trading, manufacturing and profit and loss accounts and balance sheets in any department of the Union or of the States and to report on the expenditure, transactions or accounts so audited by him.

The powers of the Comptroller and Auditor General of India are enormous. The President or Government of a State, only after consultation with him, make regulations with respect to the conduct of audit. The CAG has to prepare an annual report of each of the Governments whose accounts are audited. The report particularly points out the financial irregularities like expenditure exceeds the budgetary grants, failure to obtain necessary sanction for expenditure, non-compliance with the rules and regulations, cases of improper and wasteful expenditures, misappropriations and embezzlements etc. He submits the report before the President or the Governor as the case may be, which will be laid before their respective Legislatures.

However, due to excess pressure exerted upon the Comptroller and Auditor General of India, the system has been criticized rigorously. Realizing the difficulties of the CAG in conducting both accounting and auditing, the Government of India, in 1976, relieved him from the charge of accounting. As such nowadays, both the Accounts and Audits are separated and the CAG is required to conduct audit only. The function of accounting is given to the officer called Chief Accounting Authority (CAA). The Secretary of Finance Department acts as the CAA in India. Thus, only after 1976 the functions of CAG is shared by the CAA.

LEGISLATIVE CONTROL

Besides the Executive control over public finances, there is also another more viable and more direct method of

Parliamentary control over finance. The Parliament sanctions money to various administrative ministries for their efficient functioning. As such each administrative department should be accountable before the Legislature for the financial transactions they have made or intends to make. Normally, the Parliament exercises its control through its Committees such as Public Accounts Committee, Estimates Committee and Committee on Public Undertakings.

PUBLIC ACCOUNTS COMMITTEE (PAC)

Composition

The Public Accounts Committee is the primary Committee of the Parliament which exercises a direct control over public accounts and finances thereof.

The Public Accounts Committee came into being in 1950 after the adoption of the Constitution of India. Although the constitution is silent on the composition of the Committee, yet the Committee is composed by the members of Parliament according to Article 118(1).

Originally, the Committee consisted of 15 members all drawn from Lok Sabha. But since 1955, the Committee is enhanced to have a membership of 22 persons consisting 15 from Lok Sabha and 7 from Rajya Sabha.

The members of the PAC are elected from amongst the members of Parliament on the basis of proportional representation by means of single transferable votes.

Although the Committee is composed for one year only yet the members are eligible for re-election.

The Chairman of the Committee is appointed by the Speaker from among the members of PAC themselves. However, if the Deputy Speaker is a member of the Committee, he automatically becomes its Chairman. The Chairman presides over the PAC meetings and in his absense, another member from among the Committee is authorized by its members to act as the Chairman. The quorum of the Committee stands at 4 in order to make a meeting valid. The Chairman does not have a right to vote except in case of a tie.

Functions

The Public Accounts Committee performs the following functions:

(1) It examines the report of the Comptroller and Auditor General of India.

(2) It scrutinizes the appropriation accounts of the Government of India in the light of the CAG report.

(3) It has to examine and satisfy itself that the money shown in the accounts as having been disbursed were legally available, and applicable to the services or purposes for which it has been granted.

(4) To examine that the expenditure conforms the authority which governs it.

(5) To see that every re-appropriation has been made in accordance with the provisions of law.

(6) It examines the trading, manufacturing and profit and loss accounts and balance sheets of any department on the basis of the report of the Comptroller and Auditor General of India.

Thus, the Public Accounts Committee conducts only the 'post-mortem' examination of the accounts because they have already been audited by the CAG.

Procedure of Working of PAC

The procedure of working of PAC is very simple. The PAC considers the report of the Comptroller and Auditor General of India as the base. It considers the report of CAG, Ministry-wise and call for the officers of the concerned Ministry to clarify the points raised by the CAG in its report. Thereafter, the Committee prepares its report and make recommendations to the Government. While the report is submitted to the

Parliament, the recommendation is submitted to the Government through the Finance Ministry. On the basis of the recommendations of the Committee, the Government takes action and the Action Taken Report (ATR) is tabled before the Parliament by the Government along with the report of the PAC for further discussion by the members of Parliament.

Importance of PAC

The importance of Public Accounts Committee cannot be undermined in a democratic state having Parliamentary form of Government. It is an useful instrument of legislative control over public finances. It examines the misappropriations and the irregularities in financial transactions if any, in the light of the report of CAG and recommend suggestions to the Government to eradicate those evils. It therefore, acts as a search light for the Government. It provides a necessary check against wasteful expenditures and extravagance in financial transactions.

ESTIMATES COMMITTEE (EC)

Besides the PAC, the Estimates Committee is also an important instrument at the hands of legislature to control public finance. While PAC is concerned with the 'post mortem' activities, the Estimates Committee examines the proposals for new settings made by the various administrative departments before the proposal is actually being carried out. Therefore, the Estimates Committee, as the name suggests, examines and verifies all the estimates prepared by administrative Ministries to be placed before the Parliament.

Composition

The Estimates Committee came into operation in 1950 after the Constitution of India was adopted. However, its functions are enlarged in 1953. The Committee had its origin due to the idea of **John Mathai**, the then Finance Minister.

The Estimates Committee is consists of 30 members all

drawn from Lok Sabha. Thus, the members of Rajya Sabha did not have representation in the Estimates Committee. Initially the membership was confined to 25 only but it was only in 1953, the membership of the Committee was raised to 30.

All the members of the Committee are elected from amongst the members of Lok Sabha on the basis of proportional representation system by means of single transferable votes.

The Committee is constituted sometimes in June and it starts working from July. It prepares the plan of work for the whole year by selecting such estimates as it thinks fit to be.

Although the tenureship of the Committee is only one year, yet its members have the privilege of continuity by being re-elected time and again.

The Chairman of the Committee is appointed by the Speaker from amongst its members. However, if the Deputy Speaker is a member of the Committee, he automatically becomes its Chairman.

Functions

The Estimates Committee performs the following functions:

(1) To scrutinize any new proposal for fresh expenditures as estimated by the administrative departments.

(2) To report as to how economies consistent with the policy underlaying the estimates may be effected.

(3) To suggest to the various administrative ministries how to secure improvements in the organisation through efficiency and administrative reforms.

(4) To suggests alternative policies in order to bring about efficiency and economy in administration.

(5) To examine whether the money is well laid out within the limits of the policy implied in the estimates.

(6) To suggests the forms in which the estimates shall be presented to the Parliament.

(7) To review the schemes and projects which the administrative ministries have proposed to undertake.

The Procedure of Working of EC

The working procedure of EC is strategically different from that of PAC. The Committee select the subjects concerning the estimates of the Ministries to be examined during the year under review. They ask the Ministry to provided information to the Committee and the information provided is circulated among the members. It also seeks further information on the subject by asking additional questions. The Committee is divided into a number of sub-committees, each dealing with a particular aspect. The members of the Committee may undertake tours to examine the works at the fields. They may also summon officials of the Ministry to furnish such other information as the Committee may ask for. Evidence is also collected from non-officials of the Ministry. Then the Committee draws up a report and submit to the Lok Sabha for consideration.

Importance of EC

The importance of Estimates Committee cannot be undermined. It not only scrutinize the estimates of new proposals but also sanction allotments out of the lump sum grants. It not only provides its members the opportunity to know how administration is carried out but also make them conversant with the various problems that the Government faces. It also exercises supervisory control over the Executive so that they do not become oppressive and arbitrary. It also acts as a liaison between the government and the general public. It also helps in influencing the policies of Government.

Chapter IX

PERSONNELS IN ADMINISTRATION

Every administrative organisation has to do with getting things done and this purpose of organisation is effectively carried out only through an efficient administration. The efficiency of administration depends on the effective arrangement of man and materials in the organisation to achieve the desired objects. However, only arrangement of man and materials do not serve the purpose. It requires the technique of management of both these men and materials so that the cooperative efforts of both will be congenial for the fulfilment of the purpose of administrative organisation. Between the men and materials, high degree of importance is attached to the 'men' who are considered as the driving agent of organisation. Those 'men' who are engaged in various organisations are called *personnels*. The role of these various personnel's help the organisation to achieve its desired end.

The most important problem in the administrative organisation is how to effectively manage these personnels in administration so as to subserve the goal. The personnels, who are engaged in the organisation are to perform a diversified functions i.e. from sorting and delivering letters to advising the ministers. However, the personnels, engaged in private organisations carry on some different functions to maximize their profit. But the personnels, we are talking about are those people who are employed in the governmental organisations. These are called very aptly as the civil servants.

CIVIL SERVICE

Meaning

Civil Service in Public Administration refers to the operation of government Organisations. We know that the government exists for the sake of the people and as such any type of activity carried on by the government aims at the service of the people at large. The 'Civil Servants' are thus "those officials and employees of the government who carry out the government policies and programmes into action by rendering effective services to the people."

What it is not?

A Civil Servant is one whose main function is to administer the law of the land. He is in no way concerned with the military services or with the political services. Viewed in the sense of 'service' both the military personnel's as well as 'political' personnels are also serving the society at large. The military personnels save the country from external attack and thus make the life of the citizen vulnerable. Thus, he is also doing service to the people. But civil service and military service differs from each other on the ground that while the 'former' translates the laws of land into action for the sake of the people the later, by saving the land from external attack, provides an impetus to the former to carry out the laws without any hesitation. Therefore, military service is only a supplementary to the working of the civil service. Similarly, the 'political personnel's' being the representatives of the people, serves the society. The Civil Service, on the other hand, do not represent the people. But it also perform the same service by essentially helping those political personnels in framing the laws for the people and at the same time, by executing those framed laws into operation for the people. Therefore, civil service is essentially complements and supplements the political service.

Definitions

The term 'Civil Service' has been defined in Britain as "those servants of the Crown other than the holders of political and judicial offices, who are employed in a civil capacity, and whose remuneration is paid wholly and directly out of moneys voted by Parliament." Therefore, those people in defence forces, persons holding political office and the judicial persons, the persons who work under the government in an honorary capacity or are not paid out of public revenues are excluded from 'civil service'. According to **Finer**, "Civil Service is a professional body of officials, permanent, paid and skilled."

Types of Civil Service

In a general sense, **Finer** divided the Civil Servants into two broad categories–the higher Administrative Staffs and the lower Clerical Staffs. In the higher administrative staffs, he includes the administrative and technical staffs. The administrative officers are those civil servants who help the political heads in the formulation of policies and executing them. The technical civil servants are those officials who have specialized themselves in various technical fields and therefore devoted themselves wholly to the various technical matters, the effective functioning of which helps the government to serve the people efficiently. Example: The Doctors, Engineers, Technocrats etc.

The lower clerical staffs are termed by Finer as the manipulative civil servants who execute all the orders handed down by the first two classes by common physical activity. Example: Typist, Stenographer, Clerks etc.

The efficient functioning of government depends upon the coordination of all the three branches of Civil Servants. **Ogg** has rightly observed that "the work of the government would never be done if there were only the Secretaries of State and other heads of departments i.e. Political heads. These people cannot be expected to collect taxes, audit accounts, inspect factories, take censuses, to say nothing of keeping accounts, delivering mail and carrying messages. Such manifold task falls, rather, to the body of officials and employees known as the permanent Civil Service.... It is this body of men and women who translate the laws into action from one end of the country to the other and brings the government into its daily contacts with the people."

Therefore, Civil Servants are considered as an army of functionaries who carry on and carry out the governmental orders faithfully. Without their help, the Political heads of the State cannot move a single inch and as such they are greatly dependent on the Civil Servants.

Civil Service and Bureaucracy

Very often both the terms "the Civil Service" and the 'Bureaucracy' are used inter-changeably. However, although both refers to the body of government officials, there is a fundamental difference between the two. The term 'Civil Service' is more wide and comprehensive than bureaucracy which includes not only the bureaucrats but also the non-bureaucrats. As I told you that Civil Service consists of administrative, technical and manipulative employees of the State, or in other words, involves the higher administrative officials and the lower clerical employees who are getting money out of the public revenue. These high administrative officials are called the bureaucrats and the lower clerical officials are called the non-bureaucrats.

'Bureaucracy' on the other hand, is derived from the Latin word 'bureau' and 'cratia'. 'Bureau' means 'desk' and 'cratia' means 'administration'. Therefore bureaucracy means administration from a desk i.e. from one source. Bureaucracy has been defined by Encyclopaedia of Britanica as "the concentration of administrative powers in bureaus or departments, and undue interference by officials in matters outside the scope of State interference."

Therefore, Bureaucracy refers only to those high officials in the government who perform all the administrative functions. Viewed from this angle, bureaucracy necessarily excludes the lower level clerical staffs who do not possess administrative power. Thus, the term only signifies a narrow meaning of the term civil service. All the bureaucrats are Civil Servants, but all the Civil Servants are not, necessarily bureaucrats. Because Civil Service also includes the clerical staffs which the bureaucracy excludes from its grip.

Civil Service—A Historical Evolution

Civil Service is not a modern phenomena. It was present even before the birth of Jesus Christ in a rudimentary form in China. However, the modern concept of 'Civil Service' as a 'bureaucratic' form evolved first in Prussia during the seventeenth century A.D. The rulers of Prussia employed highly skilled, professional and paid class of administrators to strengthen the functioning of government in the State.

France also had a system of bureaucracy during the Bourbon dynasty with the help of Richelieu and Colbert. These are the class of talented, skilled and professional officials who were intensely devoted to the King. Due to their efforts a highly centralized administration came to France.

America also had a bureaucratic system even in the Nineteenth Century. But a thorough rise of bureaucracy was there in England since 1853. In India, the civil servants used to play a significant role even during the 1833's only after the efforts of Raja Rammohan Roy.

Whatever, may be the case, the Civil Servants, in these countries were appointed on 4 main principles. They are: the selling of office, patronage, spoil and merit.

(a) Principle of Selling of Office

The first principle of appointment of Civil Servants is the principle of selling of offices. These methods were followed in France. In earlier days, the public offices are annually auctioned to private parties. The interested parties who can give highest bidding bought the office. He then appoints the civil servants into these offices for efficient functioning. The fate of civil servants were at the hands of the entrepreneurs. They enjoys the office during the pleasure of the owner.

However, this system has its own demerits. There is no

security to the tenureship of the civil servants. In the next year if another party, by bidding more tender snatches away the public office from the owner, he used to vacate those officials in the office and place his own staffs in their place. The selling of public offices is advocated by the rulers of France on the ground that it brings revenue to the Public Treasury.

(b) Patronage System

Another method of appointing the civil servants was the principle of patronage system. This system was widely prevalent in Prussia. Under this system those people who are dear to the King and those people who rose to the position of closeness to the King by virtue of their own talent, capacity and sincerity, gets the public office under the patronage of the King.

However, this system has also its drawbacks. Those people who made the King happy with their good behaviour, gifts, moulded capacity and cunningness, gets the public office. The real talented people who could not make approach to the King and whose talents remained behind the screen cannot get an opportunity to hold public office.

(c) Spoil System

The spoil system has its widespread impact in USA. Here the civil servants hold the office till the satisfaction of the Chief Executive. When there is a change in the political office of the President, there also occurs a simultaneous change in the civil servants. In other words, we can say that the spoil system also advocated the patronage system. A President, who occupies the highest political office appoints his own subordinate officials in the public offices. However, if another person is elected as the President, what he does is that he banned the appointment made by his predecessor and remove all the civil servants from their position. Rather he appoints his own followers into the public offices and thus a new line of civil servants came to the forefront by spoiling out i.e. by diminishing the former line of civil servants made by the predecessor.

The demerit of this system is widely felt on the ground that the civil servants are always in a fear psychosis and therefore cannot perform their duties faithfully. They know that their service is temporary and as such they try to derive profit out of the office within his short span in the office. This facilitates bribery, corruption, hollowness and insincerity among the civil servants.

(d) Merit System

The most widely and universally accounted principle of civil service is the merit system. This system occupies a pre-eminent position first in England, then spreads to almost every corner of the world. This principle advocates that those people who have enough capacity, talent, intelligence, high calibre, farsightedness, endurance, sincerity and devotion to work are only eligible to hold the public offices. This merit of the concerned persons can be proved through an open competitive examination and those qualified in this competition should, first and foremost, be provided with the security of tenureship. It means that the office of civil servants cannot be turned down with a change in the government and administration should have continuity irrespective of governmental changeover. This will ensure efficiency in administration and also boost up the morale of the civil servants.

Characteristics of Civil Service

From the above discussion, we know that civil service is an institution of governmental organisation. The incumbents of the office are called the civil servants who enjoyed some sort of security in tenureship. **Max Weber**, the father of Sociology have talked about three types of authority such as the traditional, charismatic and the rational-legal. He considered the Civil Service as the rational-legal authority in any society. It means authority is bestowed upon the office as a whole and not on the incumbent as a person who holds the office. Weber have also highlighted the following features of bureaucratic civil service:

1. There is a separation of office and its incumbents.
2. The members are selected on the basis of merit.
3. There is fixed remuneration for the officials
4. Every official is subject to discipline and control while performing his official duty.
5. The office is hierarchically arranged.
6. Each official has been allocated different activities which he performs in order to achieve the organisational goals.
7. Each official has been entrusted with authority to discharge his functions.
8. There is a strict adherence to rules by the officials while acting in the public office.
9. The officials do not engage in activities of private profit, rather they are paid a handsome salary.
10. The office of civil servant is a career for him which once entered, has to perform till the age of retirement.
11. They are neutral in politics and remain anonymous i.e. act behind the screens.

Shortcomings of Civil Service

Although Civil Service is the most fascinated office or Career opted by a high talented person, yet it is not free from its own defects. The shortcomings of the civil service are follows:

(1) There is a lengthy procedure and round about way of doing the work. Everything revolves round formal rules and regulations and there is a routinization of work in civil service. The officials do not have their own choice in working. They have to strictly adhere to the policies and programmes of the government.

(2) There is excessive red-tapism in civil service. It means following the formal rules blindly which necessarily

involves delay in file movement. This impairs the efficiency of the working of the government.

(3) There is too much formalism in official transactions. The principle of hierarchy, unity of command and span of control are strictly to be observed. Each officials act mechanically according to the fixed norms.

(4) The civil service is irresponsible to the popular demands, instead, it is committed to the government. This defeat the very purpose of administration which stands at responding to people and popular demands as quickly as possible.

(5) It leads to despotism of the bureaucrats because the civil servants in general and bureaucrats in particular usurp the power too much. It not only fills in the details of delegated legislation but also adjudicate the administrative cases and as such it try to combine legislative and judicial powers at its hand.

(6) It leads to corruption in the social fabric because the members are generally prone to illegal extortion of money from the people before doing the work.

(7) The civil servants, in order to secure their own advantage, always prefer to become a toy at the hands of the political executive by becoming a perfect yesman to their political bosses. This leads to a vicious circle. Right or wrong, the boss is to be supported. This has greatly eroded the efficiency of administration.

Civil Service in India

Civil Service in India owes its origin to the British rule in India. Originally it consisted of only English population who were highly well-organized, well-trained, skilled and efficient. These people provided the base for British rule in India. However, with the advent of time, the Indian people were also introduced in the chain of civil service. But the Indian people remained untrained and underpaid in spite of the fact that they were intelligent.

However, reform in Indian Civil Service (ICS) was first made by Lord Clive during his second tenure as the Governor General, followed by the reforms made by Lord Wellesley. But the inclusion of Indians in the ICS was done only after 1870.

A number of Committees like the Aitchison Committee (1886), Mont-Ford Commission (1918), Lee Commission (1923) and the Government of India Act (1935) have provided for the gradual Indianization of Indian Civil Service. The real progress in Indian Civil Service was made only after India's independence.

Nowadays, Civil Service in India is divided into three wings–the All India Services; the Central Civil Services; and the State Civil Services.

The All India Services includes the Indian Administrative Service (IAS), Indian Police Service (IPS) and Indian Forest Service (IFS). These services, although recruited and controlled by the Union government, has to serve in the States as well as in Central administration. Although their conditions of service etc. are determined by the Central government, yet they may be placed under the control of State governments.

The Central Services includes those services which are not included in the All India Services. Examples: Foreign Services, Customs and Excise Services, Audit and Accounts Services etc.

The State Civil Services comprises of all the services in the line of All India Services under the State government. These members are appointed by the State governments and their conditions of service are also determined by the respective State government. Examples: Orissa Administrative Service (OAS), Orissa Police Service (OPS), Orissa Finance Service (OFS) etc.

In India, the recruitment is made through competitive examinations which are open to all graduates whether, Science, Arts or Commerce.

The recruitment age is fixed between 21 to 30 for All India Services and between 21 to 32 for State Civil Services.

All the higher posts in the sphere of administration, are in fact, given to the people belonging to Indian Administrative Services.

The salary and other allowances received by these Civil Servants are extremely high in comparison to others in the government services.

The responsibility is also high in All India level Civil Servants. They are considered to be the real backbone of the nation and as such the country seems to have enjoyed the real benefit from their talents.

The Indian Civil Service, in order to raise its position, the Administrative Reforms Commission (ARC) have suggested a number of measures which need to be implemented in the society.

RECRUITMENT

The success of administration depends on the effective utilization of the 'men' in organisation. The first and foremost task before Public Administration is to know the persons who are endowed with talents, skills and technical know-how to run the organisation. The society consists of a number of individuals, each being different in their nature, aptitude, intelligence and knowledge. Thus, the basic problem is how to secure the basic service of the best fitted personnels in administration. The method by which the office of the civil service is filled in, is called the method of recruitment.

Meaning

Recruitment, is thus a means to an end. The end, being securing the service of the talented, knowledgeable, and intelligent personnels in civil service. Thus "recruitment is defined as the process by which the service of the most suitable candidate can be secured in civil service."

People, very often, considered recruitment as the synonym of 'appointment'. However, to the student of Public Administration both the terms are different. Recruitment is a more broad and wider concept which necessarily include appointment also. Appointment, on the other hand, is a very narrow term which means filling up a vacancy in organisation. However, it does not denote the procedure by which the vacancy can be filled in and whether the person filling the vacancy is really eligible for the post or not. But this difficulty in appointment is removed through the process of recruitment. The term recruitment, in technical phraseology, means, "attracting the proper and suitable type of candidate for the post to be filled." As such, recruitment is a process of filtration which aims at weeding out the non-important and keeping with only the best. Recruitment involves a thorough and long process like publicity or advertisement, inviting applications from desirous candidates, scrutinizing, holding competitive examination, interviewing the successful candidates, appointing the most industrious one and giving him necessary training so that he will do his best in the post. Appointment, on the other hand, do not take such a recourse and limit itself only to filling up the vacancy.

Purpose

The process of recruitment is thus having a double purpose–the negative and the positive. The negative purpose of recruitment stands at keeping the rascals out of the service whereas, the positive purpose aims at securing the right persons for the job.

Viewed from this angle, recruitment believes in the principle of merit system. It want to take the service of the best, the most talented and the competent personnel so that the organisation will achieve its goal very soon without any hindrances.

Methods of Recruitment

Recruitment, in normal practice may be of two types such

as (1) the direct recruitment or recruitment through merit; and (2) indirect recruitment or recruitment through promotion.

1. Direct Recruitment

Direct recruitment is the most widely accepted method of recruitment. It is also known as the recruitment through merit. In this system, steps are always taken to secure the service of the best, talented, most knowledgeable and the most efficient persons. The talent, efficiency and their knowledge are determined on the basis of their merit. So an examination is held which provides a wide range of questions ranging from day to day life to the most developed science and technology. The basic purpose of having a direct recruitment is to know the reasoning, general aptitude and grasping capacity of the individual and to determine whether he will be the right sort of person to be appointed. Generally, the candidate belonging to lower age groups, who have completed their graduation or continuing their study qualify mostly in this direct recruitment.

Merits

Direct recruitment is having the following merits:

(a) It provides an opportunity to all the qualified persons to show their talents.

(b) It secures the service of best talented persons in the organisation.

(c) It gives new generation a scope to enter into public service and as such public office became more rational.

(d) It do not give any chance to the older persons to hold public office who are lacking in their courage, vigour and initiative.

(e) It makes administration up-to-date by bringing into limelight the new developments in the society.

Demerits

Direct recruitment has also the following demerits:

(a) It is highly expensive because a lot of money is spent in training the youths entering into public service.

(b) The administration loses the vigour of the experienced persons because they know they cannot rise to higher positions through direct recruitment.

(c) It causes jealously among the old and experienced civil servants in the service which is inimical to the progress of the organisation.

(d) There may not be effective coordination between the young bosses and the old subordinates.

2. *Indirect Recruitment*

Another method of recruitment is indirect method. It is also called recruitment through promotion. Here the posts are filled in, no doubt on the basis of intelligence, but stress is always on experience. In this method, the new entrants do not get any chance to fill up the vacancy. The vacancy is generally filled in from lower grade from among the persons who are old, more experienced and more practical in administrative affairs.

Merits

The recruitment through promotion is having the following merits:

(a) It acts as a great incentive in raising the efficiency of administration by giving scope to the more experienced persons.

(b) It helps in finding out the efficient persons more easily than direct recruitment and thus saves the time of the organisation.

(c) It is less expensive because the administration do not have to spend money on training the experienced persons.

(d) Employee's work, not examination, is the real test of

a person's efficiency. A well talented young man may not act efficiently as that of a less gifted old person who have acquired knowledge through his experience.

Demerits

However, the recruitment through promotion is not free from flaws. It has the following defects:

(a) It do not give any scope to the young generations to play their role in public services.

(b) The inclusion of only experienced and old persons in administration made the system static and unsuitable to change,

(c) It undermines the principle of equality of opportunity as it is confined to only those who are already in service.

(d) The young and talented people lose interest in public affairs because they know they could not influence the administration in any way.

There is a general problem for the students of Public Administration as to follow which of the principles and methods of recruitment. The best answer to this question is to recourse to the path of both. In India, recruitment to lower services are usually done through direct method, whereas, to fill up the higher services, the method of recruitment through promotion is adopted.

PROCEDURE OF RECRUITMENT

From the above discussion we come to know that there are two broad types of recruitment—the indirect and the direct. Besides these two types, two other types of recruitment are also found in various States. They are individual recruitment and mass recruitment. If the recruitment process categorically emphasizes on the selection of an individual to the system, it is called individual recruitment. On the other hand, if recruitment is made for the general masses to fill up a large vacancy in the organisation through competitive examinations, it is called mass recruitment. However, the normal practice is that while individual recruitment is done through promotion, mass recruitment is done through competitive examination.

Basing upon the two broad types of recruitment, there are two different procedures adopted for recruitment. They are the procedure for direct recruitment and procedure for indirect recruitment.

Procedure for Direct Recruitment

The procedure adopted for direct recruitment to fill up the vacancies is somewhat a lengthy and complicated procedure. It involves a number of stages. The various stages which are adopted in direct recruitment are follows:

(a) Advertisement

(b) Verification of documents

(c) Testing merits

(d) Certification

(e) Appointment.

(a) Advertisement

The first step for recruiting personnels to fill up the vacancies is to make advertisement. The purpose behind making advertisement is to popularize the 'Situation Vacant' through widespread publicity among the young talented persons in order to attract them towards the job.

However, the advertisement does not carry on at random. It means anybody cannot apply for the post. As the purpose of recruitment through merit is to attract the ablest individuals towards the job, so a strict qualification is prescribed for every job. The qualification requires both civil and special types. The civil qualification includes the general data like domicile, marital status, father's name, age, nationality, religion etc. The purpose of civil qualification is to comprehend the societal background of the candidates. Beside the civil qualifications, certain special qualifications are also needed for the job. It includes the educational qualification, technical knowledge and experience, if any. The purpose behind the special qualification is only to attract those suitable candidates for the post from others.

The advertisement prescribes certain limit for applying for the post. A deadline has been fixed beyond which no application would be entertained.

(b) Verification of Documents

The next step towards recruitment is to verify the applications received for the post. This verification of the documents is necessary to chalk out a list of the candidates who are qualified, better qualified and under-qualified for the post on the basis of the information sought in the application form. Generally the under-qualified persons were wiped out of selection process and the list prepared covers only the successful qualified persons. Any wrong information sought in the application, if found, may cause for the rejection of the applicant to the post.

(c) Testing of Merits

The very next step towards recruitment is to declare an examination date and hold on competitive examination in order to test the merits of the applicants. In order to test the merit, various methods are adopted by the recruitment authority. They are–written examination, interview and personality test.

(i) Written Examination

The most widespread method of testing the merits of the candidates is to hold a competitive written examination. The written examination may be of two types such as objective and subjective.

In an objective type of written examination, a candidate is to give very short answers say in one or two words. A wide range of objective questions are set in the examination like multiple choice questions, true or false, columns, blanks to be filled in, yes or no, etc. The questions ranged from day to day social life to the environment, science and technology. The objective type questions are generally asked to comprehend a candidate's general knowledge, reasoning, general English, aptitude, mental culture and general intelligence as a whole.

The subjective type of written examination may be of two types such as long answer type questions and short answer type questions. In a long answer type question, a candidate is required to write extensively and comprehensively an essay on the question asked. The purpose of holding an essay type answer is to judge the candidate's power of understanding, expression, standard of reasoning, continuity and consistency of thought.

The short-answer type question requires that the candidate should write the answer in brief more vividly and also more lucidly. Its purpose is to understand and examine the clarity of his thought, the lucidity of expression and the indepth of knowledge of the candidate.

(ii) Interview

The interview is generally followed after the written examination. Those successful candidates who has come out with flying colours in written examination are called for the interview. Therefore, written examination is a method adopted for keeping the rascals out. Interview always supplements and compliments the written examination.

The purpose behind conducting interview is to have a close watch on the activities, behaviour, dealings and orientations of the candidate. The written examination, always cannot reveal the real personality of the individual. A candidate who have done very well in written examination may lack coolness, presence of mind, initiative, decision making, social adaptability etc. which are so vital for a successful administrator. Thus, interview or oral test is intended to test the personality of the candidate.

The most common method used in interview is the 'Viva-Voce' test. 'Viva-Voce' means 'putting questions and getting answers.' The purpose of viva-voce is to obtain a look at the candidate and to detect his positive and negative qualities.

(iii) Personality Test

Still another method of testing the merit of the candidate is to go though a personality test. This is, however is most complex one because it wants to understand and comprehend an individual's psychology. It is best carried on through 'Group Discussion' where a number of candidates exchange their ideas on a given topic concerning the national and international issues. The basic purpose of conducting the personality test is to know the practical approach of a candidate to the prevailing socio-political and economic issues. It reveals the real orientation of the candidates and their aptness to eradicate the social maladies.

Besides these tests, the physical test is also carried on to know whether he is able to perform the duty effectively or not. At the same time, the performance test is also carried on to fill up the vacancies of certain technical posts.

(d) Certification

The very next step after the testing of merit is Certification. Certification means the selection of the successful candidates and preparing a list of those in order of their merit. The candidates possessing all-round achievement in written test, interview, physical test and performance test are said to have selected for the post. These are the best qualified and most talented persons required for the post to be filled in.

(e) Appointment

The final step in recruitment through merit is the appointment of the successful candidate or candidates in the post for which recruitment was held.

Procedure for Indirect Recruitment

As we know, indirect recruitment is the recruitment through promotion, the procedure for indirect recruitment is simple. Promotion is made either on the basis of seniority or on merit or on both. However, the general and most acceptable method of promotion is seniority-cum-merit basis.

Promotional recruitment is based on the following stages:

(a) Personal judgement of the appointment authority.

(b) Certificate of ability, character and education.

(c) Record of previous experiences.

(d) Examination.

(a) Personal Judgement of Authority

Promotion to higher offices are made mostly on the recommendation of the superiors. If an authority is very much pleased with the ability of his subordinate, his dealings, his initiative, his intelligence, knowledge and his good behaviour, efficiency at work etc. the superior himself recommends that he is the right type of person to get promotion because he is a man of varied talent. This makes promotion easy.

(b) Certificate of Ability

The certificate of ability, character and education lends a great deal of support for indirect recruitment. The authority writes the Confidential Character Roll (CCR) of the subordinates which acts as a basis for promotion. The efficiency rating of the person is also considered to be most important element in determining the promotion of the candidate.

(c) Record of Previous Experience

Indirect recruitment is again followed by the principle of the record of previous experiences, if any, whether educational or professional. Here the whole record of the candidate's work is regularly maintained and examined.

On the basis of above three procedures, the promotional recruitment is made in case of Seniority. However, a problem arise as to if more than one candidates are there who have equal ratings in the above three methods, how indirect recruitment is made. This is followed by the method of "Seniority-cum-Merit."

(d) Examination

Holding of an examination so to say departmental one, is the last method of indirect recruitment based on seniority-cum-merit basis. It cures the maladies of recruitment based on seniority only. The candidate who come out most successful in the examination is liable for promotion and as such the procedure of indirect recruitment ends here.

ROLE OF UNION PUBLIC SERVICE COMMISSION (UPSC)

I told you earlier that in India, the recruitment for the lower posts are made through merit while higher posts are filled in by promotion. All types of recruitment, whether through merit or promotion to Civil Services are done by the Public Service Commission. The Public Service Commission exists both at the Centre as well as the States. The Central Public Service Commission is known as the Union Public Service Commission (UPSC).

Composition

The Constitution of India provides that the Union Public Service Commission shall consists of 4 members and a Chairman. The Chairman and members of UPSC are appointed by the President for a period of six years.

Those persons who have held at least 10 years of service under the State or Central government are eligible for appointment as members of UPSC.

The salaries of the members and Chairman of UPSC are

fixed by the Constitution which cannot be altered to their disadvantage during their tenure of office.

The Constitution provides that the Chairman and members of the UPSC can be removed from their office by the President on the grounds of proven misbehaviour or incapacity to hold office only after the Supreme Court, after being made an enquiry, have reported so to the President.

The Chairman and members of UPSC cannot hold any office of profit or engage in any other profitable business with the government during their tenureship.

The Chairman and members are also ineligible to be appointed in the State or Central government after their retirement, except becoming a Chairman of any Commission.

Powers and Functions of UPSC

The Constitution provides that there are two powers of the UPSC–the administrative and the advisory powers.

(1) Administrative Powers

The UPSC has administrative powers in relation to the following:

(a) To conduct examination for appointments to all civil posts of the Union government.

(b) To frame and operate schemes of joint recruitment for any State, if requested by the concerned State government.

(c) To conduct written examinations for recruitment of cadets for admission into National Defence Academy (NDA) and Combined Defence Services (CDS).

(2) Advisory Powers of UPSC

The UPSC shall be consulted on the following matters by the government:

(a) All matters relating to methods of recruitment to Civil Services and all civil posts.

(b) The principles to be followed in making appointment, promotions and transfers in all Civil Services and civil posts.

(c) All disciplinary matters affecting a person serving under the Government of India in a civil capacity.

(d) Any claim by the Civil Servant for award of pensions due to injuries sustained by him while serving the Government of India in his civil capacity.

TRAINING

Every administrative organisation aims at maximizing the service of the personnels in order to achieve efficiency. After the recruitment of civil servants, generally question arises as to how to increase their efficiency. The answer to this question lies in training.

Meaning

Training is the most widely accepted method of increasing the efficiency of the personnels. Literally, the term 'training' means giving instruction in a particular art, profession or occupation. In the phraseology of Public Administration, 'training' can be defined as "the conscious efforts made to increase or improve an employee's skill, powers and intelligence and to develop his attitude and schemes of values in a desired direction."

Therefore, training is a continuous and systematic development of knowledge, skills and attitudes among the civil servants which contribute to the advancement and efficiency of the Organisation.

Definitions

William G. Torpey defines training as "the process of developing skills, habits, knowledge and attitudes in the employees for the purpose of increasing their effectiveness in their present governmental positions as well as preparing them for future government positions."

According to **S.B. Bapat**, training means the followings:

Firstly, it means imparting knowledge of facts into the minds of the employees.

Secondly, it means the teaching of the techniques which require coordinated handling of tools and appliances rather than of ideas.

Thirdly, it entails the formation of mental and physical habit patterns to ensure that the same stimuli would always produce the same automatic responses.

Therefore, training provides the basic foundation of the orientation and attitude formation of the employees. Only through training, an employee gets an essential information about the Organisation, its purposes and his role in the Organisation itself.

WHAT IT IS NOT?

Training is sometimes identified with education because the basic purpose of both remains overall, the same – instruction or guidance of an individual in a particular art. However, both of them are quite different in their degree which should be known by every student of Public Administration.

Training is narrow in scope than that of education. Education wants for the complete up bringing of the individual from childhood till death by necessarily helping him in the formation of character, habits, manners and of mental and physical aptitude. But training only aims at a specific angle. It aims at moulding the attitude and values of a person. It do not have anything in relation to the character of a person. It therefore aims only at increasing the skills of a person. But education, on the other hand touches each and every aspect of an individual including developing his skills.

Types of Training

Training is normally divided into the following heads –

(a) Formal and informal training

(b) Pre-entry and post entry training

(c) Short-term and long-term training

(d) Apprenticeship and general training

(e) Departmental and central training

(f) Orientation and Refresher training.

(a) Formal and Informal Training

Formal training is one which is given on the basis of prescribed rules, regulations and norms. Thus, it is a training which is carefully conceived, prearranged and conducted through and under expert guidance. Formal training is given through lectures, conferences, seminars, workshops, group discussions etc. The purpose of formal training is to inculcate the administrative skills into the employees through well defined courses.

Informal training, on the other hand, is a type of training acquired by experiences which the employee generally learns in course of his actual doing of works. Thus, no formal training is provided to any body here and the man learns from his experience only.

(b) Short-Term and Long-Term Training

The short-term training is a part of formal training which is given for a limited period of duration. Due to the short duration of the training period, it is called short-term training.

Similarly, when the duration of formal training is more, it is called the long-term training. Long-term training helps an individual to learn not only through formal activities but also from his experience.

(c) Pre-Entry and Post-Entry Training

Pre-entry training is a training imparted to the aspirants to public service before they enter into such services. In other words, pre-entry training is guiding an individual towards attainment of the jobs. Such type of training gives an individual a variety of knowledge that the job demands and thus prepares him to set himself for the job.

Post-entry training, on the other hand, is a training imparted to the civil servants after they are selected for recruitment. Thus, here all the qualified entrants to the civil service get training before they actually opt for the responsibility. It imparts training to the people about their duties, their work, their sphere of competence, the varied situations which demands prompt decision making and so on.

(d) Apprenticeship and General Training

When the training is given on a particular skill or subject and an aspirant acquires an indepth knowledge about that particular skill, it is called apprenticeship training. However, such type of training continues to ignore all other aspects of knowledge.

On the other hand, general training is imparted to the individual on a varied scale to make him know everything that comes in his way in the performance of his duties. Such type of training gives, an individual and an opportunity to acquire a variety of knowledge on different subjects, disciplines and skills instead of concentrating on one skill only.

(e) Departmental and Central Training

In a departmental training, instruction is normally given within the same department. Each department gives training to its employees in order to cater to its own specialized requirements. Such training is usually imparted to the more experienced officers of the department itself.

Central training is one where instruction is given usually

outside the departmental framework. Central training is given to the new entrants to various departments who are required to know the general problems faced by various administrative departments irrespective of the fact that they may belong to different departments.

(f) Orientation and Refresher Training

Besides the above broad categories of training, there may be another categories the orientation and the refresher training. Orientation training aims at introducing an employee to the basic concept of his job, the new work environments, organisation and its goal. Thus, it frames the orientation of the employee towards the job.

Refresher training, on the other hand, is given to an employee after he serves the job for some years. This training helps the employee to acquaint himself with the latest administrative techniques. It is thus a type of in-service training which stimulate the employees to make best efforts to improve their performances. It boosts up their morale and makes them adaptable to the newer tasks.

Importance of Training in Modern States

Training plays the most vital role in Public Administration of modern States. It is essential not only for effecting efficiency of administration but also for broadening the vision of the employees. It teaches an employee precision, makes him self-reliant and develops in him the capacity to take decisions are arrive at judgements. It enables an employee to adjust himself to new situations and comprehend the goals of the Organisation.

The Asheton Committee on Training of Civil Servants, held that training performs the followings:

(a) It produces reliable work-skill in the employees.

(b) It makes the civil servants flexible by adapting themselves to the newer tasks of a changing world.

(c) It saves an employee from mechanization by making him community conscious.

(d) It fits an employee for higher duty and responsibility.

(e) It broadens the mental ability of the civil servants by inculcating into their minds the principle of "service mentality."

(f) It maximizes the efficiency of the Organisation.

(g) It boosts up the morale of the civil servants.

(h) It help the employees to become 'people-oriented'.

(i) It improves the tone and adds to the quality of Organisation.

(j) It fosters homogeneity of outlook among the employees.

PROMOTION

Promotion occupies the most important position in administrative organisation. It is needed to boost up the morale of the staffs. Man is a creature which requires the recognition by others. After a Civil Servant is recruited and trained he generally becomes eligible to hold administrative posts. However, how long he will remain in that position? This is the most important question required to be solved in administrative organisation. It is a general fact that if a person performs his duties without any hope of changing it in a positive direction would result in static nature of organisation and thus will prove detrimental for the efficiency of the organisation itself. Thus, it has been a widely accepted phenomena that the persons working in administrative organisations should get an opportunity for emancipation i.e. from their present status to a newer one, involving new tasks and responsibilities. This is called promotion.

Meaning

The term 'promotion' is derived from the Latin word '*promovere*' which means 'to move forward'. Prof. **L.D. White** defined 'promotion' as "the means of appointment from a given position to a more difficult type of work and greater responsibility, accompanied by the change of title and usually an increase in pay."

Viewed from the angle of Public Administration, the term 'promotion' means two different things to the employees as well as to the employer. From the point of view of an employee, promotion is an advancement from a lower grade or class of the service to a higher one carrying a large salary and higher duties and responsibilities. But from the point of view of the employer, promotion means filling up the higher posts by fittest persons from within the service. However, whatever it may be, promotion is always made by taking into account the social interest rather than the individual interest of the employee.

Although promotion boosts up the morale of the employees, yet negative promotion may prove detrimental for the organisation. Negative promotion means when promotion is based on unfair means, superseding the real employee, then a general discontentment flows among the employees that injustice has been done in promotion. This is too much detrimental for the organisational structure.

Promotion is generally two types such as promotion from within and promotion from outside. Promotion from *within* means promotion made from one lower grade to a higher grade within the same class. Example: promotion from Lower Division Clerk to Higher Division Clerk etc. Promotion from *outside*, on the other hand, means promotion made from one class to another class in the higher grade. Example: from class II services to class I services, promotion of OAS officers to IAS officers etc.

WHAT IT IS NOT?

All of us know that promotion involves higher salary and change of position. But this does not mean that promotion is synonymous with that of increment or transfer.

Very often people are confused between promotion and advancement because both these things involves change or increase in the salary. However, a student of Public Administration should be more keen and conscious about the differences between these two. *Advancement* generally involves a gradual increase in the salary through increments annually. For example: an employee classified under the pay scale of 2000-60-3500, gets an annual increment of Rs. 60/- only till he reaches the maximum of Rs. 3500/-. This does not mean promotion. While advancement is gradual, *promotion* is accidental and sudden. Advancement is always automatic but promotion involves a deliberate process on part of the employer and the employee.

Again, people are confused between promotion and transfer because both the terms involves a change in the position. Both of them differ in quality only. Promotion is more comprehensive and more dynamic than transfer. *Transfer* means only a change of position from one place to another within the same grade or class. But *promotion* means a change in grade or class also along with a changeover of position. Example: A lecturer when changed from one college to another is called transfer because it involves only a change of position within the same grade. But when a lecturer is transferred as the Principal of another college, this is called promotion because it involves not only a change of place and position but also a change of grade or class.

Transfer may be made on request of the employee, but promotion cannot.

Again transfer is a routine work in the life of an employee. But promotion is not. All persons do not get promotion even though most of them retire at the same post.

Transfer is sometimes considered as a negative action to punish somebody. But promotion always involves positive actions.

Types of Promotion

Generally, there are two types of promotion, as I told earlier—the intra-departmental (within the department) and the inter-departmental (outside the department).

Intra-Departmental Promotion

Intra-departmental promotion means when promotion is made within the same department from lower grade to higher grade. For example: from lower division clerk to upper division clerk within the same department. Generally, the intra-departmental promotions are made on the basis of seniority. That means, the person who is the senior most is eligible for promotion.

However, this intra-departmental promotion involves a number of difficulties. This difficulty arise only when seniority or longer tenure is taken into account. Considering from this point, an old peon is senior to his young boss in the length of his service. So can he be considered as senior to his boss? The answer is technical one. Although he is senior to his boss in age, he is junior to him in matters of duties and responsibilities. Thus, while seniority is counted, it should be counted within the same grade i.e. among the peons, among the clerks, among the officers and so on.

Inter-Departmental Promotion

The next type of promotion is called the inter-departmental promotion. Here promotion is made on the basis of merit and not of seniority. The meritorious persons along with minimum prescribed tenure of service may come from one department and hold the post on promotion basis. However, it must be taken into mind that inter-departmental promotion is made only to fill up the vacancies of higher posts involving administrative responsibilities.

However, this inter-departmental promotion also involves a lot of difficulties. Can a junior officer in one department be promoted to another department on the basis of merit? The answer is obviously yes. But it involves a problem that can he become the boss of the department where seniors to him are still present? It involves a technical answer also. I told you earlier that inter-departmental promotions are made to administrative posts only i.e. to higher posts. If there is a senior man present in higher administrative post, who is not only senior in age but also in merit, then the officer who is transferred cannot hold the administrative office superseding that officer. Therefore, inter-departmental transfer is generally made when there is a clear cut vacancy in the administrative post.

As a matter of general principle, inter-departmental transfer is made only on three grounds:

(a) In connection with the higher administrative posts.

(b) When there is no suitable candidate available within the department to fill up the vacancy in the particular administrative post.

(c) When a new department is created or an existing department is expanded, then only inter-departmental promotion took place.

Generally, inter-departmental promotions in India are filled in through transfer-on-deputation basis i.e. the officer is transferred to the concerned department only for a specific period.

Bases of Promotion

After conceptualizing promotion, one is generally left with the feeling as to what is the base of promotion in any administrative organisation? Generally, there are two bases of promotion–

(a) through seniority; and

(b) through merit.

(a) Seniority as a base of promotion

The principle of seniority is the most traditional base of determining promotion. It means that the length of service would determine the order of precedence in making promotions. An employee who has a longer service to his credit is entitled for promotion.

However, determination of seniority is the most complex issue in any administrative organisation. If the length of service is to be considered, then, the old peon working in the department would be senior to his young boss of the department. But the reality is that length of service must be in consonance within the same grade or class. Thus, among all peons the senior most peon is entitled to promotion and among all officers in the same rank or class, the senior one is to get promotion.

This involves a second problem. That is, which is to be taken into account–seniority in service or seniority in confirmation. Sometimes, a person who is senior in service may get confirmation late than in comparison to a person who got late service but early confirmation. While in some cases, seniority in service is taken into account, in some other cases, the seniority in confirmation is also accounted for promotion.

(b) Merit as a base of promotion

Sometimes, promotion is made on the basis of merit. It means that promotion would be made on the basis of qualification and achievements of the employee irrespective of longer tenure of service. The principle of merit, as such stands in sharp contrast to the principle of seniority and advocate that the most meritorious and the best qualified are only eligible for promotion. The principle of merit provides sufficient incentive to efficient and hard working employees and this increases the morale of the employees on the one hand and the efficiency of the organisation on the other hand.

However, merit is a complex concept which cannot be determined objectively. It involves not only the intellectual attainments of a person as revealed by degrees in examinations but also the factors like personality, capacity for leadership, strength of character and so on. As a normal practice, the merit is determined on three grounds:

(i) personal judgement of the head of the department;

(ii) promotional examination; and

(iii) service ratings.

Merits of an employee is determined on the basis of personal judgement of his head of department because the head has been in constant contact with the employee in the department and as such he is in a position to appraise his personal qualities during his working in the department.

Promotional examinations are always competitive in nature which reveals the real merit of an employee. As such promotional examinations can be distinguished from departmental examination insofar as the former being competitive, whereas, the later being non-competitive in nature. The officer must pass the departmental examination in order to qualify himself for promotion. Therefore, departmental examination always have precedence over the promotional examinations.

The merits can also be determined on the basis of efficiency rating which can be calculated from the service records and service files of an employee.

In India, both the methods of seniority and merit are taken into account while opting for promotion. Generally, the higher posts are filled in through seniority whereas, the lower posts are filled in through merit.

Significance of Promotion

Promotion, whether based on seniority or on merit, has the following significance in administrative organisation:

(a) It helps in building up the efficiency and morale in the organisation.

(b) It attracts the talented persons to public service.

(c) It keeps the employees interested in the job and provides the employees with an incentive to work.

(d) It helps in procuring the best possible incumbents for the higher position.

(e) It acts as a method of rewarding the industrious and ablest persons working in the organisation.

CONDITIONS OF SERVICE OF CIVIL SERVANTS

The Civil Servants are considered as the most important instrument who make the government popular and efficient. They help in framing laws as well as formulating policies. At the same time, it is the Civil Servants who are the implementing authority of the government. The government relies heavily upon the help and assistance of the Civil Servants.

However, the Civil Servants, in order to perform their functions effectively and efficiently, must need, first and foremost peace of mind. They cannot do justice to their jobs if they have a unstable mind and they are worry of economic conditions. Therefore, the first and foremost task, before any government is to determine the conditions of service of the Civil Servants. A high and purposeful condition of service gives an individual an incentive_to work.

The conditions of service, as provided to the Civil Servants are follows:

(1) Security of Tenureship

Every Civil Servant is guaranteed with a security of tenureship throughout their service period. After their recruitment and appointment to the post, the civil servants do not entangle themselves with the worries of tenureship. A civil servant who enters into the office, got a life time tenureship till the age of retirement at the age of 58 or 60 as the case may be. This is in sharp contrast to the earlier principles followed in earlier societies relating to the office of civil servants such as the principle of sale of office, patronage system and spoil system. The security gives the civil servant an incentive to work.

(2) Appropriate Training

The persons who are qualified to be appointed as Civil Servants are given appropriate and thorough training in order to acquaint themselves with the nature of the work which they ought to perform. Training is a life long process which includes the pre-entry training, post-entry training, long-term training, short-term training, inservice training, orientation training, refresher training, formal training, informal training, departmental training, central training and so on. A Civil Servant, after thorough training, can do justice to his work because he gets an insight into the real task and responsibility involved in the work.

(3) Handsome Salary

The Civil Servants carry a very handsome salary because the nature of their job requires the most intrinsic problem of decision making. Handsome salary is provided to the Civil Servants because they should be relieved from economic worriness if they are to perform their task efficiently. An underpaid and impoverished civil service may be a liability on the government. Instead of being a guardian class, they would be a consumer class. The Fifth Pay Commission provided for a salary ranging from 8000/- to 30,000/- per month for the Civil Servants.

(4) Timely Increment

Time scale increment is another condition that govern the service of the Civil Servants. There is an annual increase in the salary of the Civil Servant by the stated amount upto the maximum of the scale fixed. The increment is automatic.

(5) Promotion

Every Civil Servant is entitled to promotion during his tenureship. An IAS officer, through promotion may move from Collector to the position of Chief Secretary moving in an upward direction in the organisational hierarchy. Each level of promotion entitles a Civil Servant increased responsibility and new tasks, more complex than the present he helds. Promotion is normally held on the basis of seniority as well as merit or as a matter of fact, a judicious combination of both.

(6) Transfer

Transfer is a part-and parcel of the life of the Civil Servants. They are bound to transfer from one post to another moving from one place to another involving various responsibilities and tasks. Transfer may be positive and negative. Positive transfer refers to promotion whereas, negative transfer means demotion and as such it involves negative change in the responsibility and tasks.

(7) City Allowances

Sometimes, it is seen that the Civil Servants belonging to the same cadre and same grade receives variation in remuneration. This variation in remuneration is in consonance with the variation in the cost of living in different places. For example: A large city like Calcutta, Bombay, Delhi etc. is more expensive to live in than smaller one. Even the smaller cities are more expensive to rural areas. Thus to meet this variation in the cost of living the Civil Servants are paid with City Allowances. The purpose of city allowance is to compensate for the hardship of service in areas where economic climate is extensively unsuitable.

(8) Bonus

Sometimes, bonus is provided to the Civil Servants once a year. This provided them a good deal of incentive to devote more into their work. Bonus is in addition to the regular scale of pay which is provided as a matter of ex-gracia payment.

(9) Adjustment of Pay to Price Level

Generally, the pay of the Civil Servants is fixed above the subsistence level. However, any change or variation in the price level also causes for the adjustment of pay scale to suit the changing circumstances. Generally, three methods are adopted in this direction. Firstly, there is a percentage increase in the salary to check the price rise. Secondly, there is a total revision of pay. Thirdly, the salary is linked with the allowances and bonus.

(10) Perks and other Allowances

Beside the above, the Civil Servants are also provided with various attractive perks and other allowances in addition to their salaries. The perk includes the non-monetary allowances whereas the allowances includes the monetary one.

The Perk includes the following:

(i) Suitable Accommodation: The Tomlin Commission in its report, held that no one can be expected to do his best work in a dingy and inconvenient office. Therefore, all sorts of privileges are provided to have a well-furnished accommodation in office where the Civil Servant performs his duties coolly and peacefully. Such type of office accommodation includes the provision of peons, chaprasis, messengers, stenographer, typist, personal assistants etc. in human side and the Air-Conditioner, Cooler, Car facilities etc. in material side.

(ii) Transport Facility: The Civil Servants are also provided with the benefit of transport facilities in order to perform their duties both in their official capacity as well as in their personal capacity. A car or jeep is provided to the civil servants and the expenditure on those transport services are incurred upon from the government.

(iii) Medical Aid: The Civil Servants are also provided with medical facility. They are allowed to take the benefit of medical facilities free of cost in return of the services they render to the government.

The Allowances of the Civil Servants includes the following:

(i) House-Rent Allowance (HRA): Generally, the Civil Servants are provided with suitable personal accommodation by the government at no extra cost, and even to some extent, with a very minimal cost. However, if the government could not able to provide the Civil Servant with housing facilities, it is bound to provide him with the house rent allowances or HRA in terms of money. The HRA is in addition to the normal salary of the civil servant. The Fourth Pay Commission has fixed the

HRA at 7.5% of the basic pay. But the Fifth Pay Commission has raised the HRA to 25% of the basic pay of the Civil Servant.

(ii) Children's Education Allowance: Sometimes, the Civil Servants in India are provided with CEA by the government in order to sustain their children's education. These are granted to the non-gazetted staffs of railway services and Ordnance factories in certain specific circumstances where there is no proper school at the station where the parent is posted and as such the children has to be sent out for schooling. Some railways maintain schools of their own for the benefit of their employee's children. The Fourth Pay Commission recommended that the State should contribute 75% of the tuition fees in case of the children of Class IV employees and 50% of the tuition fees in case of Class III employees.

(iii) Medical Allowances: The Civil Servants are also provided with medical allowances in cash for their treatment done at private health centres where the government medical have failed to do so. The total expenditure incurred is returned to the civil servant by cash by the government when he produces the requisite bills in support of his expenditure in medical treatment. Thus, there is the provision of full reimbursement of medical expenditures to the Civil Servants.

(iv) Travelling Allowances: The Civil Servants are allowed to enjoy the Travelling Allowance (TA) from the government when they are to travel on government work.

(v) Daily Allowances (D.A.): Besides the TA, the Civil Servants are entitled to receive daily allowance or DA from the government when they go outside the station in relation with a government work. The DA is in consonance with the Pay Scale of the Civil Servants. That means the lower grade civil servants are entitled to low DA, where as the higher grade officers can claim higher DA in commensurate with their Pay Scale.

(11) Leave

No employee can work mechanically without rest. He requires leave for rest and also health, during sickness or to attend to their private business. Provision is therefore, made for several kind of leaves like Casual Leave, Earning Leave, Sick Leave, Medical Leave, Leave for Private Affairs, Study Leave, Leave without Pay, Surrender Leave etc. At best, in India, a Civil Servant is allowed to enjoy 13 Casual Leaves, 2 Reserve Holidays and 30 Earning Leaves. All other leaves except the Study Leave are deducted from EL.

(12) Hours of Work

Generally, the hours of work cannot be the same in all the departments. But as a matter of convention, 8 hours per day has been fixed for the lower grade Civil Servants as working hours. But there is no such limit of working hours given to the higher grade Civil Servants. However, besides the normal working hour, an individual is allowed to have over-time for which he is paid by the government.

(13) Provident Fund

A Civil Servant is also provided with the benefit of Provident Fund. This is a sort of savings that a person can make from his salary. Nowadays the General Provident Fund (GPF) stands at minimum 10% of the Basic Pay which a person can save. The interest is given by the government on the savings.

(14) Gratuity

Gratuity is a sort of retirement benefit which is allowed to a Civil Servant by the government. The gratuity stands at full payment of one month in every year by the government. Thus, if a person retires from public life after serving 30 years, he is entitled to a gratuity of 30 months by the government with usual salary plus other allowances.

(15) Pension

After retirement the Civil Servants are provided with pension facilities in order to sustain their family in future when they have no government service. The pension stands at 50%

of the total salary provided to the pension holder till he dies. This is thus a life long incentive.

Thus, these are the various conditions of service of Civil Servants in India. This attracts a number of individuals towards government jobs.

DISCIPLINE

Discipline is the first and foremost element in organisation in order to achieve its goal. Every administrative organisation is organized on a goal. The goal gives order and meaning to each organisation. There is always a conscious effort on part of the organisation to achieve its goal. However, goals cannot be achieved unless there is sincerity among its personnels that leads to efficiency. But efficiency, is a concept which is integrated with discipline. So without discipline, there can be no sincerity which leads to demolition of efficiency of organisation.

Meaning

Discipline, as a general terminology means order. In the phraseology of public administration, discipline means subject to the orders of the superior. Thus, every government servants are required to subject themselves most systematically and thoroughly to the orders of the administrative authority. In other words, discipline involves a part of obligation on part of the government servants to behave rationally and scientifically in a way as desired by the superior authority. Thus, discipline refers to the human conduct and human behaviour in their dealing with each other and also with the superiors and subordinates in their official capacity.

Discipline keeps an individual on the path of loyalty, devotion, honesty, sincerity, integrity and industry. It makes a person humble, adaptable to societal environment and suitable for organisational goal.

Human nature is always unstable. Man is never satiable. He wants to acquire more and more even if he is provided with enough. This is the surest sign of self-centeredness which is inimical and detrimental to the effectiveness of the organisation. So what is needed is to bind the human conduct and behaviour under strict rule of a certain code of conduct which will ensure discipline among them and as such bring into efficiency in the administration.

Discipline, as such is a means to achieve efficiency in administration. It can be defined as "the process which regulates the relationship between the superior and subordinates and among the subordinates themselves in their official dealings with each other." Discipline is generally an official procedure that laid stress on the strict observance of certain code of conducts. The non-observance of those impersonal rules would inevitably followed by disciplinary action against the invader so that none of the Civil Servants will ever dare to show unfaithfulness to the official orders and official directions. Non-compliance to the administrative orders and also to the code of conduct is followed by punishment and penalties.

How to Ensure Discipline?

How to ensure discipline is the most pertinent question in administrative organisation. The answer to this is quite obvious. Discipline can be ensured best by following the civil service code of conduct. The civil service code of conduct provides for the following steps in order to ensure discipline:

(1) Every Civil Servant has to discharge his duty conscientiously in accordance with the provisions of the Constitutions and the law of the land.

(2) Every official has to obey the official orders of his superior so far as they do not contradict the law. The subordinates cannot question the reasoning of the superior's order.

(3) He must carry on his duties with sincerity and probity, with impartiality and integrity and with industriousness and care. The duties shall be

discharged without fear and favour, goodwill and hatred. He should ensure all his acts above suspicion.

(4) The Civil Servants must be truthful in their official dealings.

(5) A Civil Servant must show respect to the superior, courtesy to the subordinates and politeness to the public.

(6) He should maintain the dignity and prestige of the office by any means even if he personally feels hurt.

(7) They must observe official secrecy.

(8) They must be punctual in their work.

(9) The Civil Servants shall not take on any private trade or employment without the prior sanction of the government.

(10) Every government servant shall report to the government, if any member of his family is engaged in a private trade or business.

(11) He shall not take part in the registration, promotion and management of any bank or company registered under the Indian Companies Act, 1956, except a Cooperative Society.

(12) Neither the government servant nor any member of his family are allowed to engage in any such investment, lending and borrowings which is likely to influence him in the discharge of his official duties.

(13) The government servants should always avoid indebtedness and insolvency. If he is trapped in insolvency, he must seek the help of government.

(14) The government servants are required to seek prior permission of the government for acquiring and disposing of any movable or immovable property exceeding Rs. 1000/- only.

(15) They cannot accept gifts and any such other contributions from anybody without the approval of the government.

Non-Compliance of Orders

The non-compliance of the above rules and orders tantamounts to the breach of discipline. As such disciplinary action is taken against the invader. The disciplinary action involves for asking for explanations. If the government is not satisfied with the explanation served, then it may frame charges and as such, on investigation which is proved, inflicts penalties upon the invader.

Penalties which are inflicted as a matter of disciplinary action may be of two types–minor penalties and major penalties. Minor penalties includes censure, withholding increment or promotion and recovery from pay of the civil servant, whole or part of any pecuniary loss caused to the government by negligence or breach of orders.

Major penalties includes reduction to a lower service, grade or post, suspension from the post, removal from the service, dismissal from the service and compulsory retirement.

MORALE

Every organisation has a goal of its own and the organisation always seeks to make a conscious and coordinated effort to achieve its goal. However, organisation is nothing but the combination of men and materials. Thus, the conscious efforts on part of men and their coordinated endeavour leads an organisation to its goal. Thus, stress is always led on the human factors in organisation.

But why men will carry on conscious and coordinated efforts for the achievement of the organisational goal? Because man is a social animal. He does not live by breads alone. He needs the recognition of others in performance of his duties. Therefore, esteem serves as a powerful stimulant that drives men into action. The esteem on part of human beings are represented by high attitude, enthusiasm and loyalty towards organisation. This is called morale.

Meaning

The term 'morale' is very difficult to describe in any tangible words. It refers to a mental condition of man and as such it is a psychological phenomena. It is an inner possession of an individual or a group in the organisation. Morale is always relational because it is related with the working conditions in the organisation.

Literally, the term 'Morale' means the mental state of a body of man or army or the like. It is always related with the moral considerations like zeal, enthusiasm, spirit, hope, confidence, social service, prestige etc. Therefore, morale is somewhat, intangible concept.

Alexander Leighton defined 'morale' as the capacity of a group of people to pull together persistently and consistently in pursuit of a common purpose."

F.M. Marx defined 'morale' as 'the state of mind in which men and women voluntarily seek to develop and apply their full powers to the tasks on which they are engaged by reason of intellectual and moral satisfaction which they derive from their own self-realization, their achievements in their choosen fields and their pride in the services."

Therefore, morale is the readiness on the part of an individual to cooperate warmly in the task and functions of a given group or organisation.

In military vocabulary, morale refers to a consciousness of their strength, unity among the personnel, freedom from fear and belief in the victory over the enemy. In public administration, morale refers to a feeling of 'togetherness' among the employees on the one hand and between the employer and the employees on the other hand.

Morale, thus, is a sense of belongingness and a sense of

unity of purpose which prevails among the employees of an organisation. It is a sense of identification with and interest in the elements of one's job, working condition, fellow workers, supervisors, employers, and the company.

To sum up, morale is a state of mind or attitude that the members of an organisation have not only towards their own individual roles but also towards their work, their fellow men and the organisation to which they belong. As such morale has both individual and institutional aspects. In its individual aspect, morale refers to the opportunity for personal development by an individual. In its group or institutional aspect, morale means an opportunity to develop cooperation, coordination, fellow-feeling and unity towards each other and also towards the organisation as a whole.

An employee's morale is considered to be high if he does his work with devotion and whole heartedness not merely for the sake of emoluments attached to it, but because he feels a self-satisfaction and a sense of self-fulfillment in doing it. Such a feeling can come only to an individual if he identified himself with the goal of the organisation.

Importance of Morale

The importance of a good morale to a service cannot be over-emphasized. Its presence leads to all-round efficiency and success of the organisation. As Prof. **L.D. White** pointed out, a high morale acts both as an index of sound employment situation and a positive means of building up an efficient organisation. It fights indifferences and stimulates loyalty, cooperation, coordination, team work and fellow feelings among the members of an organisation. It induces men to far superior efforts in their respective fields of work than greed for money or fear of punishment does.

Factors Influencing Morale

Generally, three factors contribute to influence morale. They are–prestige, discipline and moral.

(a) Prestige

Prestige is one of the prime factors which influence the morale. Prestige means the dignity or the respect of appreciation that an officer or his post or the service as a whole enjoy in the estimation of the people. Morale is directly proportional to the prestige of a job or post. The lower the prestige of a job, the lower the morale and the higher the status of a job, the higher is the morale.

A research reveals that generally those offices or posts and the incumbents thereupon enjoy high prestige where there is a high income, high qualification, reputation for hard work and high social position. Therefore, morale is also simultaneously influenced by these factors.

Besides, **Dr. L.D. White** observed that morale depends a lot on the following matters:

(a) wearing of uniforms;

(b) association with well-known persons;

(c) security of tenure of the office;

(d) capacity to exercise power;

(e) high standard of skill and integrity; and

(f) the attitude of leading men of the country.

(b) Discipline

Besides prestige, discipline also influences the morale of an individual. The higher is the discipline, the higher the morale is. Only for this reason, the morale in military services is high because there is high degree of discipline in those services.

Both discipline and morale contribute for the growth of organisational efficiency. While discipline is a sort of negative instrument to attain efficiency, morale is a sort of positive instrument to attain efficiency in the organisation. While discipline tends to coercion, morale tends to persuasion and understandings.

(c) Morals

The moral behaviour also influences the morale of a person. People are sometimes confused between the two and identified the one with the other. However, moral and morale are not identical and the same. Morale refers to a sense of belongingness, a feeling of oneness among the individuals and groups. It identifies man with his work and goals of the organisation. But moral on the other hand are certain pious principles which, if observed, makes the life virtuous. It is represented by good behaviour, truthfulness, honesty, sincerity, benevolence etc. These moral behaviour definitely have a lasting impression upon the activity of the individuals. Although both of them are internal, yet while *morale* refers to the feeling of mind, *morals* refer to the external behaviour. The moral principles exert tremendous influence upon the morale of the people or the employees in the organisation.

Factors Inimical to Morale

Morale in India, is not upto the satisfaction. This definitely retards the efficiency of the organisations. The Administrative Reforms Commission has strongly felt that there was a lack of feeling of involvement among the government employees. This is due to the conglomeration of several factors. The factors which contribute for the retardation of morale in India are follows:

(1) There is lack of interest among the individual employees towards their job.

(2) There is unnecessary and undue political interference in the activities and working of organisations.

(3) There is the lack of discipline among the public servants in the organisation.

(4) The moral behaviour of the employees have degenerated to a maximum extent.

(5) The feeling of discontentment among the public employees regarding their uneven pay scale.

(6) Nepotism, favouritism and corruption have played their sinister role and steadily increasing their scope in administrative organisation.

(7) Public service failed to attract the talented men believing in the ideas of nationalism, public service, sincerity and whole heartedness.

How to Build up Morale?

The Administrative Reforms Commissions (ARC) has strongly recognized the devastating factors that contribute for the decrease in the morale of the public servants. It thus emphasized a number of strong measures to build up morale in public service. The Commission felt it strongly that in order to avoid inertness in public service, the following steps can be taken up:

(1) The government should motivate the average employees to take more interest in their work.

(2) Proper incentives should be paid to the employees in order to stimulate and sustain enthusiasm and boost up their morale.

(3) The employees should be provided with by good home conditions which will relieve them from their worriness of having unsuitable internal condition.

(4) They should be provided with proper working conditions such as security of tenure, reasonable opportunity for promotion, training, facility for leave, good office accommodation and equipments, satisfactory retirement benefits etc.

(5) They should be properly trained in the purpose of the work and organisation.

(6) They should be given a scope of sharing in the policy formulation of the organisation.

(7) The employees should be given a consultative status to improve up the organisation.

(8) The employees should have confidence over the superior in matters of impartiality, integrity and neutrality towards the employees.

(9) They should be properly trained with the code of conduct specifying what to do and what not to do by the public servants.

(10) Steps should be taken to build up a healthy and cordial atmosphere of understanding between the employer and the employees.

(11) There should be applaud appraisal of the works of the employees not only by the employing authority but also by the fellow employees. In other words, there should be recognition of the works of employees.

(12) Finally, there should be a dynamic leader to generate enthusiasm and cohesion among the employees.

If these steps could be taken then only the morale of the employees could be boosted up.

RELATION BETWEEN MINISTERS AND CIVIL SERVANTS

The successful working of Parliamentary democracy depends, to a great extent, on the harmonious relationship between the ministers and civil servants. Both of them are engaged in their endless adventure of governing men and doing their welfare. But the success of their task depends upon the proper understanding of the respective roles played by each other.

The ministers and the civil servants are complimentary to each other. While the ministers are considered to be political, amateur and non-permanent, the civil servants are considered to be non-political, expert and permanent servants of the society.

A.D. Gorwala observes "both of them are essential; one of them makes the government popular, and the other makes it efficient. The test of government lies in the successful combination of these qualities." The ministers are the professional politicians who know what people expect from the government. The Secretaries on the other hand, are men of wide administrative experiences who know how to fulfill the expectations of the people.

According to **Harold J. Laski**, "it is the duty of the secretary to tell the minister, what in his judgement, are the probable consequences of any policy for which the minister proposed to take responsibility." Each lacks what is best in the other, and therefore, supplements one-another in their mutual dealings. Thus, the ministers and civil servants are both complementary and supplementary to each other.

Who is a Minister?

A minister is one who is the representative of the people. He is either directly or indirectly comes to power through the help of the people. A minister, being a public servant, should possess the following qualities:

(a) He must be a good listener and a good learner.

(b) He must have a sound knowledge of the subject under his charge.

(c) It is his duty to see that the decision taken is a collective one.

(d) He should cultivate the habit of meeting the senior civil servants regularly and encourage frankness in discussion.

(e) He should obtain the best out of the civil servant by carefully listening to him. This also generate a feeling among the secretaries that they got a fair deal at the hands of the ministers.

Harold J. Laski observes that 'the whole difference between efficient and non-efficient administration lies in the creative use of officials by the elected representatives.'

Who is a Civil Servant?

A civil servant, on the other hand in a subordinate staff of the minister. He is elevated to the office by dint of his merit. He is a permanent, paid and skilled officer in the government. A civil servant performs the following functions:

(a) He advises the minister in any matter relating to policy formulation.

(b) He carried out the laws as passed by the legislature and makes the government efficient.

(c) He implements the governmental policies in the society whether he agrees with it or not.

(d) He made available all sorts of information and data to his political chief in order to help him in the formulation of the policies.

What should be their Relationship?

The relationship between the minister and the civil servants should be close and intimate. **Herbert Morrison** the Deputy Prime Minister in Attlee's Cabinet opined that the relationship between the ministers and the civil servants should be that of colleagues working together in a team; they should be like cooperative partners seeking to advance public interest and the efficiency of the department. Cooperation between them is an essential pre-condition of a good government.

The ministers should not interfere unnecessarily in the day to day administration of the civil servants excepts in case of grave injustice and serious default and mal-administration on part of the civil servants. Frequent and meddlesome interference by the politicians not only hampers the efficiency of the government but also shakes the morale of the civil servants.

The ministers should not be an isolated autocrat, giving orders without hearing or considering arguments for alternative courses; nor, on the other hand, should the secretary be able to treat him as a mere cipher. The partnership should be virile and alive, rival ideas and opinions should be fairly considered, and the relationship between them should be of mutual respect.

The minister should exercise a general ministerial control over the activities of the civil servants. He should direct, coordinate and control his department through persuasion and not by force. There should be frequent meeting between the minister and the secretary for consideration of the departmental problems and policies. **Morrison**, remarked, "a clumsy and inconsiderate minister can easily make the department unhappy and discouraged, whereas, what he should seek to do is to make the people live minded, happy in working for him so as to get the best out of them. . . .the greatest danger in running a governmental department is a minister who does not know how to handle the civil servants."

The Reality of Interface

The reality of relationship between the ministers and civil servants is different from the theory. The minister tries to impose their orders upon the civil servants. By using arbitrary powers of transfer, out of turn promotion, arbitrary suspension and institution of enquiry the ministers bent down the civil servants. Nowaday there is a shameful victimization of the honest and unpliable civil servants. The civil servants in order to save their position become the yesman of their political bosses. This undervalued the whole fabric of Public Administration.

Today, the civil servant has no protection against the unscrupulous politicians who view illegal money making as an essential element in the art of politics. Justice **H.R. Khanna** held that political corruption is the foster mother of administrative corruption.

Today, the advice given by the secretary to the minister is not always that which is in the best interest of the country but very often one that the minister may like.

The secretary quite often anticipates his minister's wishes and trims his sails to every wind that blows. The path set by the senior civil servants to increasingly seek the patronage of a powerful politician is widely followed and acclaimed by their juniors.

The minister oversteps his legitimate function of non-interference in the day to day affairs and takes more and keen interest on the daily administration of the department instead of laying down only policies. This sufficiently undermines the initiative and independence of civil servants.

To conclude, today the power hankering politicians and running away of the civil servants of their actual duties of rendering advice and carrying out the policies have set aside the age long tradition of civil service neutrality and anonymity on the one hand as well as the committed bureaucracy on the other hand.

RELATIONSHIP BETWEEN THE CIVIL SERVANTS AND PUBLIC

The success of administrative organisation not only depends upon the cordial relationship between the ministers and civil servants but also between the civil servants and the people. Democracy is always based upon the principle of public interest. It is often defined as the form of government of the people, by the people and for the people. In short, democracy as a form of government, always seeks and try to develop the lots of the people and as such the concept of Welfare State have emerged.

Civil servants always try to look after the general public and help them in solving their problems. It is the public that always seeks the helps of the civil servants. The civil servant helps the public right from the pre-natal stage to his death and also governs his social relationship.

The efficiency of administration can be judged by the efficient dealing of popular problems by the civil servants. If the civil servants cannot come upto the satisfaction of the general people, it is a black spot on the efficiency of administration. The civil or public servants, as the name suggests, must serve the people in order to achieve the organisational goal.

The civil servants, though a part of the general public, are categorically distinguished from them on the basis of their administrative skill and competence. These are the people who are endowed with superior qualities and as such they are called the *'elite class'* in the society. The public on the other hand, are less-gifted beings who, for each step depend on the civil servants for solution. The perfect relationship between the civil servants and the public is based on a bilineal symmetry i.e. the civil servants should help the public in solving their issues and the public should pose trust upon the civil servants in solving their issues.

Who is a Civil Servant?

A civil servant is a high ranking officials in the administrative organisation who are bestowed upon superior qualities than others and are entrusted with dealing in higher responsibilities and higher tasks. The civil servant is one who possess the following qualities:

(a) He is decisive in nature and is capable of taking firm decisions.

(b) They have a clear vision of ideas and clarity of thoughts on the problem, situation or case.

(c) They possess deep but correct farsight and can judge thing altogether by its appearance.

(d) These are the people who have organisational capacity of inviting the people to share the burden.

(e) They are progressive minded, rational and efficient leaders who can motivate the general public.

What is Public?

'Public' is an amorphous concept which lacks any precise meaning. Broadly it refers to the general masses of the society whose all round development became the basis of every Welfare State. These are numerous in numbers and less organized in any society. For the satisfaction of their wants, they do not hesitate to take the help of the civil servants. They are generally the less talented and less intelligent beings in the society. They do not have capacity to rule themselves and for that purpose, they have voted some representatives on their behalf to rule them.

What should be their Relationship?

The relationship between the public and civil servants should always be close and intimate. The civil servants should behave as the servants and not as the masters. They must devote the whole pursuit not of their own interest, but of the general well-being. They should impose self-restraint upon their activities. While dealing with the people, they should observe a high ethical standard of behaviour. They should always try to justify the public trust entrusted upon them. They should give up businessmen-like behaviour and become populist oriented. They should assume only those roles which is good enough for the community as a whole.

The civil servants should give due respect and regard to the interests and rights of the Public. As far as practicable, they should try to involve the general masses in the administrative process. In short, they should act as an instrument for the welfare of the public.

The civil servants must take steps to safeguard the dignity and worth of the human beings and to promote social progress and better standards of life. They should adjust all their activities and procedures in such a way that not even the humblest citizen is deprived of certain specific rights in relation to the public service.

The manners in which the public is dealt with by the civil servants should reflect a spirit of respect and consideration for the citizens and a desire to serve him in accordance with law and the policies of the government.

The civil servant should make personal contacts with the public and maintain public relations. They should learn about the wishes and aspirations of the public. At the same time, they should advise the public about what it should think, desire and do within the specific sphere of activity. They should cultivate a satisfactory contact between the officials and public in such a way that fearness in the public is removed. The most important function that it should take up is to keep the public informed about what the administrative agency is doing.

In short, a very cordial relation should be maintained between the public and the civil servants.

The Reality of Interface

The reality of relationship between the civil servants and people is far from agreeable. The civil servants treat themselves as masters and not servants and as such they develop a sense of superiority complex among them. The excessive procedural complexities act as a bar in the cordial relation between the civil servant and the public.

There is lack of contact with the people by the civil servants. They feel no responsibility towards public. As such the idea of service mentality has relegated to background. Money making and private interests have gained momentum in the civil servant's behaviour. The behaviour with which they deal with the public is not a behaviour of solace and solidarity rather represented by rudeness and complexity. They invariably think in terms of controlling, disciplining, mastering and lording over the people, and if they accidentally perform a service, they are apt to regard it as a act of charity instead of considering it as a part of their duty.

In short, the civil servants have become way-ward in their relation with the public. They think themselves superior to them in all respects and try to ignore the basic ethical standard which should have been there in administration.

However, they should always keep it in mind that people come to them whom they trust and think best to solve their problems. If they behave them with simplicity and sobriety and listen to their problems carefully and patiently it will boost up the morale of the general public. They will obey him as god and will prepare even dying for him for the sake of his ideals and ideology. A true civil servant, thus should always develop leadership traits and manage the affairs of the people with their cooperation without applying any external force. The people need to be persuaded by the civil servant instead of being forced to submit to the dictates of them.

Chapter X

REDRESSAL OF CITIZEN'S GRIEVANCES

The twentieth century is well recognized as a century of democracies. The democratic forms of government have a clean sweep in the world today. Every democratic state is more or less considered as a representative state because the representatives of the people rule the society. The concept of 'welfare state' have enormously increased the functioning of the government. However, the enormous expansion of public services, both in size and range, have come to affect the citizen's everyday life. This creates the problem of how to control the governmental administration so that the liberty of the people is not hampered. This brings to the limelight the concept of how to redress the citizen's grievances against the administration.

WHY REDRESSAL?

Lord Acton said, "Power corrupts and absolute power corrupts absolutely." The expansion of governmental activities have resulted in the multiplication of administrative process whereby administrative powers and discretion are vested at different levels of administration. And where there is power and discretion, there is always the possibility of abuse, especially when powers are used in the context of scarcity of commodity and pressure to spend public money.

The Law Commission of India, in its fourteenth report expressed grave concern on the point of administrative abuse of powers. It pointed out that there is a vast field of administrative action in India in which the administrative authority may act outside the strict scope of law and propriety and there is no scope for the injured citizens to obtain effective redress.

Naturally question arise what actually constitute the "*abuse of power*". The answer is obvious. Every administration necessarily stands and do work for the welfare of the citizens with due promptness. Every citizen has a right to be heard by the administrative authority of his problems and offer best help to mitigate those problems. But the concentration of power at the hands of administrative authority may sometimes results in unnecessary harassment to the citizens, malpractices and corruption in the exercise of powers. This constitutes the abuse of power.

The abuse of power in the form of harassment, malpractices (nepotism, favouritism etc.) and corruption on part of the executive creates a general feeling of discontentment among the citizens. They need the help of some authority outside the influence and control of the Executive who will not only take steps for the redress of their grievances but also will act as a check against the misuse or abuse of power.

THE INSTITUTION FOR REDRESSAL OF CITIZEN'S GRIEVANCES

The need for the redress of citizen's grievances provided for the establishment of an institution outside the influence and control of the executive. This institution serves a twin purpose–firstly, it will act as a sufficient check on the arbitrary use or misuse of power by the members of Executive. Secondly, it will arouse the confidence of the people on the democratic government as a whole and provide for best safeguard against the encroachment on the liberty of the individuals.

The institution established for the redressal of citizen's

grievances is termed in English language as the institution of 'Ombudsman.' The *Chamber's Dictionary* described Ombudsman as a 'grievance man'. In other words, Ombudsman is an officer who investigates complaints of citizens of unfair treatment meted out to them by Government Departments and suggest remedy thereof, if he finds that a complaint is justified.

The institution of Ombudsman is established by an Act of Parliament for the supervision and control of administration. He is both in the form and practice, independent from the Executive and the Legislature in the performance of his duties. The Parliament only lays down the general rules for his activities. He not only supervises the administration but also protects the rights of the individuals. It conducts informal investigations of the complaints and as such it has free access to all the files of the administrative department. He can demand explanations from the officials or authority concerned. He can intervene in all cases of illegal or improper conduct of officials. He investigates complaints against administrative decisions as well as complaints of official misbehaviour, inefficiency or negligence.

OMBUDSMAN—ITS HISTORICAL LEGACY

The institution of Ombudsman first came into being in Sweden in 1713 when the Chancellor of Justice was appointed by the King to act as an invigilator to look into the functioning of the war time government. In the year 1809, provision was made for the appointment of Ombudsman by the Legislature. The institution remained confined only to the Scandinavian countries like Finland and Denmark. In 1962, NewZealand also adopted the system of Ombudsman. Great Britain also did not lag behind and a slightly modified version of the institution called "Parliamentary Commissioner" came into being in 1967 through an Act of Parliament. This was followed by other countries such as Canada, Australia, USA, France and several newly independent countries of Asia and Africa.

A study of the system of Ombudsman or similar institutions in Sweden, United Kingdom, Zambia, and Nigeria brings into focus the fact that mainly complaints of mal-administration are looked into by the Ombudsman there and the Ministers etc., do not seem to have been brought within their purview. However, in Denmark, all administrative matters concerning all units of state administration including the Ministers have brought under the purview of Ombudsman. Norway made a bit advance when it brought the administrative aspects of acts of Ministers in the jurisdiction of Ombudsman. In Tanzania and Uganda the areas of jurisdiction for the institution that are known as Anti Corruption Squad and Inspector General of Government respectively, are mainly targeted at corruption and abuse of Public Office. The thrust of the system of Ombudsman as obtaining in these countries is mainly on redressal of public grievances arising mainly out of their complaints of mal-administration.

In India, prolonged discussions both inside the Parliament as well as outside took place and the necessity for the establishment of an institution like Ombudsman was felt for the redressal of Public grievances. However, the idea could not be formalized. In the mean while the Administrative Reforms Commission (ARC) submitted its interim report to the Parliament in 1966. It has expressed strong plea for the establishment the institution of Lokpal to investigate and report on complaints pertaining to corruption.

THE NECESSITY OF LOKPAL IN INDIA

The Administrative Reforms Commission has felt the necessity of Lokpal in India. This does not mean that prior to the recommendation of the ARC, the grievances of the people are never taken into account. The reality is that although various administrative, legislative and judicial remedies are there for the redressal of citizen's grievances, yet their utility proved to be less significant for the people. The administrative redress of grievances is done through the normal departmental machinery and procedures. There is a departmental review of both the complaints made by the citizens and the work done by the civil servants. The Central Vigilance Commission (CVC) was also there to eliminate corruption and other malaise of the civil service in India. However, the ordinary citizen cannot understand the technical operation of these administrative institutions and as such cannot get their grievances redressed.

Similarly, the legislative remedy is unknown to most of the citizens and thus proved to be a futile for the people. The Judicial remedy for redress of citizen's grievances is expensive and somewhat a lengthy procedure. Justice delayed is justice denied–this is what generally understood by the people. So they do not want to indulge in such a delaying and dilatory process. As such both the legislative and judicial remedy proved to be fallacious for the redressal of citizen's grievances.

Therefore, the ARC felt that the ultimate setup of the institution of Lokpal would lead to speedy disposal of cases and will provide the people with a redress which has not been available through the normal departmental or governmental machinery. It also strategically pointed out that the establishment of Lokpal will not absolve the department from fulfilling its obligation to the citizens for administering its affairs without generating, as far as possible, any legitimate sense of grievance. Thus, the administration itself must play the major role in reducing the area of grievances and providing remedies wherever necessary and feasible.

Therefore, the ARC has contemplated a very limited role for the proposed creation of an institution of Lokpal which would only enquire into the complaints against a specified category of persons and not be a forum to deal with all complaints of citizen's grievances.

LOKPAL IN INDIA

In its interim report on "Problem of Redress of Citizen's Grievances", submitted in 1966, the Administrative Reforms Commission recommended for the setting up of two institutions for the redressal of citizen's grievances. According to the report, "there should be one authority dealing with complaints against the administrative acts of ministers or secretaries to government at the Centre and in the States. (This is called the Lokpal institution). There should be another authority in each states and at the Centre for dealing with the complaints against the administrative acts of other officials. (This is called Lokayukta institution).

To give effect to this recommendation of the Administrative Reforms Commission, a Bill called the "Lokpal and the Lokayukta Bill, 1968" was introduced in the Fourth Lok Sabha in 1968. The bill was considered by a Joint Committee of both Houses of the Parliament, and the bill as reported by the Joint Committee, was passed by the Lok Sabha in 1969. While the bill was pending in Rajya Sabha, the Fourth Lok Sabha was dissolved and consequently the bill lapsed.

In 1971, the bill passed by the previous Lok Sabha was reintroduced in Lok Sabha as the "Lokpal and Lokayukta Bill, 1971". This also lapsed on the dissolution of the Fifth Lok Sabha.

A fresh bill called the "Lokpal Bill, 1977" was introduced in Lok Sabha in 1977. This bill was referred to a Joint Committee of both the Houses of Parliament which submitted its report in July 1978. When the bill, as reported by the Joint Committee, was under consideration of Lok Sabha, the Lok Sabha was prorogued and subsequently dissolved. Consequently that bill also lapsed.

The 'Lokpal Bill, 1985' was introduced in Lok Sabha and subsequently withdrawn. The Lokpal Bill, 1989 which sought to include the office of Prime Minister also within the jurisdiction of Lokpal, which was to be a three member body, lapsed with the dissolution of the Lok Sabha.

The "Lokpal Bill, 1996" provides for setting up the office of Lokpal with a Chairman and two other members for a fixed tenure. With a view to ensure independence of the office, the bill also provided for the appointment by President and made the removal of the members more stringent. It also provided that the Chairman and members of Lokpal shall be appointed by the President only on the recommendation of a committee. The bill provides under the scope of Lokpal purview the public functionaries like Prime Minister, members of Council of

Ministers and the members of both the Houses of Parliament. The bill also seeks to make special provisions for discouraging frivolous, vexatious and false complaints. The bill also provided for the declaration of assets by the members of Parliament and their family members, annually. On the broad objectives as outlined above, the bill was introduced in Lok Sabha on 10th September 1996.

The bill was sent for the consideration of a Joint Committee of both the Houses of Parliament and the Joint Committee, after a careful consideration reported back along with a number of recommendations on 9th May 1997. But unfortunately, when the bill was still pending in Lok Sabha, the Parliament is dissolved and the bill met the same fate along with its predecessors.

The present Vajpayee government have assured the Parliament of introducing the Lokpal Bill in the House vary soon. But he has not clarified it whether the bill will have the same features as portrayed in the "Lokpal Bill, 1996" or will have some modifications and alterations. Still we are hopeful of having the establishment of an institution of Lokpal in India very soon for enabling the citizens to have recourse to a convenient and effective forum for determination of complaints and thereby save him from pursuing his remedy through the process of courts, which may prove to be expensive or dilatory and may not facilitate in speedy determination.

General Features of Lokpal Bill 1996

The general feature of Lokpal Bill 1996, as recommended by the Joint Committee of Both the House of Parliament are as follows:

(1) The Lokpal institution is a multi-member body consisting of Chairman and two other members who are, or have been, Judges of the Supreme Court or the Chief Justice of High Courts.

(2) The Lokpal will be appointed by the President directly

or under the warrant of the hand seal on the recommendation of a Committee, consisting of the following members:

(a) Vice President of India : Chairman

(b) Prime Minister : Member

(c) Speaker of House of People : Member

(d) Leader of Opposition in Lok Sabha : Member

(e) Leader of Opposition in Rajya Sabha: Member

(3) The Lokpal shall be appointed for a period of 3 years from the date on which he enters upon his office.

(4) He can be removed from the office by an order of the President on the grounds of proven misbehaviour or incapacity to hold office after an enquiry made by the Chief Justice of India and two other senior-most Judges of Supreme Court, found the Lokpal guilty.

(5) The salary, allowances, conditions of service and pensions of the members of Lokpal shall be the same as the Chief Justice of India.

(6) The Lokpal shall conduct investigation into the complaint of corruption done by the Public functionaries like the Prime Minister, Cabinet Ministers, Ministers of State, Deputy Ministers and Members of Parliament during last 10 years.

(7) The enquiry of the Lokpal shall be informal, based on evidences and files and there shall be transparency in the enquiry and as such all transactions of the complaints shall be conducted publicly, not in camera.

(8) The investigation must be completed within 6 months and the Lokpal must make a report in writing to the competent authority and must clearly specify the action to be taken against the public functionary. The competent authority, in case of ministers is the Prime Minister and in case of all others, including the Prime

Minister, is the concerned House of which they are the members.

(9) The action must be taken by the competent authority within 30 days of receiving the report of the Lokpal.

(10) The members of Parliament shall make annual declaration of their assets before the Lokpal within 30 days of the financial year begins.

(11) The Lokpal shall make criminal charges on the persons who have made vexatious and frivolous complaints.

(12) Against the decision of the Lokpal, a public functionary or any citizen can go to the Supreme Court.

(13) The Lokpal cannot make inquiry into the complaints against the President of India, Vice-President, Speaker of the House, Chief Justice and Judges of Supreme Court, Election Commission, Comptroller and Auditor General of India & Chairman and Members of UPSC.

DISTRICT ADMINISTRATION

Administration wants to achieve the welfare of the people as a whole. For the sake of people's welfare, every administrative system tends to be diversified and decentralized so as to touch the lowest level of social organisation because administration cannot be runned from a central point situated at a far distance from the lowest unit. Therefore, every administrative structure of the government has decentralized to reach the general people. In India, there is Central government and various State governments. Each State, for administrative conveniences is divided into a number of Revenue Divisions. Each headed by a Commissioner. In Orissa, there are three such Revenue Divisions, each headed by a Revenue Divisional Commissioner. Again for convenience, each Revenue Division is divided into a number of districts, each district being headed by an officer called the District Collector. In Orissa, there are 30 districts and as such 30 District Collectors are there to implement the government policies. Looking from the executive point of view, the district represents the basic unit of administration.

Meaning of District Administration

The term "District Administration', as the name suggests refers to the administration of the District. "Administration" means 'to manage'. "District", as defined by the Chamber's Dictionary is a 'subdivision within a division'. Therefore, to manage the affairs of the district forms the very basis of the district administration.

District is the lowest unit of administration. It refers to the basic field administration. As I have told elsewhere that every administrative system has two organisations – the Headquarter and the Field. At the Headquarter, the decisions are made and administrative plans are formalized and the governmental policies are made accordingly. But the real significance of those policies are realized in the Fields where these policies are implemented by the government officials so as to bring administration to the people's reach. The district represents the basic field unit of every administrative system.

As such it is the district where the administration comes into direct contact with the people. The officials in the district administration reach the people, conceptualize their grievances and communicate them to the government. At the same time, the district officer also channelizes the governmental decisions, plans and proposals to the people which are specially devised to ameliorate their grievances and lead them to have a happy life. Thus the governmental action begin from the district.

In short, a *district* is technically the best area for geographical and functional aggregations of units and branches of administration. The administration could best be realized and felt by the people here. The goodness or badness of administration, its policies and plans is felt by the people only at the district level. The people have a direct contact with the district officer who happens to be an agent of the government. To sum up, the district level administration is strategic to both government and the people.

ORGANISATIONS OF DISTRICT ADMINISTRATION

The administration of district is a testament of governmental efficiency. As such the district covers a wide range of activities. Each activity is manned by a official.

Generally, for administrative conveniences, every district is divided into a number of sub-divisions. Each subdivision is headed by a Sub-Divisional Officer or the Sub-Collector. The sub-division is divided into a number of blocks for development purposes; a number of Tahsils for revenue purposes; and a number of police stations for law and order purposes. The Block is headed by the BDO, Tahasil, by Tahasildar and the police station by a Police Inspector. At the sub-division level, the law and order is maintained by the Sub-Divisional Police Officer (SDPO) who happens to be a man of D.S.P. rank.

At the district level, a number of departments exist. The following table will reveal a clear picture of the organisation of District Administration.

Sl. No.	*Department*	*Head at District Level*	*Head at Sub-division Level*
1.	Revenue & General Administration	District Collector	Sub-Collector or Sub-Divisional Officer
2.	Police	Superintendent of Police (S.P.)	Deputy Superintendent of Police (DSP) or (SDPO)
3.	Excise	Superintendent of Excise (SE)	Inspector of Excise
4.	Medical	Chief District Medical Officer (CDMO)	Sub-divisional Medical Officer (SDMO)
5.	Forest	Divisional Forest Officer (DFO)	Divisional Forest Officer (DFO)

(Contd.)

Sl. No.	*Department*	*Head at District Level*	*Head at Sub-division Level*
6.	Education	Circle Inspector of Schools (C.I)	District Inspector of Schools (D.I)
7.	Agriculture	District Agricultural Officer (DAO)	Agricultural Officer (AO)
8.	Horticulture	District Horticulture Officer (DHO)	Horticulture Officer (HO)
9.	Cooperative	Assistant Registrar Cooperative Societies (ARCS)	Sub-assistant Registrar, Cooperative Societies (SARCS)
10.	Veterinary	Chief District Veterinary officer (CDVO)	Sub-Divisional Veterinary officer (SDVO)
11.	Industry	District Industries officer (DIO)	-----------
12.	Information	District Public Relation Officer (DPRO)	Sub-divisional Public Relations Officer (SDPRO)
13.	Judiciary	District & Sessions Judge	Civil Judge or First Class Magistrate.

The sub-division is the basic unit of administration below the district level. It is headed by the Sub-Divisional Officer or SDO. He happens to be either a fresh trained IAS officer posted on probation basis or a comparatively experienced and old officer belonging to the State public service. On the basis of the office of the SDO, the subdivision may be broadly divided into two types such as office type sub-division and touring type sub-division. An office type Sub-division is one in which the SDO has office at the sub-division Headquarter. On the other hand, a Touring-type Sub-division is one in which the SDO does not have any office at the Headquarter. His office is located at the district headquarter and the SDO has to make tours to his subdivision daily and mix with the people. In Orissa, we have the office type Sub-divisions.

For the purpose of revenue collection, Sub-division is divided into a number of Tahsils. Each of the Tahasil is headed by a *Tahasildar*. He happens to be an experienced member of the State Public Service. Sometimes the *Tahasildar* is assisted by a *Naib-Tahasildar* in the performance of his function. Below them are the Revenue Inspectors (R.I.s) and Surveyors, Chairman etc.

For the purpose of development, each Sub-division is divided into a number of blocks. Each block is headed by the *Block Development Officer* (BDO). He is generally a member of State Public Service. He is assisted by sometimes, an Additional Block Development Officer (ABDO) in the performance of his functions.

For the purpose of maintaining law and order, each Sub-division is divided into a number of Police Stations and also a certain number of police out-posts. The Sub-Divisional Police Officer (SDPO) heads the Police department in the Sub-division. He happens to be an officer of Deputy Superintendent of Police (DSP) rank. Below him are the Circle Inspectors, Sub-Inspectors, Assistant Sub-Inspectors and Constables.

Although these various Sub-divisions are only for administrative conveniences, yet importance is always laid on 'district' which happens to be the basic unit of field administration. The district is represented by the 'District Collector' who is generally a young man within 35 years belonging to IAS rank. Otherwise, the District Collector is appointed from among the members of State Public Services on promotion basis.

The District Collector belongs to the General Administration Department of the State Government. However, he is required to exercise control and supervision over the officials belonging to various departments who remains within the district.

As such, the District Collector, being the head of the district, is involved in a network of inter-relationship with other district level functionaries as cited in the above table. The relationship among these officials and the Collector may be of following nature:

(a) Controlling, guiding and directing.

(b) Coordinating, and

(c) Resolving the disputes among them.

DISTRICT COLLECTOR

The District Collector is the pivot of district administration. It is main agency responsible for the coordination of different officials functioning in the district. He is considered as the eyes and ears of district administration i.e. the government. **Ramsay McDonald** compared the District Collector as the tortoise on whose back stood the elephant of Government of India. He is the father and mother of the Public.

The main aim of District Collector, as the name suggests, is the Collection of revenue. The term 'Collector' and its office started in India only in 1772 when the East India Company appointed the officials called 'Collectors' to supervise the revenue collection made by the Diwans'. Prior to that, the collection of revenue was the official duty of the "Kakori-Faujdar' during Mughal period. Although the District Collector was first appointed to supervise revenue collection, yet in course of time they assumed this role of collection to themselves and collected the revenue with the help of subordinate officials. As the time progressed, his functions became diversified and nowadays, he has to perform a variety of function which are quite complex in nature. It requires the ability of the authority to do with the functions.

His Duties

The District Collector has to perform a number of duties. His duties can be summed up as follows:

(a) To maintain law and order in his district, shouldering all the responsibilities upon himself.

(b) To facilitate prompt and fair collection of land revenue in his district.

(c) To supervise and carry out all the developmental plans of the government successfully in his district.

(d) To act as a link between the government and the citizens, protecting one against the possible harassment by another.

(e) To develop friendly relation with the governmental personnel operating within the district to maximize the achievement of the goal of ensuring efficient administration.

(f) To train the junior officers and to keep his office efficient.

His Functions

The functions of the District Collector is more undefined than defined. He performs all those functions which will exalt the position and performance of the government in the eyes of the people. The functions of the District Collector can be summed up in the following heads–as the District Officer, as the Collector, as the District Magistrate, as the Returning Officer and as the Miscellaneous Head.

(a) As the District Officer

The District Collector is the Chief District Officer of the district. He enjoys a superior position in relation to other district level functionaries. As such he enjoys enormous power of posting, transfer and sanctioning leave of all the gazetted officers in his district including the Tahasildars and Naib-Tahasildars.

He appoints and punishes the ministerial and menial staffs of the Collectorate, acts as the drawing and disbursing officer of the staffs as well as deals with the pension cases of the Collectorate staffs.

He prepares the estimates of works in case of revenue

buildings and is responsible for maintaining the government buildings under Revenue Department.

He complies and submits the annual administration report of the district to the government, supervises the conduct of civil suits in which, government is a party and appoints the government counsel in the district. This is all to be done by the District Officer as an agent of the government. As such he is responsible for proper implementation of government orders and looks after the interests of the government in general.

As the Chief District Officer, he acts as the Chief Protocol Officer in the district, issues tentative tour programmes of ministers and other VIPs and arranges their stay in the district.

He carried on extensive tour programmes throughout the district, meet with the people, listens to their grievances and offers best solution to mitigate them.

He maintains coordination among the activities of various public functionaries and government officials in the district, supervises, guides, controls and advises the officials to ensure efficient functioning of the administration.

(b) As a Collector

As a Collector, the District Collector is responsible for the collection of all types of land revenues, canal dues, and other governmental taxes like agricultural, income tax, sales tax, irrigation dues, stamp and court fees, excise duties of various kinds, entertainment taxes, taxes on motor vehicles and others.

He hear appeals in revenue cases against the decision of the Sub-Divisional Officer. He also deals with all matters relating to land records.

He supervises the Government Treasury and Sub-Treasury in his district and give advise to the Treasury Officers in matters relating to government money.

He also assesses the loss of crops during the natural calamities and recommend relief to the government. He also acts as an apostle in providing relief measures to the people suffered with natural calamities like Flood, Drought, Famine, Fire, Storm etc.

He is the principal agency of the government in monitoring the land acquisition work and also furnish multifarious agrarian statistics regarding rainfall, crops, flora, fauna etc., of the district.

(c) As the District Magistrate

As the District Magistrate, he controls and supervises the subordinate Magistracy. He executes the court's decisions and as such is known as the Executive Magistrate.

He orders magisterial postings during festivals and promulgates prohibitory orders if he senses any danger to the peace and tranquility in the district.

He makes Jail Inspection, and take steps for the expeditious disposal of the cases of under-trial prisoners. He is also instrumental in granting superior status to the prisoners, their premature release and their release on parole.

As the head of the criminal administration, he controls and directs the actions of the police, inspects the police station and submit the annual criminal report of the district to the government.

He also sanctions various types of license to the people and also cancels them according to the situation. He is instrumental in pacifying the labour problems, strikes and payment of compensation to workers.

(d) As the Returning Officer

The District Collector acts as the Returning Officer for the Parliamentary Elections. As the Returning Officer, he has to take steps for the appointment and training of various Presiding and Polling Officers, ensures their safety arrival at the respective polling stations and makes extensive arrangement of police and personnels for ensuring a very smooth election in his district. He also appoints a number of enumerators who carry on the counting of ballots. He also declares the results of the Parliamentary election in his district.

(e) As the Miscellaneous Head

As the miscellaneous head, the District Collector carry on Census in his district and make necessary arrangements for smooth conduct of census.

He also directs all the developmental programmes in his district and gives necessary direction to the officials for ensuring prompt action. He also listens to the grievances of the people against the government officials and takes necessary steps for their disposals.

He also takes on Press Conferences and give instructions on various works undertaken by the district administration for the welfare of the people. He also acts as the Chief Officer of Red Cross Society in the district and helps in blood donations.

Changing Role of District Collector

With the multiplication of the activities of Welfare State, the District Collector's role also is in a constant stage of flux or change. The changing role of District Collector helps in making the administration efficient.

He has to maintain perfect relation not only with his subordinate officials but also with his superiors called the Revenue Divisional Commissioner. He supervises, directs and controls the subordinates and also advises them in administrative matters. He also takes disciplinary action against them if they failed to cope with the government orders. He also keeps his superior informed of the happenings on the district administration and if necessary, seek his cooperation and advice on various issues which he finds himself difficult to deal with.

He carries on extensive tour programmes to the remotest part of the district and talks to the people about their problems. He is also responsible to see that administration reaches to every nook and corner of the district. He gives necessary instructions to the subordinate officials to mitigate the problems of the people. He also gets an insight into the real working of governmental department by his conversation with the people. The gap between the people and administration is sufficiently lowered down by frequent visit of the Collector to various areas of the district. This ensures a healthy relation between government and the people.

The District Collector is responsible for ensuring an effective and efficient Public Distribution System within his district. He maintains a strict supervision over the distribution of controlled and essential commodities. His sincere role may prove beneficial for the people and act in checking the sinister role played by the black marketeer.

He maintains a cordial relation with the Superintendent of Police and keeps a control over the police at a distance. He looks into the complaints of atrocities by the police and ensures necessary safeguard to the people by taking disciplinary action against the police official with the help of the Superintendent of Police. He takes on a stock of the situation and adopts necessary pre-cautionary actions according to the circumstances.

The District Collector, as the representative of the State government and also as the Chief Executive Officer of the district, presides over all official functions, mixes with the people, elected representatives and the press. Thereby he gets an ample scope to explain to the people the efforts to be made by the administration to remove people's difficulties as well as speak the achievements of the administration in previous years. Thus, the District Collector not only gets an insight into the grievances of the people but also provides wide publicity of the administrative efforts to provide people with a happy and self-sufficing life.

However, the last, but not the least, is the major role played by the District Collector as a coordinator between various administrative and technical departments. He acts as a catalyst for coordination and removal of conflicts, contradictions and anomalies and as such helps in strengthening development in the district.

PANCHAYATIRAJ IN INDIA

The concept of 'Panchayati Raj' has been the most fascinating topic in the field of PublicAdministration. We know that administration means the management of affairs. However, the management of public affairs is a very complex affair because it wants to deal with the human elements who are subject to passions and emotions. Any administration cannot be effective unless there is effective participation and co-operation of the people. Therefore, before aiming at achieving success, administration should seek and do utilize effectively the cooperation of the people for whom the administration do exists. The institution of Panchayati Raj only reiterate the fundamental principles of administration by trying to involve the local people of the local area to solve their local problems with the help of local resources and local efforts without looking at the government at each step.

Meaning and Evolution

The term 'Panchayati Raj' stands for the rule of the Panchayats. But what is 'Panchayat'? In traditional terminology, Panchayat means five elderly members of village who constitute a group. Due to their experience and age, these members could exercise effective control over other members of the village. In early days, when the system of judicial remedy was not known to the people, the people prefer to go to these 'Panchs' for the solution of their problems. The Panchayat used enormous powers and to some extent, it exercises the judicial prerogatives by fine and other penalties imposed on the guilty person. This system of *'rule of Panch'* was prevalent during pre-Mughal period.

However, in modern connotation, 'Panchayat' do not stand for the rule of five elderly persons. Rather it stands for the rule of the people in a democratic context. In other words, Panchayati Raj, in India refers to the rule by the local people in the solution of local problems except that involved a judicial matter.

Panchayati Raj suffered a setback during the Mughal period and also during British rule in India. However, Mahatma Gandhi, the Father of the Nation, visualized a form of state which will have the rule of Panchayats. To salute this gentleman, the Indian Constitution, after Independence, strived to incorporate a system of Panchayati Raj that will be co-terminus with the democratic institution in the State. As such Article 40 of the Indian Constitution provides that the State should take steps to organize village Panchayats and to endow them with such powers and functions so as to enable it to function as the unit of local self-government.

Panchayati Raj in Independent India

After Independence, India revived the Panchayati Raj structure prevalent during the pre-Mughal period only with a little modification i.e. election took place in Panchayats. However, the approach of the government to revive the panchayat structure was only half hearted. It did not get enough scope to function as a unit of local self-government. Without giving powers to the people at panchayat level, the government of India, launched the Community Development Project.

The Community Development Programme was started in 1952 on a pilot basis in selected areas called 'community projects.' Originally 55 community projects started functioning all over the country covering 300 villages. It was a conscious effort on part of the government to bring about an all round improvement in the living standards of rural population. To evoke popular participation, an advisory body with citizens membership were set up at various levels.

But the project suffered a cold-blooded loss at the hands of the people. The Estimates Committee of Parliament, while evaluating the programmes of community development project could came to know that the Advisory Committees set up for guiding the project continued to be ineffective and in most of the cases, became virtually non-existent. The meeting of the committee never took place and if it did so, the members devoted their time in the routine works only. Thus in short the

C.D. programmes has become leaderless and aimless. Day by day the project sink down. As such the Estimates Committee, in its report in 1956, provided for setting up of another Committee to suggest a bold measure of reforms in C.D. programmes by successfully diagonising the maladies and imbalances in C.D. programmes. As such a Committee under the leadership of Balwantrai Gopaljee Mehta was appointed which gave its report in 1957.

The Balwantrai Mehta Committee was appointed in 1956 to study and report on the Community Projects and National Extension Services with a view to ensuring economy and efficiency.

Findings

The Balwantrai Mehta Committee was struck by the following three findings:

(a) The Community Development and National Extension Service programmes had failed to evoke popular initiative;

(b) Local bodies at a level higher than the Panchayat had evinced but little enthusiasm in the community development programmes; and

(c) Even the Panchayats has not come onto the field of community development in any significant way.

To the Committee, the remedy lay in the decentralization of responsibility and power to levels below the State. It recommended "devolution of power to a body which, when created....will have the entire charge of all development works within its jurisdiction, the government...reserving to itself the functions of guidance, supervision and higher planning and where necessary, for providing extra finance."

Recommendations

The recommendations of Balwantrai Mehta Committee were as follows:

(a) There should be administrative decentralization for the effective implementation of developmental programmes.

(b) The decentralized administrative system should be under the control of the elected bodies.

(c) As regards to the organisational structure, the Committee envisaged a three tier system of rural local government, namely Village Panchayats at the village level, the Panchayat Samiti at the block level, and the Zilla Parishad at the district level.

In short, the Committee recommended for the establishment of a Panchayati Raj system in place of Community Development.

Objectives of Panchayati Raj

The objectives of Panchayati Raj system as envisaged by the Balwantrai Mehta Committee are as follows:

(1) To provide a broad base to democracy in the country by transferring powers from the Centre and the States through the districts and blocks to the villages.

(2) To enable the people to participate in democratic life of the country in a more effective way and raise their civic consciousness.

(3) To mobilize the people at the grassroot level towards nation building.

(4) To give the rural people, an opportunity which they never had before, to plan and administer their own affairs.

(5) To arouse and stimulate rural initiative towards the Community Development Projects.

(6) To create plan consciousness among the villagers, thus helping them, in turn, in the proper utilization of the available manpower and other rural resources which had remained unexploited and even unutilized.

(7) To develop a sense of community feeling, self-reliance and initiative among the villagers.

(8) To provide to the weaker sections of the community, an opportunity to participate in the management of rural affairs.

In short, the main goal of Panchayati Raj system is to achieve rural development.

Main Tenets of Panchayati Raj System

The Panchayati Raj System, as envisaged by the Balwant Rai Mehta has the following main principles to its credit:

(i) The rural local government must be a three-tier structure of local self-governing bodies from the village to the districts, these bodies being organically linked up.

(ii) Transfer of power and responsibility to these institutions must be genuine.

(iii) Resources made available to these institutions must be adequate to enable them to discharge their responsibilities efficiently.

(iv) All the developmental programmes at these levels should be channeled through these institutions.

(v) The system of rural local government evolved, should be such as will facilitate further devolution and dispersal of power and responsibility in future.

(vi) The budget of each lower Panchayati Raj structure should be scrutinized and approved by its higher structure.

The Mehta Committee on 'democratic decentralization' was considered as an historic document. **R.L. Khanna** opined that "it is a bold and imaginative attempt to inagurate a viable and virile rural self-government, an earnest effort to translate into the four square reality, Mahatma Gandhi's dream of

Panchayati Raj. It is a testament of faith in democracy, a grass root approach to administration."

With much vigour and care the institution of Panchayati Raj was first adopted by Rajasthan in 1959, followed by Andhra Pradesh, Orissa, Tamilnadu and a host of other States. We will discuss the Panchayati Raj institution later on.

In 1963, the Government of India appointed a study team to make recommendations on the strengthening of Panchayati Raj finances under the Chairmanship of K. Santhanam. The Committee realized the practical problems of finance suffered by these institutions and made strong recommendations. Besides it could realize the sinister role played by the local politicians in these institutions in order to raise their vote banks. It therefore, recommended for allowing political parties to contest the elections without their symbols.

However, during the mid-70's the Panchayati Raj institutions suffered some setbacks. It lost its early vigour on which it started functioning. Therefore, the Government of India established another Committee under the Chairmanship of Ashok Mehta to make appraisal of the functioning of Panchayati Raj in India. The Committee was appointed in December 1977 and made its recommendations in July 1978. The Committee recommended for a two tier structure of Panchayati Raj organisation–the Zilla Parishad at the district level and the Mandal Panchayats at the Mandal level. A mandal should consists of a number of blocks and would assume those functions which were assumed by the Panchayat Samiti. Besides these, the Committee also suggested for open participation of political parties in election and regularity in elections in case of supersession.

The Constitution 73rd Amendment Act, 1992, provided a constitutional status to Panchayati Raj institutions (PRIs). It made the Panchayati Raj institutions mandatory. It provided for a three tier structure instead of two.

Institutions of Panchayati Raj

Panchayati Raj stands for rural area local government. The

Panchayati Raj institutions are not the same in all the States. But more particularly in Orissa, we have a three-tier structure of Panchayati Raj institutions basing on the recommendations of the Mehta Committee. The Gram Panchayat, the Panchayat Samiti and the Zilla Parishad.

The Orissa Panchayat Samiti and Zilla Parishad Act was passed by the Orissa Legislative Assembly in 1959. Having received the assent of the governor on 15th February, 1960, the Act was enforced with effect from 26th January 1961.

The Act originally provided for the election of Sarpanch by the ward members. But the Modification Act in 1965 provided for direct election of the Sarpanch by the voters.

The Swatantra-Jana Congress coalition government which came to power in 1967, abolished the Zilla Parishad in 1968 by amending the above Act that year. However, the Biju Patnaik Government have revived the Zilla Parishad in 1993.

In the election to Gram Panchayat, Panchayat Samiti and Zilla Parishad, 30 per cent seats have been reserved for women. Besides seats have also been reserved for Scheduled Castes and Scheduled Tribes. Now-a-days political parties are allowed to field candidates in election to these local bodies.

GRAM PANCHAYAT

The Gram Panchayat consists of several villages. The population of Gram Panchayat varies ordinarily between 2000 to 10,000.

Composition

The total area of the Gram Panchayat is divided into a number of wards. Generally the number of wards in Gram Panchayat varies between 11 to 25. From each ward, a ward member is elected by the people on the basis of Universal Adult Suffrage. Beside the ward members, the Sarpanch is also directly elected by the people.

The Sarpanch presides over the meetings of the Gram Panchayat. At their first meeting, the ward members elect from among themselves a Naib-Sarpanch who performs the functions of the Sarpanch in his absence. The Government of Orissa provides that both Sarpanch and Naib-Sarpanch cannot belong to the same sex. When there is a female Sarpanch, there must be a male Naib-Sarpanch and vice versa.

The Sarpanch and Naib-Sarpanch can be removed from his office on grounds of corruption and inefficiency if two-third members of Gram Panchayat voted against him. Besides the government can also remove them for breach of law and abuse of power.

Functions

The Constitution 73rd Amendment Act provides for the following functions of Gram Panchayats:

(1) Agriculture including agricultural extension.

(2) Land improvement and soil conservation.

(3) Minor irrigation, water management and watershed development.

(4) Animal husbandry, dairy farming and poultry.

(5) Fisheries.

(6) Social forestry and farm forestry.

(7) Minor forest produce.

(8) Small scale industries including food processing industries.

(9) Khadi, Village and Cottage industries.

(10) Rural housing.

(11) Drinking water.

(12) Fuel and fodder.

(13) Roads, culverts, bridges, ferries, waterways and other means of communication.

(14) Rural electrification including distribution of electricity.

(15) Non-conventional energy sources.

(16) Poverty alleviation programmes.

(17) Education, including primary and secondary schools.

(18) Technical training and vocational education.

(19) Adult and non-formal education.

(20) Libraries.

(21) Cultural activities.

(22) Markets and fairs.

(23) Health and sanitation, including hospitals, Primary Health Centres and Dispensaries.

(24) Family welfare.

(25) Women and children development.

(26) Social welfare including the welfare of the handicapped and mentally retarded persons.

(27) Welfare of the weaker sections and, in particular, of the Scheduled Castes and Scheduled Tribes.

(28) Public distribution system.

(29) Maintenance of community assets.

Sources of Revenue

Gram Panchayat mainly obtains revenue from grants-in-aid received from State government and Central government. Besides, it also collects its own taxes to support its activities. The main sources of revenue of Gram Panchayat are as follows:

(i) House tax, water tax, lighting tax, professional tax, and taxes on vehicles.

(ii) License fee, cattle registration fee, fees for use of market sheds and slaughter house, fees for residing in Dharmasala.

(iii) Auction sale of village market, ferry, ghats and ponds.

(iv) Contribution from the public.

(v) Grants received from the government.

PANCHAYAT SAMITI

The Panchayat Samiti stands at the middle level of the Panchayati Raj system. It is the popular name of the local representatives at the block level. In Orissa, there are 314 Blocks and such there are 314 Panchayat Samiti in Orissa. Generally, the Panchayat Samiti consists of about 10 to 15 Gram Panchayats.

Composition

The total area of the block is divided into a number of wards. From each ward a 'Samiti-member' is elected on the basis of Universal Adult Suffrage. However, the Samiti members, in their first meeting, elect from among themselves one Chairman and another Vice-Chairman who constitute the political head of the Panchayat Samiti.

However, the Chairman, Vice-chairman and the Samiti members alone do not constitute the Panchayat Samiti. On the other hand, certain other persons are also the members of Panchayat Samiti.

Generally, the Panchayat Samiti consists of two types of members—the non-official members and the official members. The non-official members of the Panchayat Samiti have the right to vote. But the official members, being the representative of the government, cannot vote in the meeting although they can remain present.

The non-official members of Panchayat Samiti consists of the Chairman, Vice-chairman, Samiti members and the Sarpanchs of all the constituent Gram Panchayats.

The official members consists of the Block Development Officer and other block-level government officials in charge of education, revenue, agriculture, cooperatives etc.

Besides these two types of members, the MLAs, the MPs

and the Chairman of Municipalities and NAC's within whose constituency the Panchayat Samiti remains, constitute the ex-officio members of Panchayat Samiti.

Functions

The functions of the Panchayat Samiti may be classified in two broad areas:

(a) provision of civic amenities;

(b) fulfillment of development functions.

(a) Provision of Civic Amenities

It includes the followings:

(1) Construction and upkeeping of roads within the jurisdiction of the Panchayat Samiti but other than purely gram panchayat roads.

(2) Supply of drinking water.

(3) Opening of drains and soakage pits.

(4) Establishment of Primary Health Centres and Maternity Centres.

(5) Provision of medical and health services.

(6) Provision of establishment of primary schools, adult education centres and literacy centres.

(7) Establishment and popularization of libraries.

(8) Establishment of youth organisations, Mahila Mandals, farmer's club etc.

(b) Fulfilment of Development Functions

The Panchayat Samiti performs the following development functions:

(1) Execution of all programmes under Community Development like agriculture, animal husbandry, fisheries, cottage industries, co-operatives etc.

(2) Multiplication and distribution of improved seeds.

(3) Procurement, distribution and popularization of improved manure and fertilizers.

(4) Providing credit for agricultural purposes.

(5) Reclamation of land and conservation of soil.

(6) Providing irrigation facilities by sinking wells, repairing and digging of tanks and maintaining minor irrigation sources and supply channels.

(7) Planting of trees and growing village forests.

(8) Introducing improved breeds of cattle, sheep and poultry.

(9) Dairy farming and milk supply.

(10) Opening and development of cooperative societies in various fields.

(11) Development of Cottage, Village and Small Scale industries.

(12) Establishment and maintenance of production-cum-training centres.

(13) Implementing the poverty eradication programmes by identifying the people below poverty line and providing them with IRDP loans.

(14) Providing assistance to old-aged, sick and handicapped persons.

Sources of Income

Normally the Panchayat Samiti has the following sources of income:

(a) Grants received from the Central government as well as State government.

(b) Special grants under Community Development Programme.

(c) Contribution from public.

(d) Income from leases granted by the Panchayat Samiti to public ferries, fairs etc.

(e) Loans from the State government.

(f) Income from the trusts and endowments under it control.

ZILLA PARISHAD

Zilla Parishad constitutes the apex of the Panchayati Raj system. It is a corporate body, having perpetual succession and a common seal, can sue and be sued and is empowered to enter into contracts.

Composition

The total area of the district is divided into a number of wards and from each ward, a "Zilla-Parishad Member is elected by the people directly. The Zilla Parishad members at their first meeting, elect from among themselves a Chairman and a Vice-chairman. The Chairman being the political head of the Zilla Parishad, presides over the meetings.

Like Panchayat Samiti, Zilla Parishad also consists of non-official and official members. The non-official members of Zilla Parishad includes the Chairman, Vice-chairman and members of Zilla Parishad, the Chairman of all Panchayat Samitis, Municipalities, NACs and Corporations within the district and the members of Vidhan Sabha, Lok Sabha and Rajya Sabha from the district.

The official members include the District Collector and other district level functionaries in the district. Besides these, certain co-opted members are also there in Zilla Parishad from Co-operative societies and the members having experience in administration, public life and rural development.

The Zilla Parishad carries out its functions through various Committees. Each Committee is entrusted with a particular function. The Standing Committees of Zilla Parishad are normally constituted to look after the following programmes:

(i) Community Development.

(ii) Agriculture, Co-operative, Irrigation and Power, Animal Husbandry.

(iii) Industries including Cottage, Village and Small-Scale industries.

(iv) Education and Social welfare.

(v) Public health.

(vi) Finance and taxation.

Each Committee reviews the programmes under its disposal and makes necessary steps to improve them.

Functions

Generally the Zilla Parishad has to perform the following functions:

(1) Providing direction, guidance and advice to the Panchayat Samiti for efficient performance of their functions;

(2) Coordinate the inter-block activities;

(3) Advises the State government on all matters relating to development activities in the district;

(4) It examines and approves the budget of Panchayat Samitis;

(5) It distributes funds allocated by the State government to various Panchayat Samities in the district.

(6) It informs the District Collector and Divisional Commissioner about irregularities, if any, committed by the Panchayats and Panchayat Samitis in the district.

(7) It advises the State government on allocation of work to be made among the Panchayats and Panchayat Samities in the district.

(8) It exercises such functions and assume such powers as conferred upon them by the State government.

However, the above functions are in theory only. More peculiarly, in Orissa, there has not yet been complete transfer of powers and authorities to the Zilla Parishad by the State government. Now the Zilla Parishad just sits idle looking towards the State government for delegation of power and responsibilities to these popularly elected bodies.

Sources of Income

The Zilla Parishad normally have the following sources of income:

(1) Tax on profession, trade and employment;

(2) Tax on water;

(3) Tax on public entertainment;

(4) Grants from the State;

(5) Land revenue grant;

(6) Purposive grant;

(7) Equalization grant;

(8) Establishment grants;

(9) Plan grant;

(10) Block grant;

(11) DRDA grant;

(12) Fees on sale of goods or animals in the market;

(13) Licence fee from butchers;

(14) Income from its own property;

(15) Loans from the government.

However, the Panchayati Raj institutions require to be more strengthened in order to function effectively as a unit of local self-government.

INDEX

A

Acton, Lord, 244

Administration,
 aspects, 2
 definitions, 1, 3
 new aspects of, 136-152
 people's participation in, 146
  external, 148
  internal, 147
 personnels in, 186-243
 physiology of, 29-66

Administration at work, 104-112

Administrative adjudication, 128
 advantages, 133
 definitions, 131
 disadvantages, 134
 features, 132
 improvement, 134
 vs. judicial adjudication, 132
 what is?, 129

Administrative law, 113
 definition, 114
 importance of, 118
 meaning, 113

Administrative procedure, 113-135

Administrative structures, 67-103

Administrators,
 issues before, 143

Approaches to study, 24
 traditional, 24
  case study method, 26
  comparative, 26
  historical method, 25
  legal method, 25
  scientific method, 24
 political approach, 27
  behavioural, 27
  human relations method, 28

Appropriation Bill, 165

ARC, 95, 247, 248

Arora, Ramesh K., 138

Auxiliary organisation, 62
 functions, 63

Audit, 174
 functions of, 176
 in India, 177
 meaning, 174
 purpose, 175
 types of, 176

B

Beard, Charles, 22

Board of Directors, 111
 functions of, 111

Budget, 153
 deficit, 157
 enactment of, 165
 execution of, 170
 need of, 155
 presentation, 166
 requirements of, 156

Budgetary process in India, 158
 procedure, 159

Bureaucracy,
 role of, 144

C

CAG, 177
  appointment, 178
  historical legacy, 177
  limitations, 179
  powers and functions, 179
Central Vigilance Commission (CVC), 247
Centralisation,
  and decentralization, 52
  definition, 53
  demerits, 54
  merits of, 53
Chamber's Dictionary, 246
Chand, Ashok, 95
Changla, M.C., 95
Charlesworth, 22
Chief Executive, 104
  and general manager, 108
  dysfunction of, 106
  funtions of, 106
  types of, 105
Civil servants,
  and public, 239
  who is?, 237, 240
Civil Service, 187
  a historical evolution, 190
  and bureaucracy, 189
  characteristics of, 192
  conditions of, 220
  definition, 187
  in India, 194
  meaning, 187
  shortcomings of, 193
  types of, 188
Citizen's grievances,
  institution for, 245
  redressal of, 244-277
Clientele, 71
  demerits, 77
Command,
  unity of, 47
Control,
  functions, 44
  span of, 43
CPU, 96
  composition, 97
  evaluation, 99
  functions, 98
  jurisdiction, 98
  limitation, 98
  tenureship, 97

D

Dale, Earnest, 64
Davis, Kenneth C., 114
Decentralisation, 54
  merits of, 54
  demerits of, 55
Delegated Legislation, 119
  causes of growth of, 123
  definition, 120
  fundamental principles, 120
  limitations, 122
  negative implications, 125
  positive impact of, 124
  safeguards in, 126
  what is?, 119
Delegation, 49
  types of, 51
  merits of, 52
Department, 67
  advantages, 68
  structural pattern of, 73
Development administration, 136
  definitions, 137
  historical legacy, 136
  in India, 149
  meaning, 138
  nature, 140
  role of bureaucracy in, 142
Developmental organisaion,
  bases of, 68
Dicey's hypothesis, 116
Dimock, M.E., 4, 7, 10, 35, 84, 131

Discipline, 226
  ensuring, 227
  meaning, 226
District Administration, 252
  meaning of, 253
  organisation of, 254
District Collector, 257
  changing role of, 261
  duties of, 257
  functions of, 258
Duncan, 9
Dwidedi, 145

E

Estimates Committee, 183
  functions, 184
  importance of, 185
  procedure of working, 185
Encyclopaedia of Social Sciences, 131

F

Fayol, Henri, 8, 12, 42
Field establishments, 75
  definition, 77
  and headquarter, 79
Financial administration in India, 153-185
Finance Bill, 170
Finance,
  control over, 173
Formal and informal organisation,
  distinction between, 34
Functional base, 69
  merits of, 70
  demerits of, 70

G

Galbraith, J.K., 95
General manager, 107
  functions of, 107
Gladden, E.N., 4, 7, 11
Goodnow, F.G., 114
Gorwala, A.D., 236
Goswami, U.L., 137
Gram Panchayat, 269
  composition, 269
  functions, 270
Grange, W., 84
Gullick, Luther, 4, 7

H

Hamilton, 44
Haldane, 44
Headquarters, 74
  administrative wing, 74
  institutional wing, 75
  political wing, 74
  what is?, 77
Hierarchy,
  principles of, 39
  advantages of, 41
  disadvantages of, 42
  alternative, 42
Huxley, 23

I

Independent Regulatory Committees, 99
  characteristics, 100
  definition, 100
  functions, 102
  in India, 103

J

Jennings, Ivor, 114

K

Khanna, H.R. (Justice), 238

L

Laski, Harold J., 236
Law Commission of India, 245
Legislative control, 180
Legislature,
  as Board of Director, 110, 112

Leighton, Alexander, 230
Lepawsky, 63
Line and Auxiliary organisation
distinction between, 63
Line and staff organisation
distinction between, 64
Line organisation, 57
and staff organisation, 63
types, 57
Lokpal Bill (1996)
general features of, 250
Lokpal in India, 248
necessity of, 247

M

Marx, F.M., 3, 8, 230
McDonald, Ramsay, 257
Mcqueen, Percy, 7
Merriam, Lewis, 12
Merson, 7
Millet, J.D., 48
Milward, 31
Ministers and Civil Servants,
relation between, 235
Mitchell's, 9
Moonery, J.D., 31, 60
Morale, 229
factors influencing, 232
meaning, 230
importance, 231
Morrison, Herbert, 84, 237
Munro, W.B., 114

N

Nigro, Felix A., 3, 13

O

Organisation, 30
aspects of, 32
formal, 32
informal, 33
bases of, 36
principles of, 38
typology, 56
Ombudsman, 246
historical legacy, 246

P

Parliamentary control, 127
Panchayati Raj in India, 263
main tenets of, 267
meaning and evolution, 263
objectives of, 266
Panchayat Simiti, 272
composition, 272
sources of income, 274
Pfiffner, 4, 7, 12, 31, 34, 60, 61, 62, 84
Phillips, 128
Place, 72
minus points, 73
plus points, 73
Politics and Administration, 19
POSDCORB, 11, 12
Principles of Public Administration, 19
Private and public administration
dissimilarities, 15
similarities, 14
Process, 70
advantages, 71
disadvantages, 71
Promotion, 213
bases of, 217
meaning, 213
significance of, 219
types of, 215
Public, 240
Public Accounts Committee, (PAC), 181
functions, 184
importance of, 183
procedure of working, 182
Public Administration, 5

approaches to study, 24
traditional, 24
political, 27
approaching, 18-28
as an Art, 21
as science, 21
definitions, 6
factors of growth, 18
importance of in modern policy, 19
nature, 8
science or art, 21
scope, 10
Public Corporation, 82
and private enterprise, 86
characteristics of, 84
control over, 92
definitions, 84
role in modern states, 89
working of in India, 94
vs. govt. depts, 87
vs. Joint Stock Corp., 85

R

Recruitment, 196
meaning, 196
methods of, 197
direct, 198
indirect, 199
procedure of, 200
direct, 201
indirect, 205
purpose, 197
Redresssal, 244
Riggs, Fred W., 138
Robson, Prof, 117
Robson, W.A., 82

S

Sadan, 132
Sharma, 132
Sherwood, 34
Shukla, M.C., 84
Simon, Herbert, 4, 7, 31
Smithburg, 27
Staff and auxiliary agencie
distinction between, 65
Staff organisation, 59
functions, 59
Stone, Donald C., 138
Sundaram, L., 96

T

Taylor, F.W., 25
Tead, Ordway, 24
Training,
meaning, 208
definitions, 208
types of, 210
intradepartmental, 216
inter-departmental, 216

U

Union Public Service Commission (UPSC),
composition, 206
powers and functions, 207

V

Vieg, Z.A., 3

W

Wade, 128
Wald, Duguit, 7
Walker, 8, 12
Weidner, E.W., 137
White, L.D., 4, 7, 8, 19, 22, 31, 59, 84, 131, 214, 231
Wilson, Woodrow, 7
Willoughby, 109

Z

Zilla Parishad, 275
composition, 275
functions, 276
sources of income, 278